BUSINESS ISSUES, COMPETITION AND ENTREPRENEURSHIP

STRATEGIC RETHINKING

CONNECTING LOCAL-GLOBAL BUSINESS MODELS

BUSINESS ISSUES, COMPETITION AND ENTREPRENEURSHIP

Additional books and e-books in this series can be found on Nova's website under the Series tab.

BUSINESS ISSUES, COMPETITION AND ENTREPRENEURSHIP

STRATEGIC RETHINKING

CONNECTING LOCAL-GLOBAL BUSINESS MODELS

RAJAGOPAL
AND
DIVYA KIRTI GUPTA
EDITORS

nova
science publishers
New York

Library of Congress Cataloging-in-Publication Data

ISBN: 978-1-53616-835-8

Published by Nova Science Publishers, Inc. † New York

CONTENTS

PREFACE

The recent economic policies in the big emerging markets like India and China have given manifold boost to the business of local industries and prompted them to expand markets to new destinations. In view of the economic advantage offered to the local industries, the general reaction of corporate houses against the local business has emerged towards mergers and acquisitions to reinforce the presence of large business in the local markets. One of the core arguments this book presents is that the overall effects of local-global convergence is witnessing the Darwinian fitness in the marketplace allowing both large companies to reach the bottom-of-the-pyramid and developing the vertical thrust among local companies to grow global. Hence, this book raises one of the principal points of concerns as how sustainable is the convergence of local-global business. There are no books available until data that argue about who wins the game while exploring the red ocean against the blue ocean companies. However, the principal issue in driving companies to be fit for doing international business is how high-quality are the strategic choices to ensure competitive success? Well-managed companies meticulously develop marketing strategies to establish business in the overseas destinations. They benefit from enormous economies of scale in production, distribution, marketing, and management. Local enterprise in the global marketplace put efforts in innovation, competitiveness, and application of technology for sustainable growth.

The largest and powerful multinational business houses prefer to be aggressive to dominate over the most demanding and emerging sectors. General Motors for example is offering credit cards and supermarket groups routinely now offer gasoline, banking, pensions and saving plans apart from the manufacturing and marketing of automobiles. The privatization of the state and public sector ventures like energy, transport and communication led to industry restructuring and further allowed the multinational companies to compete in these countries. The entry to the liberalized state and public sector industries brought more professional rules and guidelines for implementing the quality standards like ISO. Nevertheless, there has been a backlash against liberalism.

Globalization has moved through several change phases from capitalistic philosophy to democratic business notions involving stakeholders in the process of business growth. Large companies are seeking to harness globalization through cooperation with the local enterprises to reach the bottom-of-the-pyramid market segment. The opportunities for global businesses are expanding with the support of rapidly emerging product markets, the global race for innovation, technology, and talent management, which tend to widen the impact of digitization. The multinational companies today are engaging with the local enterprises to exploit reverse innovations and build new business models. The successful examples of global-local business convergence in reference to India are Godrej-Boyce and GE Health Care. Some Moreover, success stories such as Airbnb Inc., and Uber Technologies Inc. are spurring the imaginations of new entrepreneurs while highlighting the vulnerability of many traditional businesses.

The scope of carrying business in emerging destinations has become wary due to protective regulations laid by governments, which allows opening more industries to multinational companies as the political philosophy for business development is leaning toward both pro-globalization and pro-localization. This conception has driven the Darwinian dynamics of 'struggle for existence' and 'survival of the fittest' among the companies leaving international business in a fix. They are defining economic security more broadly and perceiving more and more sectors to be of strategic importance such as energy, agri-business, media marketing, and defence products and services. The new phase of globalization has, so prompted the rise of state capitalism in some of the world's most important emerging markets and has altered the business fields for the multinational companies. Local companies in China and India are contributing significantly to the industrial digitization and helping to accelerate the Industry 4.0 revolution. Local entrepreneurs thus play an important role in enabling the economy to adapt to the changing conditions and to new possibilities for material improvements by creating new production organizations, and even to new industries. Because of its essential role in initiating the process of production, some economists identify entrepreneurship as a "fourth factor of production," alongside land, labor and capital. Higher efficiency of a factors of production help in generating higher revenues for the company. The global-local convergence, therefore, helps in redefining business models, economic policies, and socio-political agenda in emerging markets. Make in India initiative is another step in global-local convergence to motivate Indian companies to excel in the global workspace. The production sharing strategy, consortium manufacturing, and contract manufacturing practices of multinational companies at local workstations is a dynamic impetus driving the globalization process.

Technology is reshaping culture: Just think of the Internet. Individual choice is fragmenting the imposed uniformity of national cultures. New hybrid cultures are emerging, and regional ones re-emerging. National identity is not disappearing, but the bonds of nationality are loosening. Some of the questions that have strong hold in the debate of globalization seem to be more lashing against the western influence on pushing global trade. The questions that have emerged during the thought process of globalization may be stated as whether globalization and international trade is destroying local cultures and diversity. Does the market expand our positive liberties and increase the menu of choice? Does trade in cultural products support the artistic diversity of the world or destroy it? More generally, are market exchange and aesthetic quality allies or enemies.

This edited volume spread across fourteen distinguished articles aims at bringing together rich discussion on global-local convergence in reference to emerging markets. The impact on business-to-business and business-to-consumers imperatives, global-local convergence, and vice-versa effects that are driving the national economy are discussed through conceptual and empirical research papers. Discussions in this volume would critically analyse the convergence of technology, business practices, public policies, political ideologies, and consumer values for improving business performance at the global-local paradigm. This book will serve as a reference book to the researchers engaged in exploring the small-business development in emerging markets and the effects of expansion of multinational companies into the emerging markets. The research papers and essays complied in this volume will be enriching knowledge on business management among policy makers, corporate managers, and students of graduate management programs. In our view, graduate management students, potential researchers, and corporate managers will find this volume interesting for carrying out future research.

Rajagopal
Divya Kirti Gupta

Boston, MA
July 30, 2019

In: Strategic Rethinking
Editors: Rajagopal et al.
ISBN: 978-1-53616-835-8

Chapter 1

BUSINESS-POLITICS INTERPLAY IN GLOBAL-LOCAL BUSINESS POLICIES: A CRITICAL EXAMINATION

Rajagopal
EGADE Business School, Tecnologico de Monterrey,
Mexico City, Mexico

ABSTRACT

This article argues that introvert business diplomacy deteriorates international trade relations, affects national economy, and puts the global economy at risk. The article thus underscores that underneath the veneer of a protectionist trade policies employed by powerful nations of the world like USA and UK, the business repercussions across the trade regions could be serious. The chapter therefore argues that international relations between developed and emerging markets should be pragmatic and business-led, rather than reverse ideological driven mainly by political manifesto, economic and power imperatives, and by rhetoric notion of being big and mighty. The chapter also lays some proposition at the end of the debate for future research.

Keywords: business governance, political philosophy, enterprise management, public policy

INTRODUCTION

Business governance is an outgrowth of political ideology and public diplomacy. The nature of business and industry shifts in a country or a trade block in context of the political scenario in the countries that dominate international business. Political power dominates in trade negotiations and defines the contemporary trade philosophy for trade governance. The political framework of trade powers within their territorial boundaries influences key players in the economy comprising industries, governments, and non-government organizations. This could help in designing domestic and international policies for major customers and suppliers, concluding acquisitions and alliances, and securing financing for business from investors and banks. The political ideology and public diplomacy drive in building industry coalitions with political bodies to influence policy makers, institutional shareholders, and key opinion-leaders influencing the media and business analysts.

Many leaders exercise their public authority drawn within the political regime to influence executive decisions. However, when leaders move into positions, they direct business policies that depend more on political influence and the ability to shift the current trends in business governance. The political roles of business icons involve navigating within a business-politics matrix and driving external partners of the organizations to change the rules of business using the power of negotiation. Therefore, government agencies shift their governance system and change controls in human resources management and information technology, control budgets, and learn to practice corporate diplomacy effectively. The shifts in political ideologies leverage organizational alliances, business networks, and other business relationships in tune to the political ideology (Watkins, 2009). The socialist philosophy of business laid by Marxism principles has been realized in globalization as a global marketing practice of serving the consumers at the bottom of the pyramid to leverage their consumption pattern at par with the elite consumers.

CHRONOLOGICAL GLOBAL-LOCAL CONJUNCTIONS

Historically, the business perspectives emerged in the human mind with the generation of needs and introduction of money in the society as a tool for transactions. As needs turned into desires, the basic economics of demand and supply was enforced in the society. The business phenomenon began in the human civilization as the suppliers of food and essential products had thought of getting their share in each transaction-termed as 'profit'. The specific history of reclamation and settlement had given rise to a favorable balance of powers between state, nobility, towns, and rural communities that reduced opportunities for rent seeking and favored the rise of efficient markets. This allowed farmers, fishermen, and artisans to take full advantage of new opportunities presented by the changing economic and ecological circumstances in the late fourteenth and early fifteenth centuries (Dijkman, 2011).

Evolution of markets over the centuries has been a perennial phenomenon congruent with the shifts in social, economic, and technological knowledge in the society. The evolution of business and growth in the market have had categorical impact of two logics. On one side, economic behavior has been promoted as the basis for understanding markets, while sociologically, the arguments towards the evolution of markets have been based on an understanding that individuals are embedded in various cognitive structures involving the business activities. Shifts in the marketing processes in the society are induced by fundamental beliefs, and shared assumptions; and resemble the elements of social culture defining norms of markets, expected behavior, and thought. Such business evolution paradigms are resistant to minor discrepancies between their fundamental models and contradicting (potentially empirical) evidence. Thus, discrepancies in market behavior constitute socio-economic abnormalities, paradoxes, or puzzles in a given place and time (Hedaa and Ritter, 2005).

Malthusian trap of stagnant living standards, such as technological progress, accelerated along with the population growth. Consequently, the industrial revolution adapted to the technological progress and began to keep pace with the population. Such growth in the industrial products and services for consumption and business needs created new markets; and by the middle of the 19th century, the global transformation in product and financial markets was observed. Such phenomenal change in the global marketplace resulted into the economic dynamism in both developed and developing economies of the world. Accordingly, many countries jumped into the market fray and started to produce larger variety of products, making them more substitutable, raising the price elasticity of demand, and strengthening competition. Such market development drove higher competition to modern growth, and competitive firms aimed at larger territorial expansion at lower markups with prolonged break-even. However, in the growing market competition, small firms always face major threat from the large companies as the large firms possess more resources (physical, finance, human resources, and technology) against the smaller firms. Hence, most of the smaller firms develop cocooning attitude and confine to a niche as they cannot continue their struggle for existence in the marketplace. It has been observed that large firms often enter new market niches created by small firms through technological innovation and ingest the market share of small firms. In view of the Darwinian Theory, it may be argued that market conditions and company-specific characteristics determine entry timing and the underlying goals of the large firms, and such entry might be a continuous process for large firms in different marketplaces.

Business consortia are the alliances of individual business enterprises, specifically of small and medium size. Businesses involved in these sorts of consortia are often in the same broad field or industry, though they are rarely in direct competition with one another. Instead, members usually offer products or services that are complementary to those available through other consortium members. These alliances are not commonplace, but some analysts indicate that in future, increasing numbers of small business owners may investigate consortiums as a way of sharing common costs, increasing purchasing power, and competing with larger companies. Business consortia usually come into being for specific reasons, such as competitive threats from a common enemy (whether another business or an unwelcome economic trend), changes in competitive structures, or deregulation. Consortium of small and medium companies helps in developing the collective bargaining and purchasing power as well as marketing efforts that can provide the member firms with increased recognition and stature in the community.

The Darwinian fitness concept in market evolution argues that when the number of consumers increases, more varieties of products and services penetrate in the market driving more demand. Such market thrust in positioning products and services increases the price elasticity of demand. Some management studies exploit this feature and show, in a one-period model, how the higher elasticity of demand, due to a larger population or more liberalized trade, facilitates innovation (Desmet and Parente, 2010). As the trade liberalization continued in the global marketplace transforming the regional markets, the multidimensional growth appeared to be a strong catalytic thrust in the economy of developing countries. The multidimensional growth, in which a corporate firm manages relatively freestanding business units, was the most successful design of the marketing organizations of the twentieth century. However, some firms have evolved organizational designs that signal a new way of resolving the market competition. These firms are organized around multiple dimensions such as region, product, and services. The multidimensional growth of marketing organization is best understood as the next step in the evolution, from a resource-centric business model to a customer-centric knowledge-sharing model. It is a way of managing competitive markets that is particularly well adapted to stimulating the market leadership necessary to create economic value in complex markets (Strikwerda and Stoelhorst, 2009).

Global customer-centric organizations are becoming increasingly important with the increase in the number global customer. Yet many companies, especially those designed according to function, country, and business unit, are having difficulty in re-designing and aligning their structure according to the needs of the global customer. The reasons of the globalization of business have been revealed in many ways, the most significant ones are as listed below:

- Market saturation in home country
- Trade deficit and long disequilibrium in the balance of trade
- Increasing foreign competition
- Emergence of new markets
- Globalization and free trade zones
- Opportunities via foreign aid programs

Globalization and its impacts have profound implications for a broad range of issues important to the funding community. These issues range from the sustainable use of the worlds' resources and the protection and preservation of the environment, to the need to improve living standards, safeguard human rights, promote and protect cultures, and ensure democratic and responsive global governance.

The increasing competition in the global marketplace has induced large companies, with high market share and brand equity, to expand spatially their market operations. In this process, large companies tend to acquire smaller firms, or get themselves merged with larger organizations on win-win negotiations. Such process has been established in the global marketplace as an effective strategy for the growth of business for the larger companies, which has been considered as a survival for smaller and weak business companies in the market. In the context of global competition, this approach is considered as a process of cannibalization. At the lower end of the market, value added resellers also catalyze the cannibalization in the global market. Remanufactured products do not always cannibalize new product sales. To minimize cannibalization and create additional profits, firms need to understand how consumers value remanufactured products. This is not a static decision and should be re-evaluated over the entire product life cycle. While firms exhibit responsibility to maximize profits for the firm, this is not necessarily equivalent to maximizing new product sales. A portfolio that includes remanufactured products can enable firms to reach additional market segments and help block competition from new low-end products or third-party remanufacturers (Atasu et al., 2010).

Contextual Reviews and Research Prospects

The Governance Trend

Globalization has become functional dynamic of emerging firms in the business environment today. Most firms believe that globalization is synonymous to the business growth and invest perennial resources in developing strategy for going global. It has become one of the most pertinent issues for managers of growing firms around the world. A large number of companies in the developed countries are nourished by their huge domestic markets, but typically lag behind their European and Japanese rivals in internationalization. Companies intending to go global exhibit two apparent objectives- to take advantage of opportunities for growth and expansion; and survival in the business amidst growing competition. However, firms that fail to pursue global opportunities eventually lose their domestic markets, which are pushed aside by competitive global firms. In the middle of the twentieth century, the nature of political life changed everywhere by novel forms of political activity as the new means of mass communication, increase of popular participation in politics, and the rise of new political issues offered better understanding towards international politics and popular governance. Besides, the extension of the scope of governmental activity and other innumerable social, economic, and technical developments in the developing countries urged for stability in the government for effective implementation of the international development programs, and the trade policies have been one among the international priorities (Rajagopal, 2016).

Most of the world's political systems have experienced one or another form of internal warfare leading to violent collapse of the governments in power. Besides, certain crises seem to increase the likelihood of breakdown in the governing politics of a region or a country. In the politico-economic scenario, the economic crisis is another common stimulus to the political setbacks as witnessed in the recent Argentinean crisis. The Brazilian economy was also in decline in the late 90's due to internal economic instability. However, most companies are attracted by the comparative advantages of factors of production than the political risks, which jeopardize their manufacturing and marketing operations. Acts of political radicalism have negative consequences for intergroup relations, peaceful democratic participation, and they increase mistrust and unrest between political groups and factions within society. A sense of insecurity and uncertainty for the future, and an aggravation of the relationships among social classes also result in the politico-economic conflicts and business chaos in a country (Gøtzsche-Astrup, 2019). A severe political crisis develops distrust in the economic system of the country, triggers outbreak of revolutions in the political systems, and declines the prospects of business growth. The political unrest due to radical ideologies in a country spurs several experimental conditions for the stability of political system in extremely revealing ways that often induce either change in the political leadership or the restructuring of political governance system. Since the quality of the political leadership is often decisive, the systems that provide methods of selecting able leaders and replacing them possess important advantages towards internal and global political concerns. Many studies have shown that dealing with problems in the political arena is the principal challenge faced by international managers in developing pro political strategies to run the business successfully in the host country. It is observed that each country has its own set of national goals, but most countries also share many common objectives.

Business diplomacy addressing global concerns with domestic focus generates transnational field of cooperation and competition, in which national and international players can be integrated for a homogeneous economic growth (Kuus, 2018). Nationalism and patriotism refer to citizens' feelings about the interests of their countries. Such feelings exist in every country and the multinational firms, individually or collectively, perceived as a threat to that sovereignty. The foreign firms perceive greater threats if they are larger in size and more in number in a country. At the time of any political turmoil, the foreign firms may be targets for attack. Many countries seek "national solutions" to help troubled companies to retain what are perceived to be national champions (Rajagopal, 2016).

Business in the global marketplace moved on through capitalist, socialist, democratic, and mixed-political philosophies over centuries and had often changed governance patterns affecting the profitability, growth, and stakeholder values. Globalization has also born with such burst of political ideology, public diplomacy, and industries lookout in min-twentieth century. After a relatively long period of success of globalization with liberal trade and economy philosophy backed with the political ideology and trade diplomacy of developed countries like the USA, Britain, and European Union, the cold war driven by the protectionist ideology and public diplomacy in geopolitics is back in Twenty-first century.. Some studies reveal that state business diplomacy can be integrated with the corporate public diplomacy, which can be used to develop sustainable win-win solutions supported by the public. However, an important function of public relations is to create a perception of legitimacy; and the hope of economic and commercial diplomacy is to create a perception of attractiveness among the businesses, and public and international destination partners (Mogensen, 2017).

Businesses across the world cannot be confident of strategic status quo of a political business ideology as it is largely governed by the balances of power and international negotiations on foreign trade policies dominated by the super powers in the world. A corporate foreign policy has two components- Geopolitical due diligence, and corporate diplomacy. The former philosophy involves the assessment of local, regional, and transnational risks facing a company, while the latter aims to enhance a company's ability to operate internationally (Chipman, 2016).

Political intervention is a decision taken by the government of host country intended to force a change in the operations, policies, and strategies of a foreign firm in the interest of the country. Such interventions may range from enforcing control for complete takeover, or annexation of the foreign enterprise. The magnitude of intervention would vary according to the company's business existing in the host country and the nature of political decisions taken thereof. In countries, where foreign investment plays a significant role in the economy, the possibility of political interference in the operations of foreign firms is higher and stringent. Besides, the political system of a country like democracy, communism, or mixed economy also indicates the nature of intervention. Businesses in developed countries such as the USA and Britain are ruled largely by the government interventions as they are in reference to the public policies of the country. The political directions may also govern the functions related to transfer pricing, price ceiling and price floor, price contracts, price paid for local raw materials, and price paid for imported raw materials to be used in production in the host country. Besides, the activities of distribution and product retailing may also be subject to political interventions in many developing countries. Advertising and communication are other important areas of a multinational firm that are affected by political interference in a country.

Major structural shifts in the global economy are creating new opportunities in transaction banking, particularly in trade finance. International trade is growing faster than global GDP, and Asia is now the center of global expansion, driving trade growth in other emerging markets and in developed economies as well. An ongoing shift in global economic activity from developed to developing economies, accompanied by growth in the number of consumers in emerging markets, are the global developments that executives around the world view as most important for business and most positive for their own companies' profits over the next five years. Executives also identify two other critical positive aspects of globalization: technologies that enable free flow of information worldwide and, increasingly, global labor markets. The global economy faces significant challenges as it continues to integrate high levels of public debt in Europe and North America that are causing the fear of a negative impact on GDP growth. Emerging markets, with populations that are young and growing, will increasingly become not only the focus of rising consumption and production, but also major providers of capital, talent, and innovation. Over the trend of trade liberalization as experienced in the Latin American countries in the early decade (2001-10) of the twenty first century, the North-American Free Trade Agreement created a single market with the United

States and Canada that helped to propel Mexico into the top ranks of manufacturing exporters. (Rajagopal & Zlatev, 2017).

Political ideologies have commonly been associated with particular social classes such as, liberalism with the middle classes, conservatism with the landed aristocracy, socialism with the working class, and so forth. These ideas reflect the life experiences, interests and aspirations of a social class, and therefore help to foster a sense of belonging and solidarity. However, ideas and ideologies can also succeed in binding together divergent groups and classes within a society. A unifying set of political ideas and values can develop naturally within a society. The values of elite groups such as political and military leaders, government officials, landowners or industrialists may diverge significantly from those of the masses. Ruling governments may use political ideas to contain opposition and restrict debate through a process of ideological manipulation (Heywood, 2007). The problem today is the political aggression narrowing the business corridors on the plea of the achieving the political manifestos. Often, leaders view politics as war, where victory is paramount, and compromise several social and business interests. Such ideologies often shift the business governance from globalization to privatization on the political manifesto of making their countries great again. However, every single policy of business gateway country like the USA and China affect the global business systems and might either elevate or threaten to cripple the existing business dynamics. Revitalizing America's culture of democracy where the health of the nation comes first, above economic interest, party, and ideology plays key role (Moss, 2012).

Trends and the Ideological Shifts

In the mid-twentieth century, with the downfall of the Soviet Union, one of the super powers driving the trade and economy in the world, the American policymakers within the government and sitting at the world forums began championing the neoliberal economic policies. The new doctrine focused on ensuring capitalist philosophy in business by empowering private sector- and market-led economic growth, which prompted the government to involve only in policy-making and overpower regional trade blocks through business diplomacy and negotiations. American investment protection policy was shaped with a broader view to support domestic and global investment climate and suggest structural reforms in developing countries. Such political push had monitored the General Agreement on Trade and Tariffs (GATT), which later emerged as World Trade Organization to work on business regulations, innovations and patents, and as an international institution for resolving business conflicts. However, power-play has been indirectly affecting in such global trade institutions as well. Overtime Russia, China, USA, Japan, and France have emerged as power centers engaged in global surveillance and as policy-makers (e.g., Gretz, 2016).

Among others, there are two basic observations that come to the edge of trade diplomacy. One is the persistent divergence of income per capita across countries over a sufficiently long period of time. This effect is agitating in the developing economies, by typically exhibiting the possibilities to explore unexploited business opportunities, which allow them to grow faster than industrial nations, and falling in the trap of power play in dictating the trade diplomacy. Most countries with emerging economies tend to catch up with the political power leaders to leverage their trade and economy canvass. The other observation is that a large part of economic growth can be attributed to the efficiency with which production inputs are applied, in addition to the intensity of their use. The success of a few countries, who have managed to multiply their income levels quite rapidly, has largely resulted from booming total factor productivity. The positive or negative growth effects of a country's regulatory framework affect the economic integration, which makes factors and producers more mobile and capable of avoiding burdensome regulation. Therefore, global potential determinants of growth can be interlinked to develop a regulatory framework on growth in an integrated economy (Silberberger & Königer, 2016).

The world markets are changing rapidly promoting new emerging markets across countries. In the twenty-first century, China, India, South

Africa, Mexico, and other Latin America based economies promise new opportunities for global trade. The Pacific region has shown leap in significant Asian population, which has participated in the rapid transition in response to the global movement of trade and services since 1980. Asia may be portrayed as the fastest growing market for the top brands of western companies. At the same time, the Asian companies began penetrating the western markets at low price-high quality strategy. While the luxury and fashion goods are dominating the Asian and Far-east markets, the specialized product like electronics and automobiles from Asian Markets are trying to capture considerable market share in Europe and North American countries. In the emerging markets, the technology has homogenized with the world markets for variety of customer and industrial needs; and the reduction in the tariff barriers, duties and liberalization process worldwide has further given a stimulus to the international marketing across the regional boundaries (Rajagopal, 2017). Major shifts in business diplomacy has the following sequential effect in post-2017 global economic order:

- Globalization to protectionism (The American economy)
- Shifts in power-play (Polarization of business in Europe and Asia)
- Trade diplomacy of big-emerging markets (Attracting FDI-Make in India Program)
- Business with China and India (Incremental and reverse innovation, market diversification, curtailing imports, regional agreements)
- Manufacturing relocation and investment hubs (Playing against the theory of comparative advantage)
- Britain's exit from European Union (living in dilemma)
- Latin America for new bilateral trade negotiations (Leaning towards Asian business opportunities)
- South Africa rising as emerging market (Became a part of BRIC-SA)
- Global fragmentation in manufacturing and services (Losing market competitiveness)

- New consumption patterns across destinations (Native brands emerging)

The above discussed shifts indicate that due to the change in ideologies of the political super-powers towards international trade and economy, the globalization philosophy has fragmented and has shown isolated effects in the USA and Britain on flow of international investments, manufacturing, and services. The current philosophy of trade protection has made a small dent in the domestic economy of developed nations, but it has given a trade boost to big emerging markets like China and India to explore new markets and grow with their business agenda. By invoking the Article 50, Britain might not be able to gain a desired freedom in negotiating with the Commonwealth countries with triggering a two-year countdown to withdrawal from the European Union. This would affect the trade, economy, and industry associated with multinational companies as well (Ghemawat, 2017).

Most bilateral negotiations and free trade afreements are on the edge of strategic renegotiations in the current period (2016 onwards) in view of the critical trade and economic analysis, and the changing political ideologies. Accordingly, many countries are renegotiating within their trade blocs about eliminating or reducing the non-tariff and investment barriers. However, the protectionist political ideologies are recommending increase in the tariff barriers in international trade to develop their native markets. Such steps might dichotomize the global trade concerns, liberal trade, and economy policies of the countries that were established in the mid-twentieth century and coordinated by the World Trade Organization. The trade related negotiations among the Latin America and East Asian countries should also focus on the technical norms and standards; rules of origin, anti-dumping, subsidies, countervailing measures; other liberalization and deregulation measures (privatization); sub-regional, regional and hemispheric integration processes; and convergence and divergence between regional integration and multilateral trade regimes. The negotiations should also be dealt on simplifying the customs rules and procedures including non-transparent and inefficient infrastructures; differing customs; improper application of rules of origin, customs valuation, pre-shipment inspection and import licensing. Customs problems can be especially difficult for small and medium enterprises that have less experience and fewer resources for handling these problems (Rajagopal, 2017). Free market economies are revamping the local business governance in many emerging markets. New Zealand has experienced significant changes in local and regional development policy since the widespread adoption of neoliberal reforms in the 1980s. Policy interventions have restricted the powers of local governments. Such local governance has enlightened local communities to become more pro-active in the determination of their local economic growth options (Nel & Stevensen, 2014). Globalization policies may be re-routed by encouraging local-global convergence and improving niche business models with the multinational sectors instead of curbing globalization as most countries have customized their trade policies in tune to the liberal economic philosophy. Similarly, local and regional development has characteristically focused upon localities and regions in the historically industrialized and urbanized countries of the Global North (Pike, Rodríguez-Pose & Tomaney, 2014).

The ideological shifts in politics affecting business governance are emerging randomly across geo-demographic destinations. Ideally, political philosophy is defined by economic activity, not political borders. The major resaon behind the shift of people, capital, and business is that economic decisions are often based on the fear that the principal resources will be drained to other destinations. In emerging markets, governments prefer to give people access to the best and affordable products and defer to special interests; and try to confine business growth by restricting natural flow of products to market. They invest inefficiently, and as a result destroy wealth in the long-run. Although political leaders resist acknowledging the consequences of any ideology on business growth, the quality of international business relations is always questionable (Ohmae, 1995). The most prominent explanations, often interrelated, for the retardation in the global economic recovery include erosion of trust in institutional pillars such as public and corporate governance, the weakening consumer- and investor confidence, and the rising geopolitical risks. The weakness of fixed investment expenditure, particularly pronounced for non-residential investment, contributes significantly to the sluggish overall growth in the industrial countries. Investment expenditures play a critical role in the business cycle. There have been problems in sustaining the recovery once inventory levels werer re- established, during the recent past. Investment activity generally picks up when prospects for profitable investment opportunities increase and the utilization of existing production capacities reaches a level that calls for a further increase of these capacities (Rajagopal, 2016).

Despite reverse political ideologies, business in global marketplace is succeeding. There are debates in C-suits about why so many global strategies fail despite powerful company-industry-government triadic negotiations and other cross-border advantages. A one-size-fits-all strategy no longer stands a chance, so a single political ideology might not lead the global markets. However, cross-border differences are larger than it is commonly assumed in a trade bloc. Most economic activities including trade, virtual financial investment, tourism, and communication industry are largely affected by the political ideologies. In this pseudo-globalized political shift evidenced in the USA trade lobbies, Chinese business reactions, and emerging markets looking at the global concerns, the global businesses have been undoubtedly affected and most business economies are at surveillance.

As business has expanded beyond boundaries today, the approach to business diplomacy should be altered with geo-political trade diplomacy by matching the political, economic, social, technological, and legal (PESTL) indicators within the region. Companies can cross home-borders more profitably by basing their strategies on the geopolitical differences that matter; and identify strategies barriers to overcome the loss in business due to geo-political shifts in ideologies. Companies need to assess the cultural, administrative, geographic, and economic differences between regions at the industry level and create value. However, adaptation to policy shifts and their consequences, managing aggregation by overcoming differences, and passing through the arbitrage by exploring and exploiting differences affects the trade management process and business diplomacy (Ghemawat, 2018). The practice of regionalization is seen everywhere with social relations, including the capitalistic policies of business (Lee, Wainwright, & Glassman, 2018).

The labor market in the changing global economic order plays a significant role in determining the production patterns across regions in reference to the concerns of companies over the cost effectiveness and profit making. Accordingly, the trend of production sharing, by ways of getting the parts of products manufactured at different locations and assembled at another place, has become popular among the companies in developed countries, in order to take advantage of the low wages of skilled and unskilled labor. The effects of labor market on international fragmentation of production in the USA and Europe have been reflected in the rising trend of increase in relative labor wages and demand in industrial production since 1980s. Due to fragmentation of international trade economics and political ideology industrial production has been affected in 2010s. However, shift in the intensity of labor usage is observable in the USA and Europe, which relates to the production sharing activity. Opening up of markets can play an important role in weakening the vested interests, and reducing economic rents associated with long-standing economic and institutional arrangements. Trade can thus spur improvement in domestic institutions that otherwise would not have been possible. In addition, international agreement can be an important external anchor and catalyst for institutional change by breaking through domestic impediments to reforms. Regional or bilateral agreements may bring faster results than the multilateral process, may enable parties to conclude levels of liberalization beyond the multilateral consensus, and may be able to address specific issues that do not register on the multilateral menu. The resulting achievements in trade liberalization can be substantial complements to the WTO system, and they can be the important building blocks for future multilateral liberalization. The most powerful economic arguments against regional and bilateral trade agreements are that they can cause trade diversion and trade distortions and ultimately undermine the multilateral system because of their discriminatory nature (Rajagopal, 2016).

Trade agreements have driven the Latin American countries with enormous opportunities to explore international markets and develop market competitiveness. Besides, the trade development measures to attract foreign direct investment, and lower or eliminate the tariff barriers, have also reflected global trends in reference to the typology of these agreements. While the majority of trade agreements are bilateral, some include the free trade agreements, which have set a very comprehensive scope for trade and economic development. Notably, some free trade agreements signed by Peru, Colombia and Chile with the United States and the European Union have helped in gearing-up the trade and economy of these countries. However, the bilateral agreements signed with Asian countries, especially by Chile and Peru, pose a limited scope with regard to regulatory commitments but are very ambitious with regard to their levels of opening trade and eliminating tariffs. These agreements also have a strong potential, given the economic dynamism of this region. Other agreements are *plurilateral,* involving large number of countries on an extended geo-economic parameters like the Trans-Pacific Strategic Economic Partnership Agreement, negotiated by Chile, New Zealand, Brunei Darussalam and Singapore, which is now being broadened to include the United States within the framework of the negotiations for the Trans-Pacific Partnership Agreement (Rajagopal, 2017). As manufacturers invest in local assembly facilities in emerging economies, the nature of trade is also changing, with intermediate manufactured goods, which includes parts, components, and commodities, making up a greater share of cross-border flows of goods. Eventually, as large global manufacturers achieve scale in emerging markets, they may pull many of their suppliers to enter these regional markets, too, which could slow down the growth of trade in intermediate goods. However, there are other factors too that may reshape manufacturing flows in the future. For instance, rising labor costs in China may continue to shift more labor-intensive manufacturing to countries such as Mexico, Vietnam, and Bangladesh, which could see a resulting increase in exports (Rajagopal, 2017). The major effects of shifts in political ideology can be seen in the following business turndowns:

- Interrupted flow of factors of production
- Decline in international investments

- Ineffective trade negotiations
- Polarization of business

The policy risks broadly include administrative controls on prices, investments, and transfer of funds that affect the international business in the country. Besides, the policies on nationalization and domestication of identified industry segments, and the changing macroeconomic policies of the country carry major risk for the international business. The political instability, civil unrests, bureaucracy, and corruption are also of concerns to the inefficiency of the internal governance in a country that seriously affect the investments, manufacturing, and marketing operation of multinational companies targeting to do business in the destination country. International diplomacy also affects the exchange rates, investments, and international trade at the destination country. The political risks may be identified by analyzing contextually the political and social system of a country, its degree of openness to international trade, efficiency of the product markets, labor market dynamics, and its capital markets. By critically examining these contextual areas, companies can map the business contexts of any country and match their strategies to each of these contextual points, and they can take advantage of strengths of destination markets. However, firms need to weigh the benefits initially against the anticipated costs (Khanna et al., 2005; Rajagopal, 2016).

The current political ideology (post-2017) of restricting globalization and bringing back the collapsed politico-economic philosophy of protectionism has not only narrowed the global flow of factors of production, but also jolted the peak of business flurry in global markets. The trends in consumer and industrial products were seized for few quarters of 2016 and 2017 due to the American diplomacy and Britain exiting from the European Union. Industries and corporate houses with substantial exposure to 'Brexit' have employed contingency plans to deal with a wide range of outcomes, including unfavorable consequences due to the business diplomacy. It is expected that, the emerging parliamentary elections in Britain will be able to reframe the political ideology to handle the upcoming Brexit negotiations (Ghemawat, 2017).

General Discussion

Globalization has become a functional dynamic of emerging firms in the business environment today. Most firms believe that globalization is a synonym to the business growth and investing perennial resources in developing strategy for going global. It has become one of the most pertinent issues for managers of growing firms around the world. In the process of evolving global, many forces drive local enterprises to globalize by expanding their brand reach and participating in foreign markets through various modes of entry. In developed countries, domestic markets have turned mature and are demanding to seek international markets, while in some countries like Brazil, Russia, India, and China most companies in the present competitive marketplace are born global. A large number of companies in the United States of America are nourished by the huge domestic market but typically lag behind their European and Japanese rivals in internationalization. Born global firms hold dynamic growth in the competitive marketplace and achieve substantial international sales from an early stage in their development despite economic and technological constraints. They internationalize rapidly as the period from domestic establishment to initial foreign market entry is often three or lesser number of years. Born global firms are emerging in sizable numbers worldwide. Until recently, international business was mainly the domain of large, well-resourced multinational enterprises. The appearance of large numbers of born global firms is revolutionizing the traditional character of international business and helping to reshape the global economy (Cavusgil and Knight, 2009). Companies intending to go global exhibit two apparent objectives- to take advantage of opportunities for growth and expansion, and survival in the business amidst growing competition. However, firms that fail to pursue global opportunities eventually lose their domestic markets and may be pushed aside by stronger and more competitive global firms. In the process of going global, firms need to adopt innovative marketing strategy to sustain against competing firms. Most firms follow a global perspective to expand their business across destinations instead of adopting a country-by-country or region-by-region perspective in developing a marketing strategy (Rajagopal 2014).

Global economic activities across the developed, developing, and transitional economies have broadly strengthened during the beginning of 2010s and are expected to improve further by the end of the decade with much of the impetus for growth coming from advanced economies. Although downside risks have diminished overall, lower-than-expected inflation poses risks for advanced economies. There is increased financial volatility in emerging market economies, and the increases in the cost of capital will likely dampen investment and weigh on growth. Advanced economy policymakers need to avoid a premature withdrawal of monetary accommodation. Emerging market economy policymakers must adopt measures to changing fundamentals, facilitate external adjustment, further monetary policy tightening, and carry out structural reforms (International Monetary Fund, 2014). In emerging market and developing economies, growth picked up slightly in the second half of 2013. The weaker cyclical momentum in comparison with that in the advanced economies reflects the opposite effects of two forces on growth. On one hand, export growth increased, lifted by stronger activity in advanced economies and by currency depreciation. On the other hand, investment weakness continued, and external funding and domestic financial conditions increasingly tightened. Supply-side and other structural constraints on investment and potential output (for example, infrastructure bottlenecks) are issues in some economies.

Serving large corporates poses increasingly complex challenges as well. The expectation was that corporate needs would harmonize across countries and regions in a globalized world. However, the underlying motivation to use trade finance and the criteria used to select a service provider still differ significantly across regions. Trade services are vital to large corporates and a growing number of small and medium enterprises (SMEs) and any bank unable to support its clients' increasingly diverse and geographically extensive trading demands puts their relationships with these institutions at risk. Trade flows today encompass a broad diversity of endpoints, and no organization can aspire to cover the entire globe with adequate breadth and depth. Global banks' large, yet often thin, networks were typically designed to meet the needs of large corporate clients based in Europe or the United States, but now these networks are costly to maintain and inadequate in geographical reach. Regional and domestic banks typically enjoy strong relationships with SMEs, but they need access to an increasing number of foreign markets and want to defend against global players reaching down market. Correspondent banking and "white label" arrangements already address these gaps to some extent, but they usually provide only limited functionality within local markets, often do not cover new corridors adequately, and may expose a bank to client risks they do not understand and cannot evaluate thoroughly. Deeper technological integration among partners in various industries has opened access to underserved markets while streamlining processes and improving transparency. Technologically integrated alliances require broad client adoption of digital processes, either in parallel with the current documentary workflow or as an entirely new supply-chain interface for sourcing, financing and tracking (Rajagopal, 2017).

The companies converging global-local strategies develop business models in twenty-first century and their design has become a key driver to the performance. In fact, business model design is often associated with innovation. Increasing competition in the marketplace has driven innovation among firms and most firms recognize that they should invest resources in building ideas and capabilities for innovation at the local markets. Most firms attract tacit knowledge, diffuse on social media and within organization, and develop trust among consumers and market players on innovations in the products and services of the firm. However, for most companies, innovation is an extensive collection of initiatives and growth stimulating changes, but lack of coordination; and is managed with vacillating strategies. Firms need a balanced innovation portfolio and the ability to approach for sustainable and expected returns for the long run. In order to manage innovations, it is necessary for the firms to develop the unique capacities needed for transformational innovation finding the talent required for breakthrough of innovations and integration with the core business. Continuity in business innovation requires adequate financial and human resources as well as technology infrastructure. Innovation- related projects should be planned with a different priority in a pipeline management approach and developed through corporate growth metrics. Companies that learn how to manage for total innovation can fully harness innovation's energy and make it a reliable driver of growth (Nagji and Tuff, 2012).

CONCLUSION

Political influence in business is inevitable and has greater impact on trade, economy and business negotiations. The political power play in business drives the trend of negotiations and business expansions across destinations. The political ideology affects the manufacturing and services industries and governs the global-local convergence of business. Like manufactured goods, global commodity flows are being shaped by several trends. First, the increasing participation of emerging economies is reshaping global commodity flows as both producers and consumers. Second, digitization is enabling new efficiencies in operations, which are necessary to help navigate a world that is likely to be characterized by continuing high and volatile resource prices. Finally, increased volatility in commodity flows is expected to continue because of surging demand, supply constraints, and a higher correlation between commodity prices that stems from a more tightly interconnected world alongside of shifts in political ideologies, power-play lobbies, and peoples participation in prompting politics. Emerging economies are becoming larger participants in the global commodities markets, with rising levels of production, consumption, and investment.

References

Atasu, A., Guide V. D. R., & Wassenhove, L. N. V. (2010). So what if remanufacturing cannibalizes my new product sales? *California Management Review*, 52 (2), 56-76.

Cavusgil, S. T. & Knight, G. (2009). *Born Global Firms: A New International Enterprise*. New York: Business Expert Press.

Chipman, J. (2009). Why Your Company Needs a Foreign Policy. *Harvard Business Review*, 94 (9), 36-43.

Desmet, K. & Parente, S. L. (2010). Bigger is better: Market size, demand elasticity, and innovation. *International Economic Review*, 51 (2), 319-333.

Dijkman, J. (2011). *Shaping medieval market*s. Netherland: Brill Academic Publishers.

Ghemawat, P. (2017). *As Brexit Negotiations Start, Companies Need Contingency Plans*. HBR Web Article, Boston: MA, Harvard Business School Press.

Ghemawat, P. (2018). *Redefining Global Strategy, with a New Preface: Crossing Borders in a World Where Differences Still Matter.* Boston: MA, Harvard Business School Press.

Gøtzsche-Astrup, O. (2019). Personality moderates the relationship between uncertainty and political violence: Evidence from two large U.S. samples. *Personality and Individual Differences*, 139 (1), 102-109.

Gretz, G. (2016). *Commercial Diplomacy and American Foreign Policy*, Global Economic Governance Program, Oxford, UK: Oxford University.

International Monetary Fund (2014). *World Economic Outlook: Recovery Strengthen, Remains Uneven*. Washington, DC: International Monetary Fund.

Kuus, M. (2018). Transnational institutional fields: Positionality and generalization in the study of diplomacy. *Political Geography*, 67, 156-165.

Lee, S. O., Wainwright, J., & Glassman, J. (2018). Geopolitical economy and the production of territory: The case of US–China geopolitical-economic competition in Asia. *Environment and Planning A: Economy and Space*, 50(2), 416–436.

Mogensen, K. (2017). From public relations to corporate public diplomacy. *Public Relations Review*, 43 (3), 605-614.

Moss, D. A. (2012). Fixing What's Wrong with U.S. Politics. *Harvard Business Review*, 90 (3), 134-139.

Nagji, B. & Tuff, G. (2012). Managing your innovation portfolio. *Harvard Business Review*, 90 (5), 66-74.

Nel, E., & Stevenson, T. (2014). The catalysts of small town economic development in a free market economy: A case study of New Zealand. *Local Economy*, 29(4-5), 486–502.

Ohmae, K. (1995). Putting Global Logic First. *Harvard Business Review*, 67(2), 143-154.

Pike, A., Rodríguez-Pose, A., & Tomaney, J. (2014). Local and regional development in the Global North and South. *Progress in Development Studies*, 14(1), 21–30.

Rajagopal (2014). *Architecting Enterprise: Managing Innovation, Technology, and Global Competitiveness*. Basingstoke, UK: Palgrave Macmillan.

Rajagopal (2016). *Sustainable Growth in Global Markets: Strategic Choices and Managerial Implications*. Basingstoke, UK: Palgrave Macmillan

Rajagopal & Vladimir Zlatev (2017). *Business Dynamics in North America: Analysis of Spatial and Temporal Trade Patterns*, New York: Palgrave Macmillan.

Silberberger, M. & Königer, J. (2016). Regulation, trade and economic growth. *Economic Systems*, 40 (2), 308-322.

Strikwerda, J. & Stoelhorst, J. W. (2009). The emergence and evolution of the multidimensional organizations. *California Management Review*, 51 (4), 11-31.

Watkins, M. D. (2009). *The Corporate Diplomacy Challenge: A Leader's Guide to Navigating this Important Career Transition.* Boston, MA: Harvard Business School Press.

In: Strategic Rethinking
Editors: Rajagopal et al.
ISBN: 978-1-53616-835-8

Chapter 2

TOWARDS HARMONIC GLOBALIZATION: GLOBAL-LOCAL CONVERGENCE OF BUSINESS MODELS, ECONOMIC POLICIES, SOCIO-POLITICAL SCENARIOS THROUGH HOLISTIC CORPORATE MANAGEMENT (HCM)

Subhash Sharma
Indus Business Academy, Bangalore,
Bengaluru, Karnataka, India

ABSTRACT

World has experienced many changes. Now we have entered the VUCA (Volatile, Uncertain, Complex, Ambiguous) world. Stability paradigm has given way to VUCA environment. Disruptive technologies have disrupted many industries. In addition there has been an emergence of knowledge era and knowledge society. Further, Industry 4.0 has arrived. Artificial Intelligence (AI), Internet of Things (IOT), Automation, Data

Analytics etc. have become part of normal conversation. Corporations, Nations and individuals are also influenced by GAMA (Google, Apple, Microsoft, Amazon) effect. VUCA context requires more of creativity and imagination and we are observing a shift from rationality paradigm to creativity and imagination paradigms in business, Government and society. Innovation has become a new paradigm to beat and jump over competition. This is also leading to change in paradigm from war mindset to competition to innovation to imagination. These changes are leading us towards a search for new ideas in business models, economic policies and socio-political scenarios based on new global-local influences and convergences.

CHANGING PARADIGMS IN CORPORATE WORLD: ROLE OF CORPORATIONS

Corporates have undergone an evolutionary process and this evolutionary process can be viewed as a four stages development model (Sharma 2007). The traditional corporate model rooted in the capitalistic vision was centred around the key concepts of competition, efficiency and profit. Its primary objective was to maximize the wealth of the shareholders by maximizing profits. Subsequently the model evolved into multiple stakeholder model as it was recognized that there are many stakeholders besides shareholders. These included employees, customers, suppliers, Government and society at large. This was their second stage of evolution. In their third stage of evolution, the corporates have been conceptualized as corporate citizens. Hence, the expectation of ethics and environment concern gained importance. Corporates are expected to follow the 'principles of ethical business' and not merely 'principles of business'. In their fourth stage of evolution, corporates are turning into 'social institutions' with a dominant influence on society. Hence, the expectations have further gone up and corporates are expected to achieve synergy between efficiency, equity, ethics and ecology. While stage I model was largely an efficiency model, in stage II model, equity concerns were incorporated and in stage III model, ethics was also considered important for conduct of business. Now in their stage IV evolution, as social institutions, corporates are expected to be concerned with ecology dimension and are expected to achieve an appropriate balance between efficiency, equity and ethics and ecology and also be concerned with transcendental values of gender equality, psycho-spiritual advancement, etc. This is the New Era Model of corporates presented in Figure 1 wherein corporates are viewed as social institutions and not merely as business entities. In addition to bottom-line concerns, organizations have a social purpose, and therefore should be driven by HOPE: Higher Order Purpose of Existence. Above discussion suggests a paradigm shift in corporate management from profit maximization to value addition to values addition (reflected in corporate governance) to happiness addition (reflected in stakeholders happiness index). Thus, an overarching vision of new corporate model of social institution is represented by 4-Es model of Efficiency, Equity, Ethics and Ecology representing philosophy of Holistic Development & Management (HDM) and Holistic Corporate Management (HCM). The framework of corporates as social institutions suggests that the corporates should be driven not merely by efficiency paradigm but also by equity, ethical concerns and ecology. Thus, ethicotarian and ecological (ecotarian) views should be incorporated within the corporate philosophy. This implies adoption of the idea of 'Harmonic Globalization'.

FOUR FORCES MODEL OF HARMONIC GLOBALIZATION

Modern societies and corporations exist within the four forces context. These forces are as follows:

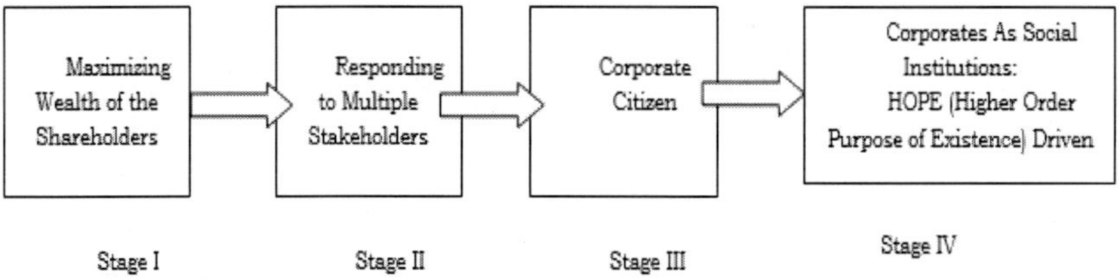

Figure 1. Four stages model of corporates' evolution ashope driven social institutions (Source: New Mantras in Corporate Corridors, Subhash Sharma, 2007 p. 501).

Dynamics of these four forces can be represented in the form of a diagram presented in Figure 2.

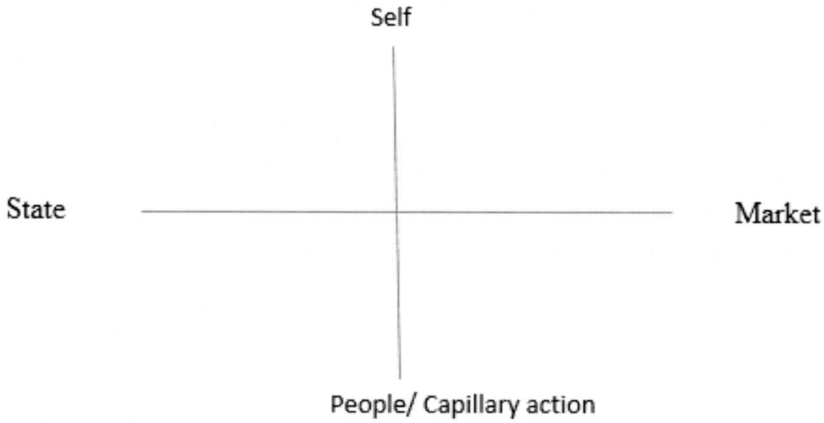

Figure 2. Four forces model for harmonic globalization (Source: New Ideas in Strategic Thinking and Management, Subhash Sharma, 2016, p. 51).

1. Force of Market
2. Force of State/ Government
3. Force of People/Capillary action
4. Force of Self

We can also refer this model as 'Four Spheres Model' of human society as society is influenced by four spheres represented by market, State, people/community and spirituality.In general we only see three lions viz. market, State and people/capillary action. However, hidden lion also plays a significant role. It represents higher consciousness and thereby spirituality. This idea is also captured through the concept of HOPE: Higher Order Purpose of existence. In ancient Indian thought Self is represented by *Triguna viz. Tamas, Rajas* and *Sattava,* wherein *Tamas* represents violent self or the lower self, *Rajas* represents vibrant self and *Sattava* represents higher self also represented by silent energy of HOPE. Strategy making can be based on *Tamas* as was the case during ancient wars, or based on Rajas as is the case in contemporary competitive times or it can be based on

Sattava as we realize the need for cooperation and innovation in strategy making.

When there is harmony among above indicated four forces, there is order, harmony and peace in society. When there is disharmony among them there is disorder, violence and conflicts in society. For brining global harmony, this model provides us a foundational basis for 'harmonic globalization' and strategy making within the domain of four forces.

In general, the social discourse is centered around the market and the State and is reflected in the ideologies of capitalism and socialism. This essentially represents x-axis of social discourse and it ignores the y-axis of people and the Self. For a holistic view, we need to consider both, x-axis representing market and the State and y-axis representing people and the Self. All the four forces should be given due importance in any social discourse.

At the level of organizations four forces model has an important lesson for Strategic Management. It implies that Strategic Management should be formulated within the framework of these four forces. Further with its focus on the role of the Self, the model suggests a need to link Spirituality with Strategy.

MOVING TOWARDS HARMONIC GLOBALIZATION THROUGH GLOBAL – LOCAL CONVERGENCE

Globalization usually implies Global Products in Local Markets. It implies multinationals entering the emerging new markets. This policy of Liberalization, Privatization and Globalization (LPG) has been followed in various nations. For example in India LPG idea was introduced in 1991. However, there is another dimension to globalization i.e., Local Products in Global Market (LPGM), indicating emergence of an outward force to balance the capture of indigenous markets by global products. For example, yoga, meditation and Indian spirituality represent arrival of the idea of Local Products in Global.

For a nation's holistic development both LPG and LPGM are needed, and policy making should aim at balancing the two.

Thus, we have following three strategies for responding to market needs and market opportunities:

- Globalization (LPG: Liberalization, Privatization, Globalization – Global Products in Local Markets)
- Glocalization e.g., Colgate's Vedshakti toothpaste
- LG (from Local to Global) - LPGM (Local Products in Global Markets)

THEORETICAL UNDERPINNINGS OF FOUR FORCES MODEL OF 'HARMONIC GLOBALIZATION'

To understand the four forces model and its link with life, nature and human beings, following discussion is presented in form of 'TCP Equations of Life, Nature and Human Beings. Following three fundamental principles and corresponding equations represent a holistic view:

1) 'T' Principle refers to the Total view of life in terms of Transactional (T1), Transformational (T2) and Transcendental (T3) approaches to relationships of human beings with others, including nature. This view of life is represented by the following equation:

   $T = T1 + T2 + T3$

2) 'C' Principle refers to the complete view of nature in terms of Competition, Cooperation and Symbiosis. In social and organizational context it is represented by Competition (C1), Cooperation (C2) and Connectivity (C3) wherein the C3 represents the inter-connectivity of human beings with everything often

captured through the concept of consciousness, particularly spiritual consciousness. Accordingly C equation is as follows:

$$C = C1 + C2 + C3$$

3) 'P' Principle refers to the human personality which displays three components viz. lower self (P1), middle self (P2) and higher self (P3). It is also displayed through three *Gunas viz. Tamas*, *Rajas* and *Sattava* representing three energies viz. Violent, Vbrant and Silent. The personality equation or the P equation is as follows:

$$P = P1 + P2 + P3$$

When these three TCP principles / equations are combined, we arrive at a comprehensive view of human beings, life and society. This view in a matrix format can be referred to as TCP matrix and is presented in Figure 3.

T	C	P	
T3	C3	P3	T3 C3 P3
T2	C2	P2	T2 C2 P2
T1	C1	P1	T1 C1 P1

Figure 3. A holistic worldview as a foundation for a new vision of holistic development & management (HDM).

It may be indicated that T1 C1 P1 describes the situation in which every dimension of life is transactionalized, worldview is competitive and lower-self finds its manifestation in terms of competition, greed and self-interest.

T2 C2 P2 describes the situation in which humanism prevails and human relationships are in transformational mode. Cooperation prevails and the middle-self moderates the lower-self and transforms it into cooperative and transformational modes.

T3 C3 P3 describes the situation in which spirituality prevails and human relationships are in transcendental mode. There is touch of altruism, harmony and connectivity. *"Vasudhaiva Kutumbakam"*, the idea of world being one big family, is the foundational concept.

When all these ideas are combined together they represent an integrative and holistic approach, leading us towards a philosophy of Holistic Development and Management (HDM) for a new social vision of 'Sacro-Civic Society'.

TCP Manifestations: Towards an Integrative and Holistic Worldview

It may be observed that T1C1P1 represents force of Market, T2C2P2 represents transformative force of Society and T3C3P3 represents the force of Self/Spirituality. These three forces represent the three forces of 'Four Forces Model of Harmonic Globalization'. Thus we arrive at an integrative and holistic vision of the world for a better future of humanity. In such a world local and global find a new domination free dialogue to create a better world.

Author's Note

This paper is based on earlier writings of the author.

FURTHER READING

Management in New Age: *Western Windows Eastern Doors*, Subhash Sharma, New Age International Publishers, New Delhi, 1996.

New Mantras in Corporate Corridors: *From Ancient Roots to Global Routes,* Subhash Sharma, New Age International Publishers, New Delhi, 2007.

New Earth Sastra: *Towards Holistic Development and Management (HDM),* Subhash Sharma, IBA Publications, Bangalore, 2012.

New Ideas in Strategic Thinking and Management: *A Knowledge Tree of New Age Mantras,* New Age International Publishers, New Delhi, 2016.

In: Strategic Rethinking
Editors: Rajagopal et al.
ISBN: 978-1-53616-835-8

Chapter 3

REDESIGNING CORPORATE SOCIAL RESPONSIBILITY FOR THE GLOBAL AGENDA: A STAKEHOLDER-CENTRIC APPROACH FOR BUSINESS SURVIVAL

Andrée Marie López-Fernández
Universidad Panamericana, Mexico City, Mexico

ABSTRACT

This chapter argues that most organizations, institutions and business, regardless of size and line of business deliver corporate social responsibility. It is fair to say that what organizational leaders mostly get wrong is the notion that corporate social responsibility is all about *giving back*; that is, either to the community, environment and, sometimes, both. Discussions in this chapter put together various concepts on redesigning corporate social responsibility in context of global agenda. A stakeholder-based approach for business survival is delineated in this chapter.

Keywords: corporate social responsibility, stakeholder management, business survival, redesigning programs

Over the past five years, the attention that organizational leaders and stakeholders have placed on firm engagement in social responsibility has significantly increased. For instance, while some firms are taking on a more active role in their overall impact on society and the environment, consumers have become much more aware of the products and services they consume, as well as brands and firms they purchase from; many have even become consumer activists. These practices are certainly beneficial as important steps taken in the right direction. That being said, there seems to be a gap between the business approach to social responsibility and the very social and environmental issues requiring immediate attention.

It is only fitting that organizations around the world are taking their impact on society and environment seriously; yet, discussions surrounding firms' engagement in corporate social responsibility tend to take a turn towards disadvantages, failures, and suspect motivations. When it comes to organizations, institutions and businesses, regardless of size and line of business, and corporate social responsibility, it is fair to say that what organizational leaders mostly get wrong is the notion that corporate social responsibility is all about *giving back*; that is, either to the community, environment and, sometimes, both. *Giving back* is a lovely sentiment, however, it is an inaccurate depiction of what corporate social responsibility engagement truly is. This oversight is significantly responsible for the misuse of the concept, as well as internal and external mismanagement. Furthermore, and importantly, it is particularly interconnected with current worldwide conditions that translate into the crises addressed by the 2030 Agenda (UN, 2019). Therefore, the very approach to corporate social responsibility needs to be reevaluated, redesigned, and revitalized.

Local Agenda

There is a wide range of social and environmental issues that permeate society, and in varying degrees of severity depending on the region, country, state, city, and small town. As such, each area has its particular problems and areas of opportunity that need to be tackled in order to account for social growth and development. A quick look at any news source paints a daunting picture; everyday journalists report on the rising humanitarian crisis caused by and the causals of, armed conflicts, poverty, inequality, natural disasters, epidemics, water crisis, famine, displacement, amongst many others. Firms operate everyday around the world in the midst of these conditions; that is, micro, small, medium, large, multinational, nongovernmental, and governmental organizations are all facing the challenges posed by operating under these circumstances; as such, these constitute each firm's local agenda. This means their business dynamics are certainly affected by them and that their actions and results impact firms in return; thus, making firms stakeholders in their local agenda. One way that firms can address these issues is by engaging in corporate social responsibility.

Corporate Social Responsibility

Corporate social responsibility (CSR) is a concept typically used to refer to organizations' impact on society and the environment. According to Moir (2001), its main purpose is responsible sustainable business growth. The concept itself has gone through a series of transformations; it emerged with the idea of responsible business practices (Dempsey, 1949), then, business responsibilities that went beyond profit and should focus on stakeholders (Abrams, 1951), to the actual coining of the term corporate social responsibility (Bowen, 1953). Therefore, the fact that firms share responsibility and ought to be accountable for their actions and environmental and community reality has been widely discussed for at least seven decades. Meaning that, it is neither a new or modern notion, nor is it considered good business to not be socially responsible.

On the bases of said work, various definitions have been developed with a focus on philanthropy, regulation, efficiency, sustainability, strategy, marketing, and good business sense, amongst others. Corporate social responsibility tends to be considered as a business process and/or a mechanism used to respond to society's needs and wants and/or environmental issues. It has been defined as an organization's commitment to internal and external stakeholders (Young and Thyil, 2009); a way for business to address and tackle social issues (Wokutch, 2014); and an organizational sense of obligation with stakeholders which leads to practices beyond legal stipulations (Grundey, 2008). No doubt many still consider corporate social responsibility to be an unnecessary cost, a mere buzzword, and/or fad.

Throughout the years, various scholars and practitioners have found that CSR is positively associated with a series of concepts and variables. For instance, it has been said to have a positive impact on profit and financial performance (Friedman, 1970; Quazi and O'Brien, 2000; Hart, 2010), market share (Ogola and Dreer, 2012), organizational performance (Margolis and Walsh, 2003; McAdam and Leonard, 2003; Okwemba et al., 2014; Zheng, et al., 2014), innovation and competitive advantage (Porter and Kramer, 2006), corporate reputation and image (Owen and Scherer, 1993), collaborator satisfaction, motivation (Mozes et al., 2011), and moral (Utting, 2005), stakeholder decision making and behavior (Alniacik et al., 2011), and consumer satisfaction (Xueming and Bhattacharya, 2006; Ogola and Dreer, 2012). Therefore, there are numerous studies that have determined that engaging in corporate social responsibility is a good and sensible practice that provides benefits for business growth.

While diverse studies increase our knowledge of the functionality of CSR, they may also be a cause of a certain degree of confusion; namely, approaches to corporate social responsibility, uncertainty of attributes, and disproportionate results. First, scholars and practitioners have been continuously developing definitions of corporate social responsibility, including but certainly not limited to: Schlusberg (1969), Wood (1991), Brown and Dacin (1997), World Business Council for Sustainable Development (WBCSD) (1999), Hopkins (1999), Moir (2001), Schwartz and Caroll (2003), Du et al., (2010), European Commission (2013), Wang et al., (2016), and Crowther and Seifi (2018), amongst many others. Second, the concept is often mistaken for others because they share attributes, such as, ethics, sustainability, citizenship (Crane and Matten, 2004), etcetera. And, third, corporate social responsibility is constantly being reduced to firms' isolated actions aimed to helping others or give back.

There are several examples of organizations that have claimed active engagement in corporate social responsibility, yet continuously fall short of the very principles of the concept. Decisions and effects of the latter tend to make the headlines which swiftly call the attention of current and potential stakeholders, which commonly leads to the viralization of said headlines. Firms around the world have been accused of corruption, modern day slavery, endangering and exploiting the environment, animal cruelty, discrimination, tax fraud, and wage theft, amongst many other unethical and questionable practices. Perhaps the current problems with CSR engagement may be illustrated with the definition, "actions that appear to further some social good, beyond the interests of the firm and that which is required by law" (McWilliams et al., 2006); the operative word being "appear."

There are too many organizations that are doing what they consider to be the bare minimum in order to be able to stick a socially responsible label on their product, service, brand, and firm. Doing so is not only misleading, but it is also a disservice to society, at least to the community surrounding the firm, and the environment, as major issues are not being addressed. A starting point, then, is to determine what corporate social responsibility is not; that is, the things or actions that are not synonymous with CSR, yet are commonly used interchangeably, including but not limited to:

- Philanthropy
- Giving back
- Helping others
- Recycling
- Paperless offices
- Training and development
- Energy saving

- Drives
- Social marketing
- Public relations strategy
- Unique selling point
- Volunteering
- Fund-raising
- Donations
- Cause-related marketing
- Family day
- Etcetera

The intent is not to say that these practices are bad, or that they should not be performed. In fact, they all may be fitted as pieces of the puzzle. The issue arises when they are used as justification that the firm performing them is socially responsible; in other words, they are certainly not the same as corporate social responsibility, especially if they are being used simply to give the idea that the firm is engaged in CSR. Take the example of a multinational firm that launches a moving and persuasive equality campaign. On the surface, the organization seems to be seeking to be and acting in a socially responsible manner; however, the same firm is also exploiting its collaborators with cost-reduction reasoning. Another common example is a firm that declares gender equality an element of their social responsibility; while women are hired for key decision making positions, they are paid less than their male counterparts. In a sense, these firms are attempting to appear to be socially responsible, yet, are in fact unethical.

Some may argue that if CSR practices are being advertised, then the firm is not genuinely socially responsible because there is an underlying objective to enhance profit. However, transparently communicating corporate social responsibility related practices is elemental (UNCTAD, 2008), as is the generation of profit (Lindgreen et al., 2009), to CSR; the problem emerges when the latter is their sole motivation. Profit enhancing objectives and strategies are by no means in conflict with business ethics, and social responsibility. Concerns increase when firms do not have a way to back up what they are communicating to the public or when it is clear that the intent is to obscure the truth. And, yes, stakeholders prefer to associate with authentic, transparent, honest, and just organizations, and are quick to call attention to those falling short of their expectations, are deceitful and misleading, and acting in an unlawful manner.

That being said, there are practices that are definitely not even close to social responsibility, yet are handled as if they were. A common example is tokenism (Kanter, 1977); it is a practice by which a minor effort is made to include a minimum number of people considered to be part of a minority group in order to appear as if there were a policy of inclusion, diversity, and equality. In other words, it is an illusion and a lie; it is discriminatory, unethical and by no means socially responsible; further, and just to be clear, meeting a quota is not better either. This practice occurs around the world, across industries, and is descriptive of an inadequate organizational structure, which is symptomatic of an ineffective corporate philosophy. Furthermore, engaging in these practices is conducive to poor corporate reputation, dissatisfied stakeholders, loss of legitimacy, and eventually profit loss. This occurs because both current and potential stakeholders eventually become aware of the latter, more so in the era of social media, and ultimately distrust the firm in question.

Therefore, although there are many organizations that have taken their role in society seriously, firms around the world are still lagging behind in their social responsibility. And, even though corporate social responsibility has become more important in developing countries (Li et al., 2010), it is still a non-issue for many organizations and countries. Of course, a first natural question is: how are firms tackling the issues of their Local Agenda? The quick answer is that they are not. Some may argue that these issues go beyond the scope of firms and that it is each government's responsibility to "fix" the problems; however, the context and conditions in which they operate compels their attention. The second question, then, comes as how can firms tackle these issues. The answer lays in a transformation of the holistic approach to corporate social responsibility in alignment with the Global Agenda.

Global Agenda

In September 2000, leaders from 189 member countries signed the Millennium Declaration (MDG-F, 2019), within which the Millennium Development Goals (MDGs) were framed. World leaders committed to the achievement of eight goals, by 2015, which aimed to: eradicate extreme poverty and hunger, achieve universal primary education, promote gender equality and empower women, reduce child mortality, improve maternal health, combat HIV/AIDS, Malaria and other diseases, ensure environmental sustainability, and attain global partnerships for development (UN, 2000), around the world. The call to world leaders' active participation and their pledge to reach these goals represented a major breakthrough in the creation of a global plan to achieve social growth and development. The Declaration was revolutionary because it was the first time development was recognized as a right; furthermore, the goals' success laid in three major characteristics: *i*) they were challenging (i.e., clear, measurable, and realist), *ii*) they provided a common language (i.e., transcended customary barriers), and *iii*) they were interdependent (i.e., significantly correlated) (WHO, 2019; SDGF, 2019). Kofi Annan, former Secretary General to the United Nations, established the UN Millennium Campaign (UNMC) in 2002 (UN System, 2017) and called citizens, organizations, business, institutions, and governments to action; therefore, the achievement of development began with the principle of inclusion.

Significant progress with the MDGs was made which led to their reassessment; in September 2015, the seventeen Sustainable Development Goals (SDGs) were established, and put into force in 2016 (UN, 2019). The goals include- no poverty, zero hunger, good health and well-being, quality education, gender equality, clean water and sanitation, affordable and clean energy, decent work and economic growth, industry innovation and infrastructure, reduced inequalities, sustainable cities and communities, responsible consumption and production, climate action, life below water, life on land, peace, justice and strong institutions, and partnerships for the goals (UN, 2019). These goals, and 169 targets, are elemental to the fulfilment of the 2030 Agenda for Sustainable Development, which is a "plan of action for people, planet and prosperity" (UN, 2015).

The SDG Action Campaign, built on the success of the UNMC, is an endeavor of António Guterres, UN Secretary General, and the UN Development Programme (UNDP) to "create awareness about the 2030 Agenda, empower and inspire people across the world to achieve the Sustainable Development Goals (SDGs) while generating political will, and help make the Goals attainable by 2030" (SDG Action Campaign, 2019). The call to action is much clearer and carries a sense of urgency like no other. The United Nations Intergovernmental Panel on Climate Change (IPCC) has stated that as global warming indicators continue to rise the year 2030 marks a deadline to prevent catastrophic effects on the planet (Miller and Croft, 2018). And, since climate change is elemental to sustainable development (UN, 2015), and the global goals are interdependent (WHO, 2019), it is imperative that the latter be met by the aforementioned deadline to counteract major effects on the planet, as well as guarantee the right to development.

Stakeholders

Stakeholders are any interested party that is affected by and can affect the dynamics of an organization (Oluwafemi and Oyatoye, 2012). The difference amongst the multiple definitions of stakeholders is that not all authors consider the same interested parties. For instance, some consider that the environment is not a stakeholder as it has no voice; however, it is argued that the environment is affected by and affects business dynamics, and most do not consider the firm as a stakeholder, yet it is argued that it has significant stake in society and the environment, as well as other stakeholders. As such, stakeholders include: collaborators, shareholders, consumers, investors, suppliers, regulatory authorities, community, environment, and the firm itself (Fernández and Rajagopal, 2014). Moreover, it is important to note that firms must consider both current and potential stakeholders, as taking only the former into account is shortsighted and, thus, impedes strategic planning and decision making. Optimal and prompt attention to potential stakeholders allows organizational leaders to anticipate needs and wants, and strategically map the steps to follow.

Stakeholders are also impacted by and impact the circumstances of the Local Agenda. It is clear that the particularities of the conditions in which they live affect their range of action and, therefore, decision making. Figure 1 illustrates the potential impact of the Local Agenda on current and potential stakeholders. For instance, a population stricken by poverty not only faces effects such as hunger, disease, poor health and sanitation, amongst others, but it is also restricted in regards to opportunities and choices. Furthermore, their possibility to actually consume products and/or services significantly decreases and, in cases of extreme poverty, consumption is moot. By any measure, ensuring the well-being of current and potential stakeholders, as well as their satisfaction with business dynamics is essential to the achievement of desired performance. Furthermore, if successful organizations tend to stakeholders' needs and wants (Werther and Chandler, 2011), and the latter include financial, environmental and social performance, then, it is clear that stakeholders ought to be central to firms' corporate and business strategy design and execution.

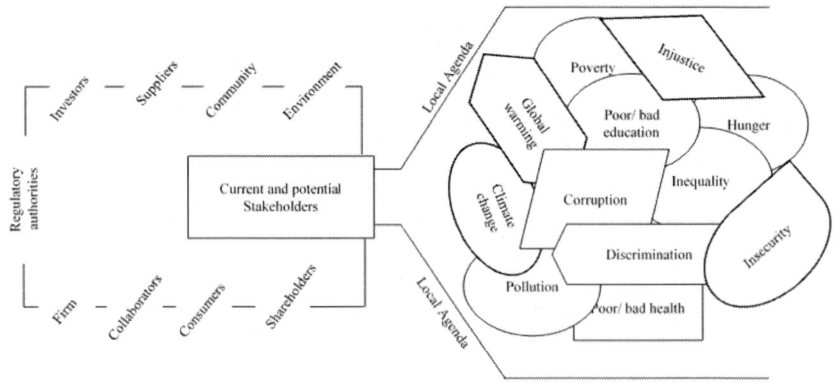

Figure 1. The local agenda and stakeholders.

So, what does *doing good business* mean today, and for the next 11 years? That is, in order to achieve the 2030 Agenda. For that matter, how do organizational leaders go about bridging the Global Agenda with business models? What has become clear is that the abovementioned call to action requests that every individual, organization, institution, business and government, proactively work towards the attainment of the seventeen Sustainable Development Goals. In such way that everyone is now considered a stakeholder in the 2030 Agenda. As a result, managing and exceeding stakeholders' expectations and needs must go beyond those related to offered products and/or services, the brand and the firm itself, and effectively incorporate indicators associated to well-being, sustainability, and prosperity. In order to do so, corporate social responsibility needs to be transformed and renovated because the current stance and approach firms are taking to be socially responsible remains ineffective.

CSR Redesign Model

A model for redesigning corporate social responsibility for a Global Agenda has been developed. The objective is to develop a definition for corporate social responsibility on the basis of a four-step process that effectively addresses imperative financial, social, and environmental issues that will lead to business and social growth and development. Figure 2 depicts the CSR redesign model for a Global Agenda. Before beginning the process, it is important that organizational leaders dispel the notion that corporate social responsibility is merely a marketing tactic aimed to greenwash and social wash the firm's brand. The model illustrates the inevitable impact of the destructive elements permeating society on stakeholders, including the firm. It then describes the steps required to internally adjust processes and procedures to tend to the firm's Local Agenda for stakeholder satisfaction and well-being, by means corporate social responsibility strategies aligned with the Global Agenda.

S_1: Examining Corporate Philosophy. A firm's corporate philosophy is its backbone; it includes the firm's mission, vision, values, objectives, strategies and tactics. It details who the organization is, its intentions and long-term plans, as well as beliefs, behavior and attitude towards internal and external stakeholders. As such, it is descriptive of the manner in which all business dynamics are performed; that is, its management approach. In a sense, it is a firm's overture which clearly depicts, amongst other things, if the firm is fit to effectively engage in corporate social responsibility. Thus, the first step in CSR redesign is the examination the firm's corporate philosophy to ensure alignment with corporate social responsibility undertakings.

S_2: Assessing the Local Agenda. Development of a global business model (Osiyevskyy at al., 2017) requires analysis of all internal and external variables that will impact and are intended to impact the achievement of strategic goals, productivity, and desired organizational performance. This requires a strategic foundation, corporate philosophy, and understanding of underlying forces, also known as the Local Agenda, and their impact on current and potential stakeholders. Meaning that, organizational leaders need to acknowledge social and environmental issues that pervade society, at least the community surrounding the firm in question. Thus, the second step in CSR redesign is the assessment of the firm's Local Agenda that is affecting and can affect stakeholder well-being and satisfaction with business dynamics.

S_3: Managing Stakeholders. The achievement of a firm's desired performance is certainly significantly correlated with stakeholder satisfaction. It has been argued that, today, a stakeholder approach definitely includes their well-being as well as their degree of satisfaction with the offered product and/or service, brand, and the firm itself. Since current and potential stakeholders' well-being is tied to the conditions that they live in, and the latter, in turn, directly impact their decision making choices and power, taking action is essential to business growth of the firm. Thus, the third step in CSR redesign is stakeholder management for the achievement of their well-being and satisfaction with the product, service, brand and firm.

S_4: Converging the Global Agenda. There are a series of external factors that negatively impact society and the environment, and although today they are a constant, there is no need for them to be perpetual. The 2030 Agenda for Sustainable Development and its call to action is a clear message that development is a right, there is no time to waste, and everyone needs to take a proactive stance for its achievement. As such, taking on the convergence of core attributes of corporate social responsibility with the seventeen Sustainable Development Goals enables the development of a business model fit for the current worldwide challenge all businesses and organizations face with no more than eleven years to overcome. This part of the process requires all internal stakeholders to engage in critical thinking in reference to current methodology for decision making. It is perhaps the most difficult task insofar as every decision needs to be questioned in function of the Global Agenda; that is, in order to ensure that the firm has effectively aligned all processes for optimal global results. Thus, the fourth step in CSR redesign is the convergence of the SDGs with corporate social responsibility strategies for the Global Agenda.

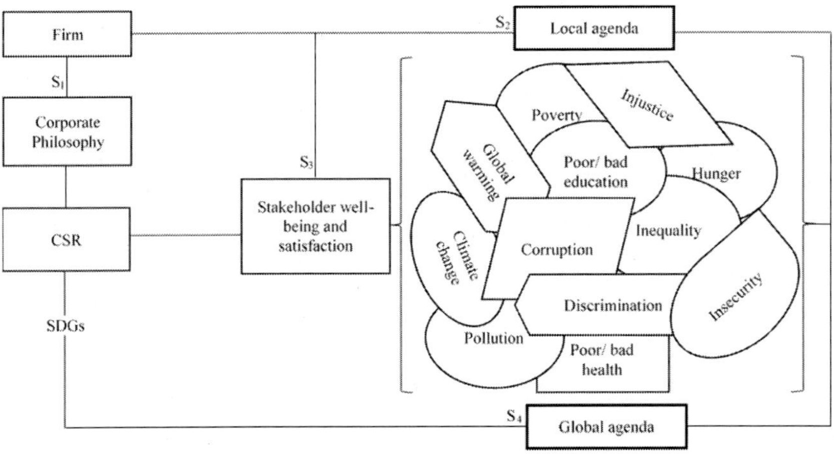

Figure 2. CSR redesign model for a global agenda.

As can be observed, the model is cyclical because each action of the process affects the next; this also means that as the firm takes action towards the alleviation of its Local Agenda, there will be a positive effect on the results of the Global Agenda. Therefore, contrary to popular belief, engaging in CSR is not a way to make firms responsible for "fixing" the world's ailments, or to free other stakeholders from their responsibility; they are not meant to change the world, but to rise to the occasion as agents of change. Hence, a redesigned holistic approach to CSR is defined as:

> The systematic process of examining a firm's corporate philosophy to ensure its suitability to be responsive to current and potential stakeholders' well-being and satisfaction by tackling the Local Agenda, by converging corporate social responsibility strategies with the Sustainable Development Goals to positively impact the Global Agenda.

CONCLUSION

In reality, corporate social responsibility mostly comes up in conversations centered on organizations that are not socially responsible or are caught engaging in unethical or questionable practices. Current and potential stakeholders are constantly being bombarded with news of both effects and impacts of humanitarian crises, and poor business decision making that ultimately worsens the latter. Every piece of information and data informs their decision making, attitude and behavior, and every environmental and societal setback dictates their scope of action. The issue is exceptionally straightforward, as the subject matter involves human beings and the planet; it is incomplex to decide to minimize the negative impacts, do no harm, and strive for successful outcomes that do not happen at the expense of the others.

The proposed model is able to bridge local and global objectives because of three particular elements, that is, it is holistic, stakeholder-centric, and cyclical. Adopting a holistic approach to CSR means taking everyone and every variable into account for decision making. Embracing a stakeholder approach to CSR means that their needs, wants, well-being, and satisfaction are priority; and, since the firm itself is also a stakeholder, there is no reason why it should not benefit in terms of productivity, performance, enhanced corporate reputation, and, of course, increased profit. In addition, appreciating the principle of causality means that every effort made internally to be responsive towards the alleviation of the Local Agenda, has a direct and positive impact on the results of the Global Agenda. Redesigning CSR in this manner, then, is in all interested parties' best interest, since not meeting the 2030 Agenda will certainly affect the very survival of businesses around the world. In other words, doing good business today means locally achieving business and social growth and development, for global social growth and development.

References

Abrams, F. K. (1951). Management's responsibilities in a complex world. *Harvard Business Review, XXIX*, 29-34.

Alniacik, U., Alniacik, E., & Genc, N. (2011, July-August). How corporate social responsibility information influences stakeholders' intentions. *Corporate Social Responsibility and Environmental Management, 18*(4), 234-245.

Bowen, H. R. (1953). *Social responsibilities of the businessman.* New York: Harper & Row.

Brown, T. J., & Dacin, P. A. (1997, January). The company and the product: Corporate associations and consumer product responses. *Journal of Marketing, 61*(1), 68-84.

Crane, A., & Matten, D. (2004, December). Questioning the domain of the business ethics curriculum. *Journal of Business Ethics, 54*(4), 357-369.

Crowther, D., & Seifi, S. (2018). *Redefining corporate social responsibility.* Bingley: Emerald Publishing Limited.

Dempsey, B. W. (1949, July). The roots of business responsibility. *Harvard Business review, 27*, 393-404.

Du, S., Bhattacharya, C. B., & Sen, S. (2010). Maximizing business returns to corporate social responsibility (CSR): The role of CSR communication. *International Journal of Management Reviews, 12*(1), 8-19.

European Commission. (2013, March 19). *A guide to communicating about CSR.* Retrieved October 2013, from http://ec.europa.eu/enterprise/policies/sustainable-business/files/csr/campaign/documentation/download/guide_en.pdf.

Fernández, A. M., & Rajagopal. (2014). Convergence of corporate social responsibility and business growth: An analytical framework. *International Journal of Business Excellence, 7*(6), 791-806.

Friedman, M. (1970, September 13). The social responsibility of business is to increase its profits. *The New York Times Magazine*.

Grundey, D. (2008). Applying sustainability principles in the economy. *Technological and Economic Development of Economy, 14*(2), 101-106.

Hart, S. M. (2010, April). Self-regulation, corporate social responsibility, and the business case: Do they work in achieving workplace equality and safety? *Journal of Business Ethics, 92*(4), 585-600.

Hopkins, M. J. (1999). *The planetary bargain: Corporate social responsibility comes of age.* London: Palgrave Macmillan.

Kanter, R. M. (1977). *Men and women of the corporation.* New York: Basic Books.

Li, S., Alon, I., Fetscherin, M., & Lattemann, C. (2010, October). Corporate social responsibility in emerging markets. *Management International Review, 50*(5), 635-654.

Lindgreen, A., Swaen, V., & Johnston, W. J. (2009, April). Corporate social responsibility: An empirical investigation of U.S. organizations. *Journal of Business Ethics, 85*(Suppl 2), 303-323.

Margolis, J. D., & Walsh, J. P. (2003). Misery loves companies: rethinking social initiatives by business. *Administrative Science Quarterly, 48*(2), 268-305.

McAdam, R., & Leonard, D. (2003). Corporate social responsibility in a total quality management context: opportunities for sustainable growth. *Corporate Governance, 3*(4), 36-45.

McWilliams, A., Siegel, D. S., & Wright, P. M. (2006). Corporate social responsibility: Strategic implications. *Journal of Management Studies, 43*(1), 1-18.

MDG-F. (2019). *What do we do. Millennium Development Goals*. Retrieved June 10, 2019, from MDG Achievement Fund: http://www.mdgfund.org/node/922.

Miller, B., & Croft, J. (2018, October 8). *Planet has only until 2030 to stem catastrophic climate change, experts warn*. Retrieved June 10, 2019, from CNN: https://edition.cnn.com/2018/10/07/world/climate-change-new-ipcc-report-wxc/index.html.

Moir, L. (2001). What do we mean by social corporate responsibility. *Corporate Governance, 1*(2), 16-22.

Mozes, M., Josman, Z., & Yaniv, E. (2011). Corporate social responsibility organizational identification and motivation. *Social Responsibility Journal, 7*(2), 311-314.

Ogola, F. O., & Dreer, T. (2012). Market share as an indicator for corporate social responsibility (CSR) spending: The study of Coca Cola's market. *African Journal of Business Management, 6*(6), 2234-2247.

Okwemba, E. M., Chitiavi, M. S., Egessa, R., Douglas, M., & Musiega, M. G. (2014, April). Effect of corporate social responsibility on organisation performance; Banking industry kenya, Kakamega County. *International Journal of Business and Management Invention, 3*(4), 37-51.

Oluwafemi, O. j., & Oyatoye, E. O. (2012). Corporate social responsibility: are firms in Nigeria actually giving back or giving away? *International Journal of Business Excellence, 5*(1/2), 116 - 129.

Osiyevskyy, O., Troshkova, M., & Bao, Y. (2017). What makes a global bsiness model? In A. Presenza, & L. R. Sheehan, *Geopolitics and strategic management in the global economy* (pp. 19-39). IGI Global.

Owen, C. L., & Scherer, R. F. (1993, June). Social responsibility and market share. *Review of Business, 15*(1), 11-16.

Porter, M. E., & Kramer, M. R. (2006, December). Strategy and society. The link between competitive advantage and corporate social responsibility. *Harvard Business Review, 84*(12), 78-92.

Quazi, A. M., & O'Brien, D. (2000, May). An empirical test of a cross-national model of corporate social responsibility. *Journal of Business Ethics, 15*(1), 33-51.

Schlusberg, M. (1969). Corporate legitimacy and social responsibility: The role of law. *California Management Review, 12*(1), 65-76.

Schwartz, M. S., & Carroll, A. B. (2003, October). Corporate social responsibility: A three-domain approach. *Business Ethics Quarterly, 13*(4), 503-530.

SDG Action Campaign. (2019). *Sustainable Development Goals Action Campaign*. Retrieved June 10, 2019, from About us: https://sdgactioncampaign.org/about-2/.

SDGF. (2019). *Millennium Development Goals*. Retrieved June 10, 2019, from Sustainable Development Goals Fund: https://www.sdgfund.org/mdgs-sdgs.

UN. (2000, September 8). *Millennium Summit of the United Nations*. Retrieved September 12, 2018, from Millenium Declaration: http://www.un.org/en/development/devagenda/millennium.shtml.

UN. (2015, September 25). *Transforming our world: The 2030 Agenda for Sustainable Development.* Retrieved June 10, 2019, from Resolution adopted by the General Assembly: https://www.un.org/ga/search/view_doc.asp?symbol=A/RES/70/1&Lang=E.

UN. (2019). *The Sustainable Development Agenda*. Retrieved June 10, 2019, from About: https://www.un.org/sustainabledevelopment/development-agenda/.

UN System. (2017, February 23). *United Nations Millennium Campaign*. Retrieved June 10, 2019, from United Nations: https://www.unsystem.org/content/united-nations-millennium-campaign.

UNCTAD. (2008). *Guidance on corporate responsibility indicators in annual reports.* New York & Geneva: United Nations Publication.

Utting, P. (2005). Corporate responsibility and the movement of business. *Development in Practice, 15*(3 & 4), 380-386.

Wang, H., Tong, L., Takeuchi, R., & George, G. (2016). Corporate social responsibility: An overview and new research directions. *Academy of Management Journal, 59*(2), 534-544.

WBCSD. (1999). *Sustainable consumption facts and trends. From a business perspective.* Retrieved June 8, 2019, from World Business Council for Sustainable Development. Business solutions for a sustainable world: http://www.wbcsd.org/pages/edocument/edocument details.aspx?id=142.

Werther Jr., W. B., & Chandler, D. (2011). Part I. Strategic corporate social responsibility. In W. B. Werther Jr., & D. Chandler, *Corporate social responsibility. Stakeholders in a Global Environment* (Second ed., pp. 1-19). California: SAGE Publications, Inc.

WHO. (2019). *Millennium Development Goals (MDGs)*. Retrieved June 10, 2019, from World Health Organization: https://www.who.int/ topics/millennium_development_goals/about/cn/.

Wokutch, R. E. (2014, December). Corporate social responsibility Japanese style, revisited. *The Journal of Corporate Citizenship*(56), 11-30.

Wood, D. J. (1991, October). Corporate social performance revisited. *The Academy of Management Review, 16*(4), 691-718.

Xueming, L., & Bhattacharya, C. B. (2006, October). Corporate social responsibility, customer satisfaction, and market value. *Journal of Marketing, 70*(4), 1-18.

Young, S., & Thyil, V. (2009, July). Governance, employees and CSR: Integration is the key to unlocking value. *Asia Pacific Journal of Human Resources, 47*(2), 67-185.

Zheng, Q., Luo, Y., & Wang, S. L. (2014, March). Moral degradation, business ethics, and corporate social responsibility in a transitional economy. *Journal of Business Ethics, 120*(3), 405-421.

In: Strategic Rethinking
Editors: Rajagopal et al.
ISBN: 978-1-53616-835-8

Chapter 4

RETHINKING AND TRANSFORMING LOCAL-GLOBAL CONVERGENCE: UPHOLDING OUR WORLD, REGENERATING OUR EARTH AND THE CALLING OF A PLANETARY *LOKASAMGRAHA*

Ananta Kumar Giri
Madras Institute of Development Studies,
Chennai, Tamil Nadu, India

ABSTRACT

Local-global convergence in business is linked to new ways of thinking about and constituting relations in self, culture society and the world including creating new pathways of relationship between business and society. It is helped by building upon alternative philosophical and cultural world views other than the dominant logic of profit maximization. This dominant logic of convergence in the name of globalization is leading to destruction of communities as well as Nature and no wonder today backlash against such policies of convergence are growing leading to movements of delinking and disruption in the global political economy. It is in this context that this chapter offers alternative ways of conceptualizing our visions and practices of local-global convergence by bringing the calling of upholding our world to our discourse. It argues that local-global convergence in business should help us uphold our world rather than destroy it in the name of profit maximization and market share. It also submits that such convergences should help us regenerate our Earth as our Earth is also dying in the face of climate change and other pressures. Upholding our world and regenerating Earth today is an act of right conduct today which is the other name of *Dharma*. I discuss the calling of Dharma below and suggest local-global business convergences should be attentive not only to narrow interpretations of law but also to calling of right conduct or *Dharma*.Local-global convergence can help to bring people from different backgrounds come together in a spirit of mutual enrichment including enrichment of knowledge and livelihood and for this we can build upon the vision and practice of *Lokasamgraha.* I offer these modes of thinking and practice below without a detailed discussion of their implications for local-global convergence. I offer these broad ways of thinking with a hope that scholars and practitioners of local-global convergence in business can have some alternative ways of thinking about and practicing these concerns.

Keywords: Globalization, local governance, spirituality, mind and cognition, management

UPHOLDING THE WORLD: *DHARMA* AND THE CALLING OF AN INTEGRAL PURSURARTHA

Upholding the world calls for a life of *Dharma*—right conduct and right living on the part of individuals as well as society. Dharma in Indic thought also has a cosmic dimension. *Dharma* is part of *Purusartha*—four fold end or goal of life characterized by *Dharma* (right conduct and right living), *Artha* (which means wealth as well as meaning giving rise to the challenge of meaningful wealth), *Kama* (desire) and *Moksha* (salvation). *Dharma* refers to modes of right conduct and thinking which is different from righteousness as a fixed system of classification between right and wrong especially imprisoned within a political and religious system of classification between righteous self and the unrighteous other. Upholding our world depends upon our living a life of *Dharma* and cultivating it in the lives of self and society and in our transactions such as business.It challenges us to understand the relationship between *Dharma* and law as well as justice and *Dharma* (Giri 2013) as *Dharma* challenges us to go beyond an anthropocentric *reduction* of justice and dignity and realize our responsibility not only to human beings but also to the non-humans[1]. Here we also need to explore the link between *Kama* and *Dharma*, desire and *Dharma* and cultivate integral Purusartha where elements of Purusartha such as Dharma and Kama are related to each other rather than isolated and delinked from each other leading to destruction and violence (see Kashyap 2001; Krishna 1991, 1997; Parel 2016 & Sri Aurobindo 2000). We can critically rethink our epics such as Mahabharata and Gilgamesh to understand the violence of *Kama* (desire) when it is not guided by *Dharma*. The burning of Khandava forest in Mahabharata is a manifestation of destructive desire of Agni, the god of fire. In the epic, Krishna and Arjuna instead of interrogating the desire of Agni to consume the forest of Khandava became an accomplish to this which constitutes the originary violence in Mahabharata[2]. Similar is the killing of Humamba, the guardian god of forest in the epic Gilgamish from Sumerian civilization, the earliest epic of humanity (Rifkin 2009). Our dominant models and practice of development, management and business practices are being accompanied by destruction of forests and Nature which today has brought us to the tipping point of climate change. It is a product of work of our *Karma* (action) and

---

[1]Gurucharan Das describes this need to cultivate dharma vis-a-vis in our relationship to non-humans in his interpretation of Mahabharata (see Das 2009).

[2] As the story goes, Agni wanted to consume the forest of Khandava and every time He would try to do, Indra would send rain and the nefarious desire of Agni could not be realized. Once Krishna, Arjuna and their friends were having a feast and Agni came in the disguise of a Brahmin and asked for food. Krishna and Arjuna agreed to this but then Agni showed his true self and asked for Khandava forest as his food. Krishna and Arjuna did not interrogate this desire of Agni rather became an accomplish in the fulfillment of his desire. As a result, the whole of Khandava forest was burnt and all the plants and animals were brutally killed. Only one snake Takhaka escaped. Taskaka wanted to take revenge and he helped to build the beautiful palace of the Pandavas in Hastinapuri seeing which Duryodhana became so envious that he wanted to overtake them by hook or by the crook. He invited Yudhishtira for the play of dice which as is well-known led not only to the loss of kingdom of the Pandavas but also to the attempt to disrobe Draupadi. Without the originary violence of the burning of Khadava the war of Mahaharata which led to the destruction and violence from both sides would not have happened (see Karve 1968).

Kama (desire) not restrained and uplifted by the spirit of *Dharma*. Today the survival of humanity itself is in question which urgently calls for transformation of such a destructive and violent model of development including business practices of local-convergence to be undertaken. In this context, we need to preserve both Nature and Humanity, biodiversity and cultural diversity in creative ways which can only secure true happiness for us what spiritually attuned scientist M.S. Swaminathan (2011) calls biohappiness. Biohappiness can make a creative link between *Anna* (food) and *Ananda* (bliss) which help us to nurture and uphold our body, soul, self, other and the world.Local-global convergence should aim at increasing biohappiness of people and community by creating a proper balance between economics and ecology and contributing to preservation and flourishing of cultural and biodiversity (see Sahi 2017).

Regenerating Our Earth

Upholding our word is accompanied by manifold efforts of regenerating our Earth. Our Earth today has been under stress and with climate change it is now bereft of green cover in many parts of our world which threaten human life on Earth. Our Earth is our Mother but sometimes we look at Earth as only a dead Matter and with inspiration from Gaia cosmology which also touches science and religious and spiritual traditions of the world we can relate to Earth with sacredness. This is the spirit of Pope Francis' (2015) encyclical *Laudato Si* and Dallmayr's (2011) meditation in his *Return to Nature?* It also calls us to plant seeds of trees and life on and with Earth. Regenerating our earth is connected to climate care movement in which we all can take part (Swaminathan 2011).It calls for creative discovery of our roots and also a cross-fertilization between roots and routes. Regenerating our Earth calls for regenerating our both roots and routes in creative and transformative ways and creating a new Earth Sastra where Arthasastra (the knowledge of wealth) would work in accordance with the spirit of Earth Sastra (knowledge and reverence for Earth (Giri 2019; Sharma 2013). It calls for new ways of Earth work which also consists of new ways of memory works and memory meditations in which we can hear the groaning of our Mother Earth and contribute to Her healings especially as ravaged by war and climate change.

LOKASAMGRAHA

Lokasamgraha is an important invitation for self, social and cosmic transformation from the Indic tradition and it appears briefly in Srimad Bhagvad Gita twice. It is usually translated as well-being of all but it also refers to the process of gathering—gathering or collecting of *loka*—people[3]. It is creative and critical gathering of people and the accompanying process of mutual care that leads to well-being of people. As a process of gathering it is not just confined to the public, the public sphere—or public political processes. It also involves in an integrally inter-linked manner gathering of soul—*atmasamgraha.Lokasamgraha* and *atmasamgraha*—gathering of soul and people—lead to a creative gathering of society not just as a mechanical entity but as a living process of critique, creativity and transformation. It also leads to creative regeneration of commons and a cosmic mobilization of energy. As K.B. Rao writes: "If the term *Samgraha* is taken as a verb, it stands for the act or process. But taken as a noun it stands for Reality in its dynamic Being." *Lokasamgraha* challenges us to realize that our life, self, society and the world have a cosmic dimension and our cosmos is not just a dead entity but a living evolving process. *Lokasamgraha* challenges us for a transformation of our cosmology from a

---

[3] As K.B. Rao writes:

The term occurs twice in the third chapter of the Gita, the Karma Yoga (3.20, 25). Here are some of the most prominent readings:

Holding people together (Sri Aurobindo).
World Maintenance, i.e. the world order (Radhakrisnan).
Integration of the World (Natarajaguru).
Performing Action with an Eye to Universal Action (B.G. Tilak).
Extending loka-samgraha to include salvation for all.
Establishing *Ahimsa* as essential to Loka-samgraha (Gandhi).

mechanical one to a living and a spiritual one.[4] *Lokasamgraha* is not confined among human beings, it includes all beings and therefore challenges us to go beyond an anthropocentric concept of welfare and to "widen the implications of *lokasamgraha* to cover the universal order of Being" (Rao 2016).

Lokasamgraha challenges us to realize well-being and happiness for all but for this we are all invited to be creative in our strivings and struggles and it can not be left to the others, society and state. At the heart of *Lokasamgraha* is care and responsibility which connects the vision and practice of *Lokasamgraha* in the Western political traditions such as in the works of Hannah Arendt and in the Chinese philosophy of *Tian-Xia*—All Under Heaven (Dallmayr 2015).

Lokasamgraha challenges us not only to maintain the world but to uphold it. This upholding is crucially dependent upon right living in self and society which is facilitated by appropriate social policy and public actions as well as by the strivings and preparation of the soul.

It also challenges us to regenerate our earth by planting new seeds and trees of life in the landscape of despair and destruction especially of climate change.

---

[4] Lokasamgraha appears in Bhagavad Gita and here what K.B. Rao writes deserves our careful consideration:

The cue for the philosophy of the Bhagavad Gita is concealed behind a most significant expression which is used only twice in the text, but which sums up the whole perspective not only of the philosophy of the Gita but Reality as such, namely *loka-samgraha*. This is yet another significant term, which stands for the same, if divested of the narrow colorings put upon it, and that is *dharma-sangraha*, which the Lord [Lord Sri Krishna] terms dharma-samsthapana (4.8). If taken in its widest sense against the background of the philosophy of the text itself and of the personality who says he has incarnated to achieve it. It is not simply overcoming the dissipating forces of irreligion and immortality and stabilizing righteousness of a certain kingdom at a given time, but has behind it the very basic truth of consolidating the more fundamental truth, viz., universal order, harmony and growth, transcending the limits of relative grievances and feelings, misunderstanding as well as understandings, customs, practices and even their laxities, linking all these with the larger sinews of Reality operating outside and around human living and extending it into the possibilities of all existence. Dharma is not only *Rta*, but also *Satya*. It is order and Reality. In addition, how are we to understand the dynamics of it in its being and continuance of being, i.e. in its eternality, other than by the most apt expression *loka-samgraha*?

The Calling of *Lokasamgraha*

Loka means both space and time and *Lokasamgraha* calls a creative gathering of space and time with and beyond their contemporary capitalist production as commodities and alienating entities. *Lokasamgraha* challenges us for creative rethinking and reconstitution of space and time where we can gather together without anxiety and help each other realize our potential—our evolutionry potential (see Giri 2012, 2013).Our space and time in modernity as well as in contemporary late modern times are determined by logics of capital but *Lokasamgraha* challenges us to nurture our space and time as pregnant capable of generating new lives and relationships and not just reproduce the capitalist relations of power and profit. *Lokasamgraha* is also a process of knowing about each other and knowing oneself. It involves creative epistemic practices of mutual knowing and knowing self, other and the world. It also involves ontological processes of self-realization, co-realizations, self-development as well as co-development. Processes of being together in *Lokasamgraha* involve manifold creative movements of ontological epistemology of participation going beyond the dualism of epistemology and ontology which bedevils modernist science, subjectivity and politics (Giri 2017).*Lokasamagraha* also involves movements across our initial positions and locations so that we do not become fixed and imprisoned within our positions and we can stand, seat and meditate in other positions and others' positions. Such transpsitional movements create possibility of a new subject formation what be called a transpoistional subjectivation rather than only a positioned subjectivity. Similarly objectivity in *Lokasamgraha* is also not fixed; it emerges out of transpositional movements across positions. *Lokasamgraha* calls for cultivation of a new subjectivity and objectivity which can be called transpositional subjectobjectivity (Giri 2016). It challenges us to go beyond the dualism of subjectivity and objectivity, ontology and epistemology. Going beyond the dualistic logic of modernity, *Lokasamgraha* calls for cultivation of a non-dual logic and path of living, a multi-valued logic and path of living of autonomy and interpenetrations (Mohanty 2000; Giri 2017).

Upholding our World and Regenerating Our Worth: Planetary *Lokasamagraha* and New Politics and Spirituality of Co-Creativity and Co-Creation

Lokasamgraha is related to generation of well-being and thus is at the root of this heart- touching aspiration and prayer: *Lokah Samastah Sukhino Bhavantu* which means let all people and all being be happy. But how can we be happy? What is the meaning of happiness when it becomes a slave of quick satisfaction and consumption. Can we be happy without being creative? Creativity may be the foundation of well-being, creative self and creative society. Thus along with the familiar prayer *Lokah Samastah Sukhino Bhavantu* we can strive and pray new prayers*: Lokah Samastah Srujana Bhavantu*—let all people be creativity, *Lokah Samastah Srata Bhavantu*—let all people be creators, *Lokah Samastah Saha Srasta Bhavantu*—let all people be co-creators. *Lokasamgraha* calls for multi-dimensional co-creative movements in self, society and cosmos to be creative in self and society, religion, politics, spirituality and every day. It also challenges to envision and practice local-global practices including practices of convergence in ways which lead to upholding our world, regenerating our earth and realization of *Lokasamgraha*.

References

Agarwala, S.P. 1995. *The Social Message of the Gita Symbolized as Lokasamgraha.* Delhi: Motilal Benarasidass.

Dallmayr, Fred. 2011. *Return to Nature?* An Ecological Counter History. Lexington: University of Kentucky Press.

Dallmayr, Fred. 2015. *Against the Apocalypse: Recovering Humanity's Wholeness.* Lanham, MD: Lexington Books.

Das, Gurucharan. 2009.*The Difficulty of Being Good.* Delhi: Penguin.

Giri, Ananta Kumar. 2019. *Weaving New Hats: Our Half Birthdays*. Delhi: Studera Press.

Giri, Ananta Kumar. 2016. *"Transforming the Subjective and the Objective: The Calling of Transpositional Subjectobjectivity"*. Madras Institute of Development Studies: Paper.

Giri, Ananta Kumar. 2013. *Knowledge and Human Liberation: Towards Planetary Realizations*. London: Anthem Press.

Giri, Ananta Kumar. 2012. *Sociology and Beyond: Windows and Horizons*. Jaipur: Rawat Publications.

Giri, Ananta Kumar. (ed.) 2017. *Pathways of Creative Research: Towards a Festival of Dialogues*. Delhi: Primus.

Giri, Ananta Kumar. (ed.) 2019. *Cross-Fertilizing Roots and Routes*. New York. Palgrave Macmillan.

Karve, Irawati. 1968. *Yuganta: The End of An Epoch*. Pune.

Kashyap, Anand. 2001.*Sociological Concerns: Issues in Cognitive and Development Anthropology*. Jaipur: Book Enclave.

Krishna, Daya. 1997. *Prolegomena to Any Future Historiography of Cultures and Civilizations*. New Delhi: Project of History of Indian Science, Philosophy and Culture and Munshiram Manoharlal.

Krishna, Daya. 1991. *"Time, Truth and Transcendence"*. In History, Culture and Truth: Essays Presented to DP Chattopadhyaya (eds.), Daya Krishna and K. Satchidananda Murty, pp. 323-326. Delhi: Kalki Prakashan.

Mohanty, J.N. 2000. *Self and Other: Philosophical Essays*. Delhi: Oxford U. Press.

Parel, Anthony J. 2016. *Pax Gandhiana: The Political Philosophy of Mahatma Gandhi*. New York: Oxford University Press.

Pope Francis. 2015. *Encyclical Letter Laudato Si of the Holy Father on Care for our Common Home*. Rome: Vatican.

Rao, K.B. 2016. *The Bhagavad Gita As The Philosophy of Loka-Samgraha or Cosmic Consolidation*. Bengaluru: Darpan Books.

Rifkin, Jeremy. 2009. *Empathic Civilization: The Race to Global Consciousness in a World in Crisis*. New York: Jeremy P. Tarcherer.

Sahi, Jyoti. 2017. *"Art and Ecological Sustainability: Sustaining the Imagination"*. In Cultural Spaces for Sustainable Futures (ed.) Siddhartha. Bangalore: Pippal Tree.

Sharma, Subhash. 2013. *A New Earth Sastra.* Bangalore: IBA Publications.

Swaminathan, M.S. 2011. *In Search of Biohappiness: Biodiversity and Food, Health and Livelihood Security*. Singapore: World Scientific.

Sri Aurobindo. 2000. *Thoughts and Aphorisms*. Pondicherry: Sri Aurobindo Ashram.

In: Strategic Rethinking
Editors: Rajagopal et al.
ISBN: 978-1-53616-835-8

Chapter 5

BUSINESS MODEL *VS.* LEAN CANVAS IN THE GLOBAL – LOCAL SCENARIO: A CONCEPTUAL STUDY

M. Pushpa[*] *and Y. Lakshman Kumar*[†]
Hyderabad Business School, GITAM (Deemed to be University),
Hyderabad, India

ABSTRACT

Entrepreneurship is the buzzing word in this modern era which is a dream role for many people globally but very few of them transform their dreams to reality. There are many factors towards the success and survival of the micro and small business. The very first step in any startup is to have a blue print of the business that gives an idea about the credentials required to start business and succeed, which is called as Business Modelwhich is the key for any startups. The paper tells about the factors that are important

[*] Corresponding Author's Email: pushpa.machani1234@gmail.com; M. Pushpa, Research Scholar, Hyderabad Business School, GITAM.
[†] Corresponding Author's Email: lakshman7@gmail.com; Y. Lakshman Kumar, Dean and Director of GITAM Hyderabad Business School.

towards the success and sustainability towards the entrepreneurial business and the type of plan required for each business according to the complexity levels. Paper emphasizes on the importance of Business Model and Lean canvas. The Study on the scenarios where Business Model and Lean Canvas play major role is discussed. Researcher suggests with a framework that exhibits the importance of the Business Model and the Lean Canvas at various scenarios.Finally the paper suggests the conceptual model for 'Ease of Business in Micro and Small Enterprises'.

Keywords: Entrepreneurship, business model and lean canvas

INTRODUCTION

In the current global scenario every individual want to not only be economically independent but also tries to be a job giver than a job seeker. Thus entrepreneurship has been chosen as a career by many throughout the world. Entrepreneurship not only helps in creating employment opportunities but also becomes a helping hand in economic development of the country. An entrepreneur aspirant to be a successful person in his career should plan carefully about the business which is going to be started.

There are many factors which transform an entrepreneurial aspirant to an entrepreneur. Business Model is being one of them. Business Model is a document act as a blue print that depicts the roadmap of the proposed business in detail. Business Model plays an important role in an entrepreneurs' life without which the business may not take-off. A Business Model rationalizes towards the conceptual structure, the viability of the product or the service and provides the information about organizational operations, money making and value achievement. Lean Canvas is the simple problem-solution fit with back envelop calculations that take very little time to draft. There is no such hard and fast rule that startup should follow a particular business model or should follow only Lean Canvas. Any startup can impart either Business Model or the Lean Canvas according to the need and the requirement.Main purpose of the paper is to explore on various factors that contributes towards setting up various businesses, success and sustainability of the business. Next level of the study focuses towards the importance of Lean Canvas and Business Model. Thus a detailed study on the Business Model and Lean Canvas is made in order to identify whether Business Plan or Lean Canvas suits best for the micro and small business. Study continues with an objective of distinguishing Lean Canvas and Business Model. Literature from various aspects of entrepreneurship was reviewed in the further process.

LITERATURE REVIEW

Thorough literature review was focused on gaining the knowledge in various important factors contributing for the business startup, development, success and sustainability. Kulkarni (2018) surveyed that in the 'Global Entrepreneurship Development Institute' (GEDI) 137 countries were ranked as per the Global Entrepreneurship Index. All the countries were ranked on the criteria of 14 parameters that include: risk capital availability, Go global, intension towards growth, innovation in the process, innovation in the product, overcome competition in the market, manpower, technology updating, opportunity identification, cultural support, network building, risk acceptance and startup skills. GEDI stated that India was ranked 68 out of 137 countries thus considering a "middling" performance. Added to this he also mentioned that as per the Asia Pacific region, India is again in the middle position, 14th out of 28 countries. Leadingplayers include Australia being the first position, Hong Kong holds the second position and Taiwan at third position. India falls below China (9th) and more established regional economies such as Korea (4th) and Japan (6th) in the region.

Afandi *et al.* (2016) explored the role played by social capital in entrepreneurship includi ng the multidimensional and multi stage entrepreneurial process like trust, norms and networks. Their study revealed that social capital is not always solely unique to the various stages of the entrepreneurial process. They also mentioned that social networks of an individual play the most important role in the entire process of entrepreneurship. Babalola et al. (2016) examined various factors which hinder the micro and small business growth amongst the rural entrepreneurs and found out that there should be a collaborative network with the individual entrepreneurs, government agencies and entrepreneurial associations for resolving typical barriers. A study on various factors and their influence on the farmers' ecological behaviors were made by (Ji-xue et al. 2018). Their study showed that, the ecological protection behavior includes five paths namely: ecological emotion, ecological knowledge, ecological perceived severity effects, indigenous factors role and perception of individuals affected by the ecological attitudes.

A study towards the successful entrepreneurial management by Kirchenhofer and Lechner (2011) says that a successful entrepreneurial management depends on the entrepreneurs and the investors. They also highlighted that the importance of parties should resist to the inducement of the popular saying "never change a winning team" and emphasized towards the importance of having appropriate competencies for every new venture which means that the habitual entrepreneurs can have the possibility of entrepreneurial experience usage. Fisher et al. (2014), recognized the presence of both individual and macro level indicators. Their study says that macro and micro level indicators recognize an important relationship between the entrepreneur and their venture. Impact of personal and environmental factors on the success of an entrepreneur is given by Gomezelj (2013). He mentioned that political, cultural, social, and demographical factors also have an equal impact on entrepreneurial success. He identified certain personality traits like desire towards independence, self-confidence, locus of control, thrive towards achievement, propensity of risk taking, information and knowledge and finally opportunity recognition which contribute the micro and small business success. He identified that financial support from the government in the form of programs and policies, education and training to start and run the business, professional infrastructure to run the business, openness and competitiveness towards the local market, access towards physical infrastructure and finally norms and social culture are important for starting the business.

Venugopal (2015) says that women play a significant role in continuing their firm life cycle by benefiting from active involvement in their micro and small ventures by their family. According to Chen and Chang (2013), the entrepreneurial success competence of an entrepreneur plays a vital role where competence is understood in terms of leadership, skill, experience and manpower. They also mentioned motivation as another important component which requires innovation and pioneering. Hence, it may be inferred that the creative factor of an entrepreneur lies in the opportunities of technology and market, effective application of scarce resources, enduring risk, ambiguity and uncertainty. It was outlined from them that entrepreneurial experience, manpower and creativity has a positive relation towards venture profitability. He also supported many reasons for the human capital importance in the creation of a new venture, its performance and enhancement.

A research model for the 'New Product Success' (NPS) was proposed by Wang (2014) based on 'Environmental Turbulence' (ET) and 'Entrepreneurial Orientation' (EO) which includes risk taking and innovativeness. He mentioned that ET in business terms means any unpredictable and the highly varied event occurs in the environment for the industry in which the business operates. Thus he mentioned that the main objective of any new product development lies in the steady market tapping which generates sufficient revenue for the business growth. It can be inferred that ET was found to be the one, which exerts strong and positive influence on risk taking, innovativeness and pro-activeness which is also called as EO, finally leading to the NPS in an entrepreneurial journey for a new venture (Fisher et al. 2014) conceptualized the entrepreneurial success with the help of certain indicators. Indicators proposed by him include: satisfaction towards the life and the business, continuous growth, passion, need for achievement, locus of control, personal involvement in the operations of the business, achievement focused, reactive towards interpersonal constraints and thrive towards business sustainability. Babalola (2016) selected a few factors that impede the growth of rural entrepreneurs. They are: operational challenges with respect to the business like transportation and roads, poor location of business premises which are the part of the infrastructure. He also mentioned a few challenges with respect to the skill development like fail to employ the skillful people and challenges with respect to the support which means that no resources for assisting the small business growth and absence of small business education, challenges with respect to the workforce like not capable of retaining the young employees. He highlighted certain personal challenges like time pressure which leads to the imbalance of work and family, failed to prepare the Business Model in order to gain the financial support from banks due to accounts and management skill deficiency.

Amrita (2017) considered a few factors to measure the success rate of women entrepreneurs in the micro and small business sector. They are:

> Government factors: Government assistance, policies and programs, training, subsidies and financial support by the government.Individual factors: family commitment, knowledge, skill and competence, labor attitudes, problem solving capability, work life balance, leadership and working, creativity and innovation, risk taking ability and work ethics. Social Factors: Inspiration and support from the society, empower entrepreneurial activity, drive and sustain, societal perception bout the women entrepreneurs and networking management in entrepreneurship. Economic and social factors: Profit generation capability,Cost control, production opportunities, Project resources, innovation and Research and Development. Market related factors: capacity to pay, value relationship with the customers, customer assistance, new product introduction, differentiation among the products and services, market acceptance, political and social environment and effective coordination among various stake holders. Technological and infrastructural Factors: state-of-art and access to the new technology, innovation, Information and communication Technology for facilitating the resource allocations, technological infrastructure creation,network development activities, websites and communication material.Management Factors: gender empowerment, Qualitative recruitment, talent management, mentoring, motivation, decision making skills and training.

Gasper (2017) from his research found out that many factors either drive or depress the entrepreneurial activities. He mentioned that large firms promote the monopolistic interests in order to elite the entrepreneurial class where a dynamic system should come in to the market with free competition and creativity. Thus he says that entrepreneurs need many resources including infrastructure, qualitative information and communication technology and research and development for business activity engagement.

Osborne (1995) identified a few essential elements for the success of an entrepreneurial firm with a classic entrepreneurial strategy. He stated that resourceful entrepreneurial opportunities lead in different directions that focus on linking the firm innovatively. Few essential elements highlighted in his study include: customers life style, productivity performance, job creation and expansion of the existing firms, entrepreneurs themselves who has the potential to create and reinvest wealth for their benefit, competitors whose approach is to respond dynamically for the strategies of any social trends and demographic patterns. Environmental and personal factor influence on the entrepreneur performance was studied by (Gomezelj 2013). It was found that there are many reasons for the personal factors arise from individualslike traits of each individual and personality traits which are the root cause for the establishment of the firm. He also mentioned in his study that therc could be various contexts through which environmental factors arise in the political, social and cultural context.

(Scarmozzino and Corvello 2016) researched the importance of Professional Social Networking Websites (PSNW) as learning for the entrepreneurs in high-tech startups. He says that the most valuable and intangible asset for any operations and dynamic learning is knowledge through which startups can gain the opportunity of initiating knowledge acquisition practice thus facilitating knowledge seeking for entrepreneurial learning contribution. (Melendez and Lorenzo 2017) identified certain factors as inhibitors and enablers of female indigenous micro and small Entrepreneurs along with the role of social capital that include: Societal Level in which cultural and institutional dimensions were considered, Community Level in which social capital and opportunity identification along with the values as dimensions. Individual Level that comprises of education and family along with personality traits were considered (Fischer 2017) researched on various motivational aspects of entrepreneurial success and the study revealed that motivation is one of the important factors for the sustainability.

Business Model is a very important strategic tool for the entrepreneurs for the success of their entrepreneurial journey. Messmer (2016) in his study found that Business Model helps an entrepreneur in raising the money for the business, helps in making decisions at the right time, supports in identifying the potential weakness and able to communicate the business ideas with stakeholders (Cremades 2016) opined in his study that it is not mandatory to have a Business Model at the initial stage to get funding. He further added that traditional Business Model may not work at times unless there is more clarity regarding the business that has to be started.

According to the Harvard Business Review (HBR) Entrepreneurs succeed when they are flexible enough to respond the opportunities. They should also start their business after getting the clarity towards original customer. These could be few reasons where Business Model written at the initial stage and ends up being fable.

Right way to design a Business Model is to conduct a pilot study at the initial stage for gaining the market knowledge says Nienhaus (2015). He also mentioned in his study that if the result is positive then the financial part should focus on the customers count organization is expecting to attract, finally the revenue and profit. Adding further he mentioned in his study that pilot study helps in bridging the gap where market information needs to prove the financial stability which helps in understanding the customers and the market thus helps towards the improvement of a product/service. Xie and Jiuchang (2016) explores in their research that for the entrepreneurial activities female entrepreneurs play a significant source of growth. They stated that female techpreneurs are prioritized due to labor market's nature where their role is to promote stability and prosperity of the economy which has a positive effect on the performance of new venture (Rantso 2015) in his research found out that rural, non-farm and small scale enterprises face many challenges which results in their poor performance. He also mentioned about few challenges they face which include networks, local market production, unskilled labor, capital scarcity, scattered business and so on. He opined that global market should focus on less developed countries so that micro and small businesses rely strong towards competitive advantage which finally leads to market strengths, technology and efficient production process.

Structure, culture, learning, coordination, stress and control are the marketing specific linkages in addressing the New Product Development (NPD) says (Menon 2002). He mentioned that outcomes of NPD are related to traditional metrics of performance which are important drivers in Organization Learning process for micro and small business. He also told that from the management perspective organizational learning is a cumulative experience. Ethics plays an important role in the business sustainability, at the same time business plan is more important for any entrepreneur to start the venture as opined by (Connor 2015). The below figure 1 depicts the final pilot study outcome which tells the ability to generate profit will be tested and concludes if the Business Plan is workable or not. Lean Canvas is an adaptation of Business Model Canvas by Alexander Osterwalder which *AshMaurya* created in the Lean Startup spirit. Lean Canvas empathizes on actionable and entrepreneur-focused Business Model.

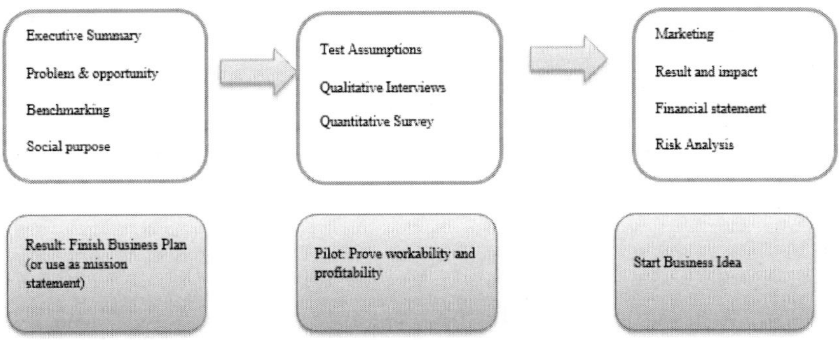

Figure 1. Pilot study output of a business plan (Source: Nienhaus 2016).

It focuses on '9 blocks' include: I) Problem, II) Most Viable Product, III) Unfair advantage, IV) Key metrics V) Customer segments, VI) Channels, VII) Unique Value Proposition, VIII) Cost structure and IX) Revenue streams.

(Maurya 2012) explains each block in the canvas as:

- **Problem** is the primary one to be identified for any business without which a business cannot proceed forward.

- Once the problem is identified corresponding list of alternative solutions have to be listed and the final solution is considered based on the **MVP**(Most Viable Product) which means the reason for the customer has to pay for the product or service that is offered.
- **Unfair Advantage** tells about the way one will defend from their competitors, which means that what is the key advantage which one has that cannot be copied or extracted from the competitors.
- **Key Metrics** are the core activities of the business which plays a crucial role that right metric identification carry the business towards the success path
- **Customer Segments** is the customer to be targeted whose needs are going to be satisfied.
- **Channels** are the ways through which the products or services reach the customers.
- **Unique Value Proposition** says that how the product or service is different from the competitor products or services
- **Cost structure** in the canvas is not in detailed but can be back envelop calculations which give a rough estimate of the cost that is going to be incurred in the business.
- **Revenue Streams** tells about the channels through which revenue gets generated once the business gets started.

Lean Canvas gives defensibility of the business in the form of unfair advantage, market size in the form of customer segments, Traction in the form of Key Metrics and Margins in the form of Cost Structure and Revenue Streams. Thus Lean Canvas plays an important role for any business start-up at its initial stages for the smooth functioning of the operations.

BUSINESS MODEL *VS.* LEAN CANVAS

(Mourya 2015) narrated the below points about Business Model and Lean Canvas in the context of Lean Startup Spirit. The points serve as important indicators and may be used by the entrepreneurs for their new ventures. His contributions focused towards the importance of Business Model and Lean Canvas and the way they gain advantages over each other:

- To prepare a Business Model at least 8 weeks of time is required. Traditional plan follows the waterfall model, where the analysis of the market has to be done, then planning has to be done based on the outcome of the market analysis and finally the plan gets executed. Modern days' Business Model is a continuous process where the model prioritizes and tests at each phase. Lean Canvas is a fast approach that takes 20 minutes where a concise distilling of the business essence is incorporated in a single sheet with the back envelops calculations and portable in nature.
- Lean canvas is a replacement of Business Model. It is a single sheet with nine blocks whereasthe Business Model runs into pages in which the content of the plan is in detail.
- Stakeholders wish to see the quantifiable objective i.e., detailed financials in the plan which is there in Business Model but missing in Lean Canvas.
- Business Model holds good if the entrepreneurs' needs to raise the capital from the investors, needs support from the consultants, investors and advisors. Lean Canvas purely focuses towards entrepreneurial activities alone.
- Lean Canvas meant purely for the startups whereas Business Model works for boththe new and the existing businesses. Business Model lays emphases on customer relationships, customer segments and channels through which entrepreneur can approach the customers. Lean canvas emphasizes more towards customer segments and channels but doesn't focus on the customer relationship.
- Business Model gives the clear picture of the list of the financial sources required, infrastructure needed, details of the manpower, layout plan and so on. Lean canvas doesn't focus on any of these which are considered to be the core activities for the medium and the large business.

- Lean canvas includes an important block called unfair advantage that tells about the unique strength of the business that cannot be copied by the competitors whereas the Business Model doesn't include the same.
- Business Model adopts constructive analysis, discussion and creativity whereas Lean canvas is a simple problem-solution approach that entrepreneur follows step wise.

Thus it can be inferred that though Business Plan and Lean Canvas serve the same purpose and have many similarities, they slightly differ in certain scenarios. Next section focuses towards the scope of the study to figure out areas in which study is explored.

Scope of the Study

The paper draws inputs for Lean canvas from the review of the existing literature. The analysis in this paper is from the literature of various studies. There could be limitations from the data that is to be mentioned as important.

This paper gives conceptual information which can further be extended to the empirical research. Two models that are mentioned in the paper i.e., Business Model and Lean Canvas can be applicable to the startups of various business in different sectors and can also be experimented with various businesses bifurcated according to the scalability confined to particular geographical location. A comparative study can be made on the Business Model and Lean Canvas with empirical data of various businesses at different geographical locations.

Objectives of the Study

- Comprehend the differences between Business Model and Lean canvas.

➢ Analyze the types of the suitability of the Business Model and Lean Canvas for the type of the business.

Below figure depicts the importance of Business Model and Lean Canvas. It also gives the clarity about the advantages of each Business Model vs. Lean Canvas:

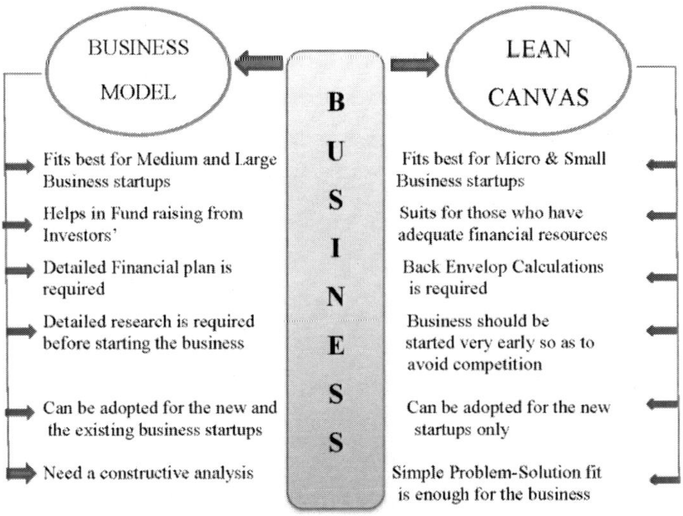

Figure 2. Comparision between business model and lean canvas.

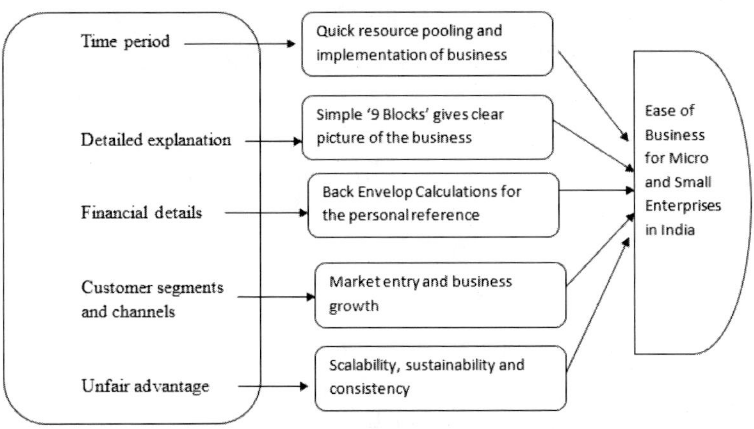

Figure 3. Conceptual model for ease of business for micro and small enterprises in India.

The above figure gives a clear picture about the importance of Business Model and Lean Canvas. It highlights the areas in which both Business Model and Lean Canvas plays a vital role and how they are differentiated from each other. The above figure imparts more information about the appropriation of each style with respect to the type of the business. The above figure gives a clear picture about the model that can be implemented in Micro and Small Enterprises in order to have the ease of business. It articulates that for small and micro businesses quick resource pooling with the precise business blueprint with nine blocks and simple back envelop calculations is enough. Most of the times Small and Micro business doesn't depend on any financial companies for fund raising, so, inspite of having detailed financials, it is enough to have back envelop calculations. Market entry and business growth strategies should be simple and straight with their unfair advantage as a highlight. The above model can be tested for the new micro and small startups in India.

DISCUSSION

From the above model it is clear that Business Model suits for the medium and large startups. As those startup entrepreneurs need to raise fund from the investors they prepare a detailed financial plan to impress the investors. Whereas Lean Canvas fits in to the micro and small businesses that do not require any financial assistance from the external people and can proceed with simple back envelop calculations. To start a medium or large scale business, detailed research on various factors such as environment, competitors, available substitute products or services need to be studied and the same should be part of the Business Model. Lean canvas doesn't require all these because small entrepreneurs start the business very early in order to avoid competition. Business Model suits for the new and the existing businesses where as Lean Canvas suits for the new business alone. Business Model is a constructive analysis which takes at least two months dedicated time to prepare where as Lean Canvas takes hardly 20 minutes for its preparation.

FUTURE RESEARCH IMPLICATIONS

This framework can be considered for all the businesses irrespective of the type, scalability, industry and so on. An extension to the same can be considered for the empirical research. Lean canvas can be prepared for the small businesses and Business Model for the medium or the large business in various industries. Same study can be made as a comparative study.

CONCLUSION

Lean Canvas and Business Model are important in their own style and are significance in the business thus, playing a crucial role in either new startups or the already existing businesses. Each of them fits in different type of businesses which depend on various parameters like type of the business, scalability of the business, size of the business, requirement of the resources and so on. Lean Canvas is the best fit for the new small business whereas the Business Model for the new or the existing medium and large businesses.

ACKNOWLEDGMENTS

We would like to thank Dr. Divya Keerthi Gupta, Associate Professor, GITAM- Hyderabad Business School, Hyderabad and Prof. K. V. S. Krishnamohan, Adjunct Professor, GITAM-Hyderabad Business School, Hyderabad. They became my helping hand when I ran into trouble spot and steered me in right direction.

REFERENCES

Afandi, Elvin and Majid Kermani and Fuad Mammadov, 2017. "Social capital and entrepreneurial process", *International Entrepreneurship and Management Journal,* Springer, vol. 13(3), pages 685 - 716, September.

Amrita, K., Garg, C. P. and Singh, S. (2018). Modelling the critical success factors of women entrepreneurship using fuzzy AHP framework. *Journal of Entrepreneurship in Emerging Economies*, *10*(1), 81 - 116.

Babalola, S. S. and Agbenyegah, A. T. (2016). Rural entrepreneurship: an insight into impeding factors influencing micro-entrepreneurial growth.

Chen, M. H. and Chang, Y. Y. (2013). The impacts of human capital in enhancing new venture's performance: Competence, motivation and creativity. *Journal of Knowledge-based Innovation in China*, *5*(2), 146 - 168.

Cremades, A. (2016). *The art of startup fundraising: pitching investors, negotiating the deal, and everything else entrepreneurs need to know*. John Wiley & Sons.

Fischer, D., Mauer, R. and Brettel, M. (2018). Regulatory focus theory and sustainable entrepreneurship. *International Journal of Entrepreneurial Behavior and Research*, *24*(2), 408 - 428.

Fisher, R., Maritz, A. and Lobo, A. (2014).Evaluating entrepreneurs' perception of success: Development of a measurement scale. *International Journal of Entrepreneurial Behavior and Research*, *20*(5), 478 - 492.

Gaspar, R. E. (2017). Large firm dominance on country's entrepreneurship potentials. *Journal of Global Entrepreneurship Research*, *7*(1), 1.

Kam-Sing Wong, S. (2014). Impacts of environmental turbulence on entrepreneurial orientation and new product success. *European Journal of Innovation Management*, *17*(2), 229 - 249.

Kirschenhofer, F. and Lechner, C. (2012). Performance drivers of serial entrepreneurs: Entrepreneurial and team experience. *International Journal of Entrepreneurial Behavior and Research*, *18*(3), 305 - 329.

Maurya, A. (2012). Why lean canvas vs. business model canvas. *Available in: http://practicetrumpstheory. com/why-lean-canvas.*

Menon, A. and Lukas, B. A. (2004). Antecedents and outcomes of new product development speed: A propositional inventory germane to marketing. *European Journal of Marketing*, *38*(1/2), 209 - 223.

Nienhaus, M. (2016). *Social smoothie importance of a business plan pre-startup planning* (Doctoral dissertation).

O'Connor, A. (2015). Questioning the Ethics of University Entrepreneurship Curriculum. In *The Challenges of Ethics and Entrepreneurship in the Global Environment* (pp. 79 - 107). Emerald Group Publishing Limited.

Omerzel Gomezelj, D. and Kušce, I. (2013). The influence of personal and environmental factors on entrepreneurs' performance. *Kybernetes*, *42*(6), 906 927.

Osborne, R. L. (1995). The essence of entrepreneurial success. *Management Decision*, *33*(7), 4 - 9.

Padilla-Meléndez, A. and Ciruela-Lorenzo, A. M. (2018, August). Female indigenous entrepreneurs, culture, and social capital. The case of the Quechua community of Tiquipaya (Bolivia). In *Women's Studies International Forum* (Vol. 69, pp. 159 - 170). Pergamon.

Perrotta, S. G. M. International Journal of Gender and Entrepreneurship. *Journal of Gender and Entrepreneurship*, *8*(1), 28 - 47.

Rantšo, T. A. (2016). Factors affecting performance/success of small-scale rural non-farm enterprises in Lesotho. *Journal of Enterprising Communities: People and Places in the Global Economy*, *10*(3), 226 - 248.

Scarmozzino, E., Corvello, V. and Grimaldi, M. (2017). Entrepreneurial learning through online social networking in high-tech startups. *International Journal of Entrepreneurial Behavior and Research*, *23*(3), 406 - 425.

Smørsgård, N. M. (2016). *The Jenga Tower Framework-A Qualitative Study of Lean Startup in the Large Company Context* (Master's thesis, NTNU).

Xie, X. and Lv, J. (2016). Social networks of female tech-entrepreneurs and new venture performance: the moderating effects of entrepreneurial alertness and gender discrimination. *International entrepreneurship and management journal*, *12*(4), 963 - 983.

Xue, Y. J., Deng, T. and Mao, K. (2018). Influencing Factors on the Ecological Protection Behaviors of Entrepreneurial Farmers in Chinese Forest Zones. *Sustainability*, *10*(6), 1827.

Web Resources

Cremades, A. (2016). *The Art of Startup Fundraising: Pitching Investors, Negotiating the Deal and Everything Else Entrepreneurs Need to Know.* https://the-eye.eu/public/Books/HumbleBundle/theartofstartup fundraising.pdf.

Four Reasons why a Business Plan is important. https://www.iafrikan.com/2016/06/15/4-reasons-why-a-business-plan-is-important/.

Kulkarni, A. (2015, Jan.). *Entrepreneurship in India: A global perspective.* https://m.dailyhunt.in/news/india/english/the+indian+economist-epaper-indecono/entrepreneurship+in+india+a+global+perspective-newsid-80370992.

Mebmer, R. (2016, June).

Maurya, A (2012, Feb.). Why Lean Canvas VS. Business Model Canvas. https://blog.leanstack.com/why-lean-canvas-vs-business-model-canvas-af62c0f250f0.

Nienhaus, M. A. (2015). Social Smoothie Importance of a Business Plan for Pre-Startup Planning. https://run.unl.pt/bitstream/10362/17299/1/Nienhaus_2016.pdf.

Roos, S. P. Business Model Canvas VS. Lean Canvas. https://canvanizer.com/how-to-use/business-model-canvas-vs-lean-canvas.

In: Strategic Rethinking
Editors: Rajagopal et al.
ISBN: 978-1-53616-835-8

Chapter 6

DETERMINANTS STIMULATING CUSTOMER SENSORY EXPERIENCE OF GLOBAL AND LOCAL COFFEE CHAINS

Sadhvi Mehrotra*[1,*]*, PhD and Divya Kirti Gupta*[2]*, PhD
[1]Dayanand Academy of Management Studies,
Kanpur, Uttar Pradesh
[2]GITAM Hyderabad Business School,
GITAM (Deemed to be University),
Hyderabad, Telangana State, India

ABSTRACT

Marketers have moved from traditional marketing practices towards innovation procedures and sensory inclusions using various techniques that stimulate and influence the customers. There is a colossal shift from customer satisfaction towards customer experience. Marketers are studying the role of customer experience on customer perception of a brand. While purchasing and consuming the product, people are still relying on their experience, guided by their senses, previous purchases and

* Corresponding Author's Email: sadhvimehrotra@gmail.com.

knowledge. For marketers, sensory marketing is emerging as a solution. A beautiful, spotless café, expertly crafted cup of coffee, dark antique furniture, low lighting, jazz music and strong aroma of freshly grounded coffee; all these experiences stimulate a customer's senses. The paper attempts to understand the role of human senses in customer experience of coffee. It also looks at the sensory marketing practices that are currently being employed by coffee retail chains. Two leading coffee brands in India have been studied in this paper - Starbucks and Cafe Coffee Day. Further, the paper presents the 'Sensory Marketing Framework for Coffee Brands' which will help companies in understanding the impact of senses on customer experience of coffee, and how the experience contributes to customer perception of the coffee brand and subsequently impacts the purchase intent.

Keywords: sensory marketing, customer experience, senses, Starbucks, Café Coffee Day

INTRODUCTION

Sensory marketing is a relatively new area in marketing and is defined as "marketing that engages the consumer's senses and affects their behaviors" Krishna (2011). Human senses include sight, smell, sound, touch and taste, and the important role of the senses in consumer marketing is however, only just being acknowledged. Since there is a link between marketing and human senses, Krishna (2011) encourages marketers to ask questions like - How do we get to know that our senses can judge products and tell us the products that we like, and can one sensory aspect of a product impact how a person perceives a different sensory aspect of the product?

Schmitt (1999) opined that sensory marketing, if applied to marketing, would generate studies on feelings that the product provides to the consumer, where human senses play an important role. He further says that consumption of products is a holistic experience, where customers are emotional and rational beings and are in search of experiences. Today, the shift in consumer behavior gives us new space to understand and adopt a new marketing strategy - Sensory Marketing (Manenti, 2013).

Salaga et al., (2015) are of the view that a strong brand is an asset to the company and a very effective tool in the battle among competitors. Brand value is created on the customer's perception and is measured on his or her willingness to buy and get associated with the brand.

McKinscy in its 2014 report mentions that companies which focused on maximizing satisfaction, with regard to the entire customer experience, have the potential to increase customer satisfaction by 20% (Mckinsey & Co., 2014). In today's competitive world (Sheth &Parvatiyar, 2000) customer experience is an important point of differentiation from the competitors. Customer experience (Meyer & Schwager, 2007) is about not only how the company answered or addressed the issue of the customer, but it is also defined by the interaction process and how customer felt about the hours of operation. Sensory space (Zwei, 2014) works on all the five senses. Hence, sensory evaluation is a holistic approach to assess the product.

Café Culture is developing in India and it is becoming a fashion symbol. Thi Truc Ly & Tien Minh (2015) said that no industry focuses more on olfactory senses than coffee industry. Taste and aroma are the important senses for evaluating a cup of coffee. Olfactory sense contributes a lot to taste. In the design of a coffee roaster and the space engages people with all their senses. Smell of coffee beans, bean crunching, taste of food, open kitchen and products to touch near customer zone may all contribute to the sensory experience of the brand.

There are two objectives of the present study. The first is to understand the sensory variables on which experience of coffee can be judged, and the second is to understand the effect of sensory marketing on the customer's experience of coffee, which eventually leads to the customer perception of coffee brands and repurchase intent. For this, the authors propose a 'Sensory Marketing Framework for Coffee Brands.' The two brands being considered for the study are Starbucks and Café Coffee Day, which are leading coffee brands in India.

Coffee Market and Sensory Marketing: Literature Review

The acceptance of the coffee has increased due to premium coffee stores such as Starbucks, Costa Coffee, Café Coffee Day, Barista etc. and all are taken as primary hangout places (Bushan & Chakravart, 2014). According to Grand View Research (2018), increase in disposable income and influence of western culture witnessed global exposure of foreign brands in Indian market. Coffee chains scaled up their standardization by adopting many differential strategies like store ambience, assortment of food and aspect of sensory inclusion (Grand View research, 2018).

The new trend in multinational companies is to have a strong brand and connect with the customers. Currently, it's not only about customer satisfaction, but companies are striving for customer experience which carries a lot of weight on buying behavior. Companies are trying to attract the customers by providing different kind of experiences resulting from various triggered simulations (Klaus and Maklan, 2007) because as Griffin (2005) says, a satisfied customer does not account for being a loyal customer. Customer experience is the antecedent of customer loyalty (Klaus and Maklan, 2007). Experience is related to the company's offering. Berry et al., (2002) enumerate that whenever customer buys a product the experience of a customer can be good, bad or indifferent. Consumers do not make decisions on rational basis, but they also focus on emotions. Customer experience includes both conscious and unconscious side of the human mind, where it is expressed in form of emotional and rational decision towards company's offering (Shaw et al., 2010).

According to International trade (2011), coffee is an important beverage and its production is important for world's economy. According to the studies coffee has many species, but only two are of real economic importance: Arabica and Robusta. Mordor Intelligence Report in 2019 stated that Arabica holds 70% of the global coffee market, while the Robusta and Liberica hold 27% and 3% respectively. The coffee market is divided on various parameters (Tucker, 2011) like product type and is segmented into powder, whole bean, instant coffee etc. The demand for ready to drink coffee is rising. Liquid instant coffee and nitro coffee is the new buzz in the market. Two players that are majorly into the game of nitro coffee are Starbucks and Dunkin Donuts (Maynard, 2017).

In 1971, Starbucks opened its first store in Seattle's historic Pike Place Market, United States and offered the world's finest freshly roasted whole bean coffees (Paryani, 2011). Today the company connects with its millions of customers with 24000 retail stores in 70 countries. Since inception of the Starbucks, customer experience was one thing that was most important part of the company's business plan. From selling coffee bean to perfect cup of espresso, the company focused on customer service, quality coffee, ambience and atmosphere of the store and co-creation of the value. Starbucks is not only known for serving a perfect cup of coffee but it also provides an ambience and place to experience a good cup of coffee (Larson, 2008). For enriching experience of its customers, company focuses on quality control of the products. When Starbucks thought of providing enriching customer experience; the most important parameter for enhancing experience was employee satisfaction. Schultz (2011) in his book 'Onward' quotes that company focuses on employee's salary, health benefits and stock options.

Café Coffee Day (CCD), which started much later in 1996 in Bangalore, India, is now known as India's favorite hangout for coffee lovers, and today it serves worldwide with more than 1530 outlets and has opened many subsidiaries (Sachitanand & Balasubramanyam, 2014). The company has realized the importance of change in marketing trends and shift towards customer experience (Agrawal, 2009) but, in terms of implementing sensory marketing and enhancing customer experience, CCD is in a nascent stage.

Though Starbucks is an older brand, it is comparatively new to the Indian market. The company opened its first outlet in India in 2012. Kanuuri (2013) is of the opinion that though Starbucks has considerable experience in the coffee industry, but it is new to Indian market, whereas CCD could easily expand being an established player in India.

Barlow (2013) says that as Starbucks marked its success in China, it was eager to repeat the same performance in the Indian market. In case of Indian market, Starbucks faced some strategic problems in 2012. The first among them (Larson, 2008) was that Starbucks was compared to fast food and restaurants, as cafes were not achieving huge sales back then. Secondly, due to location of the stores, the rentals are very high and the national players were drifting towards shutting down of their stores. Strategically it is difficult to run a cafe because of high rentals and expenses (Srivastava, 2012).

Numerous industry experts predicted (Wang, 2012, August 10) that successful entry of Starbucks in India would be possible through a local partner with long-term commitment and a tactful strategy to market the brand. Then Starbucks entered into a joint venture with Tata Beverages in India (Starbucks Media, 2016, June 26). Gupta et al., (2018) mention that today Starbucks joint venture with Tata Beverages is still overcoming all strategic problems and is targeting a niche crowd, which is giving a tough competition to the other competitors. Tata proved to be a valuable partner as it helped in getting prime locations for Starbucks and is providing an experience to the customers (Gupta et al., 2018).

According to Alsitrawi (2016), to create experiential branding Starbucks has focused on three components: Firstly, they promised to provide highest quality coffee and to maintain the quality they worked directly with the suppliers. Secondly, they wanted to inspire the customer with an experience when they walked into the store; loyal customers visit 18 times a month on an average. Third, they wanted to create the store atmosphere, which was calm and relaxing, so that customer stayed for a longer time.

Howard Schultz (Bartiromo, 2013) in his interview said that they had cracked the code of universal relevance, as they made Starbucks as third important place for people in the country after home and work. However, Indian market is crowded with national & international players in coffee industry, but the main competitor to Starbucks is homegrown player - Cafe Coffee Day (Madonna, 2013). The vision of Café Coffee day is to be the best café in the county by offering world class coffee experience at affordable prices. To enhance the customer experience CCD opened new outlets with the facility of book café and music lounge (Joshi, 2011).

For defining customer experience today, both Starbucks and Café Coffee Day are using all these aspects in different ways. Clegg (2003) said that the brands that practice sensory marketing have the charisma to attract the customers and maintain long term relationships with them. Starbucks and CCD carry the charisma to instigate the five senses and create right combination of emotional response.

Several researchers, who explored it from sociological, psychological and marketing point of view, research the concept of sensory marketing. American Professor Aradhana Krishna (Krishna, 2010) is considered as a pioneer in sensory marketing mentions in one of her work, 'Sensory Marketing: Research on the Sensuality of Products' that how all the five senses affect our emotions, liking and consumption of the products. Hulten (2009) enumerate the shift of companies from mass marketing to sensory marketing. Hulten (2009) developed a sensory marketing model known as SM model, which focused on the relation between the human senses and the multi-sensory brand experience. The conclusion of this model was that there is significant contribution of multi-sensory brand experience and it will help the brands to differentiate and position easily in the human mind.

Sensory marketing is helping the marketers to influence the consumption pattern of customers by impacting their senses and emotional influence (Randhir et al., 2016). Practices that are being adopted by the companies till today focus on sight and colors to trigger senses. For example, purple color used by restaurants portrays luxury and red is for the appetite. A colossal shift in the concept of brand management occurred when companies started focusing on brand experience rather than just to create a brand. Earlier, companies focused on logos, color, design elements, but now they create experience by invigorating senses. In his research, Kumar (2013) mentions that Indian marketers are now adopting concept of sensory marketing. Few years back, high end magazines used to carry advertisements for fragrances and perfumes by pasting strips. Those fragrant strips used to invigorate the sense of smell. In 2010, Volkswagen in India had put up an audio advertisement in Times of India newspaper, wherein a small audio was inserted with the print advertisement and the record played as soon as the reader opened the Volkswagan ad page (ET Bureau, 2010).

According to study done by Oklahoma State University in 2016, it was found that 83% of human sight sense reacts, its 3.5% for touch, 11% for hearing, 1% for taste and 1.5% for smell.

Schmitt (1999) stated that experiences provided sensory, emotional thinking, behavioral and related values based hedonistic perspective. Sheth & Parvatiyar (2000) proposed that three variables construct customer experiences: stimulus variable – perceiving sensory and information, context variable influenced by the context of the stimulus, and situational variable- perceptions are influenced by individual prior experience with a particular product or service. Starbucks coffee experience can be differentiated on customer's sensory experience. Schmitt (1999) defines customer experience as sensing, acting, thinking and feeling. These days the customer's emotions are been aroused by the five senses in the competitive scenario and that is why companies are focusing on sensory marketing.

Krishna (2011) is of the opinion that sensory marketing can be used in various aspects: Sight for vision, Olfaction for smell, Audition for sound, Tactile for touch and Gustative for taste. The marketers for generating brand awareness use sight sense.

Thurston et al., (2013) enumerate descriptors of coffee as body, flavor, acidity, aroma etc. when added to the cup of coffee they add uniqueness and complexity. The scoring of the coffee is done on many characteristics specifying unique attribute (Specialty Coffee Association of America, 2015). Barwise & Meehan (2004) said that companies need to focus on long lasting relationships with the customers now and they should move from traditional marketing to use of creative advertising and marketing communications. Hence, reinventing the product or the brand with unique selling proposition and experiences is what company should focus on to make customer feel special.

Starbucks is successfully using sensory marketing in four steps. The company focuses on how to position its brand, then design the right sensory element, test the sensory element and increase the element by critical touch points (Yalch & Spangenberg, 1990). Lindstorm (2005) states how companies can hold their marketing strategies to appeal the five senses.

Huang & Lu (2013) state that the colour of the drink and food has effects on customer's exceptions and emotions.

A memorable brand experience is created by triggering all the five senses of the customer's mind (sight, touch, smell, taste and sound). The further discussion is done for each type of human sense and its use in sensory marketing, in general and in relation to coffee.

Sight and Sensory Marketing

The most seductive out of all the senses is Sight. Issanchou (1996) mentions that to create the brand image the most powerful sense is sight. Marketers focus on sight sense for generating brand awareness and memorable sight experience (Hulten, 2017). Kotler (1973) mentions that any individual's main visual dimensions are brightness, size, color and shape. Customers identify the brands through its shape, color, architecture and themes (Kumar, 2017). For generating customer experience, companies spend a lot on choosing the color and theme related to the product or service. According to Shabgou & Daryani (2014) 6.1 percent of sight sense has impact on consumer behavior. Sight stimulates the highest percentage of sensory stimulus. A sensory cue stating 'Touch me' can alone have an impact on customer's mind to touch the product (Eriksson and Larsson, 2011).

Sight sense also creates perception about the brand. Choosing colors and designing a logo is a crucial aspect because its helps to impact a customer for a long time. To understand the environment of the coffee retail stores, presentation is the important aspect. Lindstorm (2005) said that visual experience is the primary foundation for sensory stimulations. Larson (2008) in his strategic analysis of Starbucks said that the company through its logo defines the importance of the color green and how that logo is associated with the values of the brand.

Kang (2009) quoted that sight affects the pleasure of emotions. Hulten (2011) multi-sensory brand experience model enumerates that sensory expressions drawn from sight sense are graphic, interior and exterior, theme, color, light, style, packaging and design. CCD is trying to change the interiors of its outlets to give a modern look and vibe to the customers (Dalal, 2014). It is focusing on vibrant colors and artifacts. Company has also launched digital menu application, which focuses on interactive touch screen display which makes viewing a pleasure.

Smell and Sensory Marketing

Olfaction focuses on smell. Rodriguez (2004) said that among all the senses, smell is the one, which has direct link with the brain, and it is 10000 times more receptive than taste. Taste factor is deeply connected with the sense of smell. To determine the flavor of the food, smell is as much important as taste. The sense of smell includes the smell of the object and the environment. Paul et al., (2000) say that the smell of an object conveys the attribute evaluation of the objects and helps in judging the quality. The smell of the environment is not totally dependent on the object. Scent marketing helps in creating good mood, ambience and it impacts the purchase decision. For example, these days' restaurants focus more on the smell and scent of restrooms (Elangovan & Padma, 2017). In fact, odors help in lasting memory of a brand. According to Spangenberg et al., (1996) a pleasant smell influences the point of sale.

Vlahos (2007, September 9) stated that smell of the brand should be same all over the globe. The sense of smell should start from starting of packaging till its retail counter. Clarke et al., (2012) found that lighting and smell positively influence the customer's in-store experience. The sensory expressions that are invigorated by the sense of smell can be product intensity, atmosphere and signature scent (Shabgou & Daryani, 2014). So, the coffee shops should focus on signature smells that persuade the customer to buy, feel relax and nostalgic.

Starbucks focuses a lot on this factor. It roasts the coffee beans specifically in its outlets because it wants that customers should smell the aroma of coffee (Larson, 2008) which gives a richer experience to the customers. Employees of the Starbucks are strictly instructed that they cannot carry any perfume, deodorants or smoke as that smell can affect the fragrance of the coffee (Upadhyaya, 2017). CCD is working on coffee aromas and the fragrance of coffee which will make the customer feel relaxed and help them to rejuvenate.

Touch and Sensory Marketing

Tactile focuses on touch. As humans, our touch factor is an important link between our brains and the reality. The receptors of our body help us to explore the objects in the surrounding. When we come across a haptic sensation i.e., a pleasant touch, the brain releases a hormone called as oxytocin, which leads to sense of calmness and well-being. The marketers think that customers, who feel and touch the product are more likely to purchase it (Dalesio et al., 2018). Our sensory receptors are more than 4,000,000 that can be targeted easily by the companies (Randhir et al., 2016) and companies focus on ease, smoothness and package of the product (Mckinsey & Co., 2017).

According to Rieunier (2002), the perception of the customer about restaurant depends mostly by the weight of the cutleries, comfort of the chairs and softness of the napkins. Touch sense builds a relationship between product and the consumer, which is formed through contact.

Larson (2008) mentions that Starbucks focuses on customized message embedded on the glasses, the comfort of the furniture and the atmospherics. Starbucks believe that customers should make the company their third most important place after home and office. Kasliwal (2008) enumerates that CCD has also worked on many aspects - changed the feel of its cups, switching from plastics to rough and embedded cups, have made use of the advancement in the technology by introducing touch screens, so that customer can have a deeper attachment with the product or brand. All the touch screens introduced by CCD had interactive displays.

Sound and Sensory Marketing

Music relates to the auditory sense and helps the customer to remember the brands (Ghodeswar, 2008). Studies had been made to find what kind of music fits the best with the different kinds of places- for example, if it's a wine cellar then classical music will raise the quality of sensation (Areni & Kim, 1993). Music also helps in building up the sales environment (Ford, 2013 & Wei, 2014). Typaldos (2016) enumerates that Starbucks gives an atmosphere of light music with some message related to Starbucks.

Simulation of sound can persuade the customer to avoid certain products or to purchase specific products or services and Andringa & Lanser (2013) say that customers can be attracted towards the pleasant sound and they can get bothered by annoying sounds. Sensory branding was pioneered by automobile industry. Krishna (2010) writes that sound and smell used by automobile industry impact the prospective buyers. She supplements it with an example by saying that the sound of the door of a car states the durability and solid engineering of the car.

Recently, Business Wire (2018) on CCD stated that to change the perception of customers and to make company one of the leading hangout coffee places, CCD came up with the idea of wireless charging. It has tied-up with power solutions and they installed more than 300 spots across the leading cities. Sachitanand & Balasubramanyam (2014) say that music played in CCD also persuades the customers to spend more time in the cafes. Starbucks invest its money in various music programs for customization of its music.

Taste and Sensory Marketing

Gustative refers to taste (Kikut-Ligaj & Trzcielińska-Lorych, 2015). Science specifies five tastes: savoury, salty, sweet, sour and bitter (Erickson, 2008). In sensory marketing, companies are focusing on these to convince customers. Customers link four basic gustative sensations i.e., sour, sweet, salty and bitter with colors (Celier, 2004). So companies focus on what they are offerings and they relate with colors. Both, Starbucks and CCD focus on all the aspects of taste sense by providing a rich cup of coffee. Garwaite et al., (2017) stated in their case study that the only difference between the two companies is that the Starbucks provides customization with special reference to taste.

Louzada Pereira et al., (2017) mention that coffee expert tasters conduct cup test that helps to assess the strength and the weakness of the coffee. The descriptors used to evaluate the sensory aspects of the coffee are: aroma, fragrance, bitterness, sweetness, roasting, body etc. (James et al., 2015).

Overall atmosphere of the retail outlet is also important. The perception of atmosphere is through senses, and there is a difference between perceived and intended atmosphere (Pallasmaa, 2014). The intended atmosphere is the atmosphere that coffee chains intend to offer to their customers and the perceived atmosphere is the one that customer feels and relates to. The perceived atmosphere varies on the basis of culture, values, beliefs, sound and smell. Elangovan & Padma (2017) stated in his research that atmosphere plays an important part in aiming and making distinction between the social classes and lifestyle buyers. Starbucks focuses on the niche segment, and also believes that the values what the company follows are comprehended by the customers. The company organizes various programs to stay connected with its customers like tasting of coffee and tea. Sachitanand & Balasubramanyam (2014) mention that the segment of customer visiting Starbucks enjoys every sip of coffee and the knowledge function related to the products work with buying behavior of the customers. CCD focuses on youth segment and the customers try to perceive CCD as a café to spend time with friends and to have formal meetings (Mishra, 2013). The perceived atmospheres of both the brands are different and focus on different segments of the society.

After reviewing various studies done on sensory marketing, including those on coffee brands, the variables that can help to invigorate customer's senses, as identified by various researchers, are presented in tabulated form in Table 1.

Table 1. Sensory variables identified by different researchers

Contribution	Sight	Smell	Touch	Sound	Taste
Kotler (1973)	Color, Brightness, Size and Shape	Scent, Freshness	Smoothness, Temperature	Volume, Pitch	
Hulten (2011)	Graphic, Interior and Exterior, Theme, Light, Style, Packaging and Design				
Spangenberg et al., (1996)		Pleasant			
Rieunier (2002)			Weight of the cutleries, Comfort of the chair, Softness of the napkins		
Areni & Kim (1993)				Kind of Music	
Erickson (2008)					Taste as Savory, Salty, Sweet, Sour and Bitter
Infocafes (2009)		Aroma			Sweetness, Bitterness
J. J. Kellaris, R. J. Kent (1994)				Organized sound	

Contribution	Sight	Smell	Touch	Sound	Taste
R. E. Milliman (1986)				Slow music lead customer to stay longer	
Middlestadt (1990)	Color				
T. A. Summers, P. R. Hebert (2001)	Light				
Gumperz (1977)				Power of music	
DeNora (1986)				Music	
Rieunier (2002)	Color, material, Light and Layout	Natural smells and Artificial smells	Material and Temperature	Music and Noises	
Belk (1975)	Location, Décor, lighting			Sound	
Gomez & Garcia (2012)	Color & Light, Interior & Exterior Design of store				
Bruner (1990)				Time, Pitch, Rhythm, Volume & Texture of music	
Solomon (2008)	Color	Odor of Product/Store		Background Music	Flavor houses
Schmitt (1999)	Aesthetic design			Jazz music	
Soars (2009)		Fragrance			

Source: Primary Data.

The scoring of the coffee is done on many characteristics specifying unique attributes (Specialty Coffee Association of America, 2015). Identifying the variables under each of the five senses shall help to understand their effect on customer experience, which subsequently leads to formation of customer perception of the coffee brands. The variables identified are from literature review. Table 2 presents the summary of 'variables that invigorate senses' towards coffee experience and is prepared on the basis of the review of existing literature.

Table 2. Variables invigorating senses at a coffee outlet

Sight	**Sound**	**Touch**	**Smell**	**Taste**
Ambience Color Emotions Appearance Cleanliness Spotless café	Atmospherics Music Conversation &Greetings	Mouth Feel Temperature Feel of Furniture, Upholstery, Cutlery, Astringency Body (viscosity and texture)	Coffee Aroma	Bitterness Sweetness Acidic Flavor

Source: Primary Data.

Based on the review of literature, the authors propose a conceptual framework on 'Sensory Marketing of Coffee Brands' in the next section. The framework shall be tested later using the above variables for which Starbucks and CCD will be studied on five senses i.e., sight (visual), sound (audition), touch (tactile), smell (olfaction) and taste (gustative).

SENSORY MARKETING OF COFFEE BRANDS: A CONCEPTUAL FRAMEWORK

The emergence of sensory marketing is helping marketers and the companies to catch on the different attributes of the products and services. Since human senses help individuals to know and feel about the product and service, they impact how people view and feel about a particular brand.

Knowing customer better is an art and a challenge. Sensory marketing is helping organizations to understand the preferences and shifts in the purchasing pattern of the coffee customers. For the customers, the overall experience of a coffee brand is important. However, it is not easy to crack down the customer experience code, but Starbucks and CCD are using sensory marketing to take concrete in that direction. Companies are building their sensory signatures.

To accelerate growth and retain customer loyalty in comparison to its competitors, both companies have focused on continuous innovation. Starbucks and CCD continue to make changes in their store formats and marketing strategies to know how their products are been perceived by the customers. Both are attempting to know the depths of linkage between marketing and the senses.

To understand the effect of sensory marketing on the customer experience of retail coffee chains, an attempt has been made to understand the ways in which the five senses impact coffee customers. With the help of literature review, the authors could identify the variables that invigorate the senses for coffee, and in a limited way, could identify how Starbucks and CCD are enriching the customer's experience using sensory marketing.

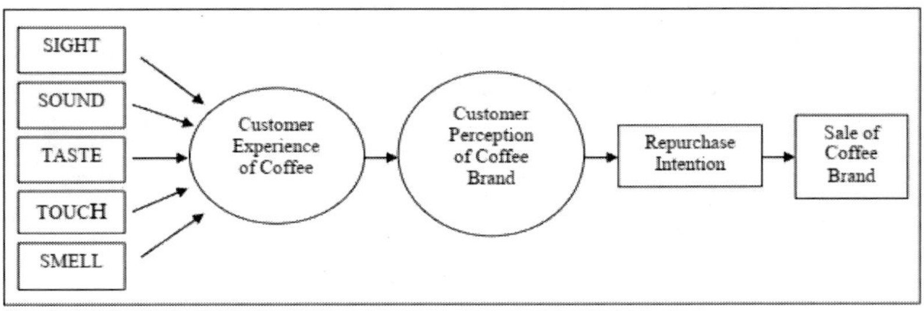

Figure 1. Sensory marketing framework for coffee brands.

A conceptual framework is proposed (Figure 1) by the authors. It connects customer experience of a coffee brand to the customer perception. It further proposes that customer perception subsequently affects the customer decisions (purchase intent) in the form of 'repurchase intention' affecting the sales of the coffee brands.

The framework below shall be used to build further research output in the area of sensory marketing, which shall enrich the understanding of growth of coffee brands in India and outside.

REFERENCES

Agrawal, R. (2009). Threat of a "me too" perception: a case of Café Coffee Day, *The Marketing Review*. 9. pp. 251-271.

Alsitrawi, A. (2016). Starbucks: Creating a Unique Customer Experience, *International Journal of Scientific & Engineering Research*, 7(4), ISSN 2229.

Andringa, T. C., & Lanser, J. J. (2013). How pleasant sounds promote and annoying sounds impede health: a cognitive approach. *International journal of environmental research and public health*, *10*(4), 1439–1461. doi:10.3390/ijerph10041439.

Areni, C. S. & Kim, D. (1993). "The Influence of background music on shopping behaviour: Classical versus Top-Forty Music in a Wine Store," in NA – *Advances in Consumer Research Vol. 20 (Eds).* Leigh Mc Alister and Michael L. Rothschild, Provo, UT: *Association of Consumer Research,* 336-340.

Barlow, N. (2013, October 9). China's coffee industry is booming. *China Briefing*, Retrieved from https://www.china-briefing.com/news/chinas-coffee-industry-is-brewing.

Bartiromo, M. (2013). Starbucks Schultz eye's global growth. USA Today.

Barwise, P. & Meehan, S. (2004). *Simply Better: Winning and keeping customers by delivering what matters most.* Boston: Harvard Business School Press.

Berry, L. L., Carbone, L. P. & Haeckel, S. H. (2002), "Managing the total customer experience," *MIT Sloan Management Review*, vol. 43, no. 3, pp. 85.

Business Wire (2018, September 25). Cafe Coffee Day Enhances in-cafe Experience with Future-Forward Digital Technology. Retrieved from https://www.businesswireindia.com/cafe-coffee-day-enhances-in-cafe-experience-with-future-forward-digital-technology.html.

Celier, P. (2004). *Le marketing sensorial (Sensory Marketing). Mohammedia ENSET School.*

Clarke, D. W., Perry, P. & Denson, H. (2012). The sensory retail environment of small fashion boutiques. *Journal of Fashion Marketing*, 16(4): 492-510.

Clegg, B. (2003). *Capturing customers' hearts: leave the competition to chase their pockets:* Prentice Hall.

Dalesio, N. M., Ortiz, B., Pluznick, J. L. & Berkowitz D. E., (2018, November 27). Olfactory, Taste, and Photo Sensory Receptors in Non-sensory Organs: It Just Makes Sense. Retrieved from https://doi.org/10.3389/fphys.2018.01673.

Dalal, M. (2014, April 23). Café Coffee Day to revamp look, menu. Retrieved from https://www.livemint.com/Companies/hp77tRfVHFyfHjIOfuX9bI/Caf-Coffee-Day-to-revamp-look-menu.html.

Elangovan, N. & Padma, C. (2017). Impact of Multi Sensory Marketing on Consumer behavior in Restaurant. *International Journal of Business and Management Invention*. ISSN (Online): 2319 – 8028, ISSN (Print): 2319 – 801X. Volume 6 Issue 2 || February. 2017 || PP—01-09.

Erickson, P. (2008). A study of the science of taste: On the origins and influence of the core ideas, *Behavioral & Brain Sciences*, 31, 59–105.

ET Bureau (2010, September 22). 'Talking' Volkswagen Vento print advertisement becomes talk of the town. Retrieved from https://economictimes.indiatimes.com/industry/services/advertising/talking-volkswagen-vento-print-advertisement-becomes-talk-of-the-town/articleshow/6603554.cms.

Ford, M. (2013, July 15). The Psychology of Music: Why music plays a big role in what you buy. Retrived from http://blog.motivemetrics.com/The-Psychology-of-Music-Why-Music-Plays-a-Big-Role-in-What-You-Buy.

Ghodeswar, M. B. (2008). Building brand identity in competitive markets: a conceptual model. *Journal of Product and Brand management.* 17/1 (2008) 4-12.

Grand View Research (2018). *India Coffee Retail Chains Market Size, Share & Trends Analysis Report, by Type (Dine In, Take Away), by Region (North India, South India, West India, East India), Competitive Landscape, And Segment Forecasts, 2018 - 2025.* GVR-2-68038-141-2. [online] p.50. Available at: https://www.grandviewresearch.com/industry-analysis/india-coffee-retail-chains-market.

Griffin, J. (2005). Twelve Laws of Loyalty, The Canadian Manager, Summer. Pp. 28-92.

Gupta, P., Nagpal, A. &Malik, D. (2018) "Starbucks: global brand in emerging markets," Emerald Emerging Markets Case Studies. Retrieved from https://www.emeraldinsight.com/doi/abs/10.1108/EEMCS-03-2018-0044.

Huang, L., & Lu, J. (2013). When color meets health: The impact of package colors on the perception of food healthiness and purchase intention. In S. Botti & A. Labroo (Eds.), *Advances in Consumer Research* (Vol. 41, pp. 625-626). Duluth, MN: *Association for Consumer Research.*

Hulten, B., Broweus, N., & Van Dijk, M. (2009). *Sensory Marketing*, Palgrave Macmillan, London.

Hulten, B. (2011). Sensory Marketing: The Multisensory Experience Concept. *European Business Review*. 23(3): 256-273.

Hulten, B. (2017). Branding by the five senses: A sensory branding framework. *Journal of Brand Strategy*. 6. 1-12.

Issanchou, S. (1996). Consumer Expectations and Perceptions of Meat and Meat Product Quality. *Meat Science,* 43(S): S5-S19.

James, E.M.S., Torres, I.B. & Pérez-Villarreal, H.H. (2015) 'Sensory evaluation of commercial coffee brands in Colombia,'*International Journal of Business and Systems Research*, Vol. 9(3). pp. 195–213.

Joshi, M. (2011). Café Coffee Day (CCD): A Case Analysis, Article *in SSRN Electronic Journal*, doi: 10.2139/ssrn.1920827.

Kang, E. (2009). *The impact of Sensory Environments on Spagoers' Emotion and Behavioural Intention.* Houston: University of Houston.

Kasliwal, N. (2008). Brewing the Brand- A Case Study of Cafe Coffee Day. International Conference on Brand Management. Retrieved from https://www.researchgate.net/publication/280875326_Brewing_the_Brand-_A_Case_Study_of_Cafe_Coffee_Day.

Kikut-Ligaj, D. & Trzcielińska-Lorych, J. (2015). How taste works: Cells, receptors and gustatory perception. *Cellular & Molecular biology letters*. 20. 10.1515/cmble-2015-0042.

Klaus, P. and Maklan, S. (2007), "The role of brands in a service-dominated world," *Journal of Brand Management*, Vol. 15 No. 2, pp. 115-22.

Krishna, A. (2010) Sensory Marketing: Research on the Sensuality of Products. Routledge, New York.

Krishna, A. (2011). An integrative review of sensory marketing: Engaging the senses to affect perception, judgment and behavior, *Journal of Consumer Psychology*.

Kotler, P. (1973). Atmospherics as a marketing tool. *Journal of retailing*, *49*(4), 48-64.

Kumar, S. J. (2017). Analyzing the Impact of Sensory Marketing on Consumers: A Case Study of KFC. *Journal of US-China Public Administration,* April 2016, Vol. 13, No. 4, 278-292 doi: 10.17265/1548-6591/2016.04.007.

Kumar, P. (2013). Multisensory Marketing: Creating New Sustainability Perspective in Hospitality Sector. Atna J Tou Stu, 8, 1 (2013), 43-55 ISSN 0975-3281|doi:10.12727/ajts.9.4.

Larson, R.C. (2008). *Starbucks a Strategic Analysis, Past Decisions and Future Options*. Retrieved from https://www.biu.ac.il/soc/sb/stfhome/bijaoui/891/case/2009/starbuck08full.pdf.

Louzada Pereira, L., Cardoso, W., Guarçoni, R., Francisco Almeida da Fonseca, A., Moreira, T., & Caten, C. (2017). The consistency in the sensory analysis of coffees using Q-graders. European Food Research and Technology. 10.1007/s00217-017-2863-9.

Madonna, A. B., Raghubir. (2013). If we find something attractive we will look at it, Business Standard.

Manenti, M. (2013). *An analysis of the sensorial marketing methods in the fashion retail sector* (Master's thesis, Dublin Business School, Ireland). Retrieved from https://esource.dbs.ie/bitstream/handle/10788/1775/ma_manenti_m_2013.pdf?sequence=1&isAllowed=y.

Maynard, M. (2017, July 14). Starbucks goes big into cold brew coffee on Tap; could it fizzle like fizzio? Retrieved from www.forbes.com/sites/michelinemaynard/2017/07/14.

Mckinsey & Co. (2014). The three C's of Customer Satisfaction: consistency, consistency and consistency. Retrieved from https://www.mckinsey.com/industries/retail/our-insights/the-three-cs-of-customer-satisfaction-consistency-consistency-consistency.

McKinsey & Co. (2017). 'Customer experience: new capabilities, new audiences, new opportunities. Number 2. June 2017. Retrieved from https://www.mckinsey.com/~/media/mckinsey/featured%20insights/customer%20experience/cx%20compendium%202017/customer-experience-compendium-july-2017.ashx.

Mishra, A. (2013). Business model for Indian retail sector: The Café Coffee Day case. *IIMB management review*. Vol 25(3). September 2013. Pp. 160-170.

Mordor Intelligence. (2019). Coffee market – Growth, Trends and Forecasts (2019-2024). Retrieved from https://www.mordorintelligence.com/industry-reports/coffee-market.

n.d. (2014, August 8). *Creating a sensory experience*. Retrieved from https://www.cafeculture.com/general-interest/creating-a-sensory-experience.

Pallasmaa, J. (2014). Space, place and atmosphere: Emotion and peripheral perception in architectural experience. Lebenswelt: Aesthetics and Philosophy of Experience. 10.13130/2240-9599/4202.

Paryani, K. (2011). Product, quality, service reliability and management of operations at Starbucks, *International Journal of Engineering, Science and Technology*, Vol.3, no.7, 2011, pp. 1-14.

Randhir, R., Latasha, K., Tooraiven, P. and Monishan, B. (2016). Analyzing the Impact of Sensory Marketing on Consumers A Case Study of KFC. Ebene, *Mauritius: International Conference on Tourism, Hospitality and Marketing*, pp.978-1-943579-19-8.

Rieunier, S. (2002). Le marketing sensoriel du point de vente. *Recherche et Applications en Marketing*, *17*(4).

Rodriguez, G. (2004). 'The sense of smell: a powerful sense.' *Reprinted from reSources, Spring 2004, Volume 11, Number 2 with permission from California Deaf-Blind Services http://www.sfsu.edu/~cadbs.*

Sachitanand, R. & Balasubramanyam, K. (2014). *How Starbucks and Cafe Coffee Day are squaring up for control of India's coffee retailing market. E T Bureau.* [online] Available at: https://economictimes.indiatimes.com/industry/services/retail/how-starbucks-and-cafe-coffee-day-are-squaring-up-for-control-of-indias-coffee-retailing-market/articleshow/36219229.cms?from=mdr.

Salaga, J., Bartosova, V. & Kicova, E. (2015). Economic Value Added as a measurement tool of financial performance. In *4th World Conference on Business, Economics and Management (WCBEM), Conference proceedings*, 219-226.

Schmitt, B. H. (1999). *Experiential Marketing: How to Get Customer to Sense, Feel, Think, Act, and Relate to Your Company and Brands*, New York, NY: The Free Press.

Schultz, H. (2011). *Onward – How Starbucks fought for its life without losing its soul,* Wiley publication, United Kingdom.

Shabgou, M., & Daryani, S. M. (2014). Towards the Sensory Marketing: Stimulating the Five Senses (Sight, Hearing, Smell, Touch and Taste) and its Impact on Consumer Behaviour. *Indian Journal of Fundamental and Applied Life Sciences, ISSN:2231-6345 (Online).*

Shaw, C., Dibeehi, Q. & Walden, S. (2010). *Customer experience: Future trends and insights.* Basingstoke, Palgrave Macmillan. 199 p.

Sheth, J.N. & Parvatiyar, A. (2000). Handbook of Relationship Marketing, Sage, London.

Spangenberg, E. R., Crowley, A. E. & Henderson, P. W. (1996). Improving the Store Environment: Do Olfactory Cues Affect Evaluations and Behaviors? *Journal of Marketing*, 60(2), 67–80.

Specialty Coffee Association of America. (2015). SCAA protocols — Cupping specialty coffee. Retrieved from SCAA Protocols https://www.scaa.org/PDF/resources/cupping-protocols.pdf.

Srivastava, S. (2012, November 12). Starbucks India isn't celebrating yet, *ForbesIndia Staff*, retrieved from http://www.forbesindia.com/article/cross-border/starbucks-india-isnt-celebrating-yet/34105/1.

Starbucks Media (2016, June 26). The Tata group and Starbucks Coffee Company Strengthen Global Partnership with Multiple New Commitments. Retrieved from http://tataglobalbeverages.com/media/news/2016/06/27/the-tata-group-and-starbucks-coffee-company - strengthen-global-partnership-with-multiple-new-commitments.

Thi Truc Ly, P. & Tien Minh, D. (2015). *An Emerging Marketing Technology: Sensory marketing applied in Retail industry.*

Thurston, R., Morris, J., & Steiman, S. (2013). *Coffee: A comprehensive guide to the bean, the beverage, and the industry.* Plymouth, UK: Rowman & Littlefield.

Tucker, M. C. (2011). *Coffee Culture: Local Experiences, Global connections*. New York. Routledge.

Upadhyaya, M. (2017) Emotional Connect between Brand and Consumer through Sensory Branding. *American Journal of Industrial and Business Management,* 7, 352-359. https://doi.org/10.4236/ajibm.2017.74025.

Vlahos, J. (2007, September 9) *Scent and Sensibility: Can Smell Sell?* New York Times. Retrieved from https://www.nytimes.com/2007/09/09/realestate/keymagazine/909SCENT-txt.html.

Wang, H. (2012, August 10). Five things Starbucks did to get china right, *Forbes.* Retrieved from https://www.forbes.com/sites/helenwang/2012/08/10/five-things-starbucks-did-to-get-china-right/#4467c8fe53 af.

Yalch, R. F. & Spangenberg, E. (1990). Effects of Store Music on Shopping Behavior. *Journal of Consumer Marketing*, 7 (Spring), 55–63.

In: Strategic Rethinking
Editors: Rajagopal et al.
ISBN: 978-1-53616-835-8

Chapter 7

A Study on Internet Banking (IB) Experience: The Role of Demographics in the Indian Context

Thirupathi Chellapalli and D. V. Srinivas Kumar
School of Management Studies (SMS), University of Hyderabad

Abstract

With the advent of the 21st century, the service organizations realized that offering quality services is no longer sufficient for establishing a long-lasting competitive advantage. In today's rapidly changing economic and competitive environment, survival is no longer confined to low prices and innovative products/services. To be competitive, the organizations need to recognize the uniqueness of each customer. In this world, everyone has different attitudes, values, preferences, beliefs, personality, backgrounds. Therefore, each person gains experience through his/her personal lens. In the face of post modernity, these experiences of the customer play a significant role in the growth and survival of any organization. Hence, to compete effectively the business organizations have entered in an era of customer experience. With regards to our economy, banking self-service technologies (e.g., Internet banking, Mobile banking, ATM banking, etc.) are emerging as one of the major infrastructural constituents and many service sectors have realized the significance of customer experience. For such purpose, understanding the role of demographics of each customer imperative and it has been creating a paramount importance to retail banking industry in this context the study undertaken has been designed a questionnaire to collect the responses of the customers from four select cities namely Hyderabad, Delhi, Mumbai, and Kolkata.

Keywords: internet-banking experience, demographics, customer experience, Internet banking usage, etc.

INTERNET BANKING – AN INTRODUCTION

Globalization and liberalization of the economy have resulted in several new prospects and challenges for the banking industry. The banking sector is at the crossroads and is continually advancing by adopting to the changes brought in by the innovations in technology. Retail banking sector has witnessed enormous growth and emerged as a major driver of the overall banking industry. This sector gives banking services to the individual customers. At present, Indian financial players are adopting innovative approaches to enhance their customer base and enhance market share. To gain competitive advantage and to meet the new challenges, organizations need to focus on customer experiences. About Indian economy, banking self-service technologies (SSTs) are emerging as one of the major infrastructural constituents and many service sectors have realized the significance of customer experience.

Internet plays a vital role between banks and customers to receive and deliver information; this form of banking is described as Internet banking (Reserve Bank of India, 2001). "The process in which internet and computer device are used as a medium to facilitate banking services is termed as Internet banking". "Internet banking is a web-based service that enables the banks to authorize customers to access their account information". "It permits the customers to log on to the bank's website with the help of bank's issued identification and personal identification number (PIN)". Online services were started in New York in 1981 by Citi bank, Chase Manhattan, Chemical & Manufacturers Hanover offered home banking services using the videotext system. In India, ICICI (Industrial Credit and Investment Corporation) was the pioneer to introduce E-banking in 1997.

In internet banking system, the bank has a centralized database that is web-enabled. All the services that the bank has permitted on the internet are displayed in the menu. Any of the permitted services can be selected, and further interaction is directed by the nature of service. It would a borderless entity permitting anytime, and anywhere and anyhow banking. Internet banking provides a number of benefits to its customers. Some of the benefits are as follows: It removes the traditional geographical barriers for customers. The customer can access their account anytime, and from any part of the world, Due to new innovative and convenient facility it attracts new customers who are using traditional banking system so far. It facilitates the offering of more services because this is internet based services which is time saving and customer can access and regulate his/her account himself/herself. However, regardless of the fact, it is vital on the part of every customer to undertake few precautionary measures while transacting online. According to a report drafted by Facebook and the Boston Consulting Group (BCG), "the number of users opting for online banking is expected to double to reach 150 million mark by 2020, from the current 45 million active urban online banking users in India". (Financial Express June 22, 2017)

LITERATURE REVIEW

The concept of customer experience was initially conceived in the mid -1980s. As opined by Lawrence Abbott (1955) "what people really desire are not products, but also satisfying experiences. People want products because they want experience which they hope the products will render". According to Bitner (2000) the traditional "high-touch and low-tech" personal encounters have now been supplemented by the "high-tech and low-touch" technology interfaces.

As per Bitner, Brown & Meuter, (2000) within technology-based self-services, (banking sector has been witnessing a new paradigm known as technology-based self-services which include online banking, ATM banking, Mobile banking, etc.), man-to-man interaction to a greater extent is substituted by man-to-machine interaction. According to Meuter et al., (2000) self-service technologies (e.g., Internet banking, mobile banking, ATMs, etc.) are technological interfaces that enable customers to produce a service independent of direct service employee involvement.

The nature of service encounter highly significant to the customers. Due to intangible nature of the delivered services, the customer not just purchase the service but also accumulate the experience Bateson (1995). Pine and Gilmore (1998) opined, experiences are a distinct economic offering, as different from services and goods. Meyer and Schwager (2007) Defined, customer experience are the internal and subjective response customers have to any direct or indirect contact with a company. Creating and delivering superior customer experience has become one of the prime objectives of organizations (Verhoef et al., 2009).

Research Objective

This paper aims at examining the role of demographics (geographic locations, education, occupations, age, income, gender and marital status) on customer experience in the usage of Internet banking experience. The study explores whether Demographics play a role in customer experience with regards to usage of Internet banking.

Research Hypotheses

H1: There is a significant difference among the respondents of different geographic locations in terms of Internet banking experience.

H2: There is a significant difference among the respondents with different levels of education in terms of Internet banking experience.

H3: There is a significant difference among the respondents with different occupations in terms of Internet banking experience.

H4: There is a significant difference among the respondents of various age groups in terms of Internet banking experience.

H5: There is a significant difference among the respondents with various income levels in terms of Internet banking experience.

H6: There is a significant difference between male and female respondents in terms Internet banking experience.

H7: There is a significant difference between married and unmarried respondents in terms of Internet banking experience

RESULTS AND DISCUSSIONS

Table 1 represents city wise sample distribution of internet banking users in the select four cities in India. The Distribution results indicate that approximately 25% of samples are drawn from each of the cities. Hyderabad 105 (25.1%), Delhi 105 (25.1%), Mumbai 104 (24.9%), Kolkata 103 (24.7%).

Table 2 represents gender wise sample distribution of Internet banking users in four select cities in India. The distribution indicates 208 males (49.8%), 210 females (50.2%) respondents.

Table 3 represents marital status wise sample distribution of Internet banking users in four select cities in India. The distribution indicates 257 married (61.4%), and 161 Unmarried (38.9%) respondents.

Table 1. Internet Banking (IB) users city-wise sample distribution

City	Frequency	Percent
Hyderabad	105	25.1
Delhi	105	25.1
Mumbai	104	24.9
Kolkata	103	24.7
Total	417	100

Table 2. Internet Banking (IB) users gender-wise sample distribution

Gender	Frequency	Percent
Male	208	49.8
Female	209	50.2
Total	417	100

Table 3. Internet Banking (IB) users marital status-wise sample distribution

Marital Status	Frequency	Percent
Married	257	61.4
Unmarried	161	38.6

Table 4 represents age wise sample distribution of Internet banking users in four select cities in India. A majority of the respondents (33%) belong to the age group under 25 years followed by 30.4% of respondents belonging to the age group 42 years to 50 years and 24% belonging to the age group 26 years to 41 years. Rest of the respondents were spread across age groups 34-41 years, above 60 years.

Table 5 represents education wise sample distribution of Internet banking users in four select cities in India. A majority of the respondents (46%) belong to the bachelor degree holders followed by 35.2% of respondents belonging to the master degree holders and 10% belonging to the M.Phil./Ph.D. Rest of the respondents were spread across (6.2%) Intermediate, (2.6%) High School & Below.

Table 6 represents monthly income wise sample distribution of Internet banking users in four select cities in India. A majority of the respondents (34.4%) belong to the income group of > Rs.45, 000 followed by 23.4% of the respondents belonging to the income group of Rs.35, 001-Rs.45, 000 and 18.6% belonging to the income group of Rs. 25, 001-Rs. 35, 000. Rest of the respondents were spread across income groups of (15.3%) Rs.15, 001-Rs.25, 000 (8.3%) up to Rs. 15,000.

Table 4. Internet Banking (IB) users age-wise sample distribution

Age	Frequency	Percent
Under 25	138	33.0
26-33	100	24.0
34-41	44	10.5
42-50	127	30.4
51-60	-	-
Above 60	8	1.9
Total	417	100

Table 5. Internet Banking (IB) users education-wise sample distribution

Education	Frequency	Percent
High School & Below	11	2.6
Intermediate	26	6.2
Bachelor degree	191	46.0
Master degree	147	35.2
M.Phil./Ph.D.	42	10.0
Total	417	100

Table 6. Internet Banking (IB) users monthly income-wise sample distribution

Monthly Income	Frequency	Percent
Up to 15000	35	8.3
15001-25000	64	15.3
25001-35000	76	18.6
35001-45000	98	23.4
>45000	144	34.4
Total	417	100

Table 7 represents occupation wise sample distribution of Internet users in four select cities in India. A majority of the respondents (37.3%) belong to the private employees followed by (21.8%) of the respondents belonging to the government employees and (17%) were business owners. Rest of the respondents (16.3%) were students and (7.6%) of the respondents belonging to the self-employed.

INTERNET BANKING EXPERIENCE - CITY WISE ANALYSIS

It is observed that there is no significant difference in Internet-banking experience among respondents of the cities in which the study was conducted. Hence, the Null hypothesis is accepted. It can be concluded that there is no significant difference in Internet-banking experience among respondents across various cities selected for the study. In simple terms, Internet-banking experience more or less same in the cities selected for the study.

Table 7. Internet Banking (IB) users occupation-wise sample distribution

Occupation	Frequency	Percent
Self-employed	32	7.6
Student	68	16.3
Private Employee	156	37.3
Govt. Employee	91	21.8
Business Owners	70	17.0
Total	417	100

Table 8. ANOVA results for internet-banking experience by city

	Sum of Squares	df	Mean Square	F	Sig.
Between Groups	.581	3	.194	.001	1.000
	Sum of Squares	df	Mean Square	F	Sig.
Within Groups	107540.893	414	259.761		
Total	107541.474	417			

ANOVA results show that the variance in Internet-banking experience city-wise is statistically insignificant. In other words, Internet-banking experience more or less same in case of four cities selected for the study.

Internet Banking Experience - Gender Wise Analysis

It has been identified that there is no significant difference in Internet-banking experience based on the gender of the respondents. Hence, the Null hypothesis is accepted. It can be concluded that Internet-banking experience does not differ by gender. In simple terms, Internet-banking experience does not vary in terms, of male and female respondents.

Independent samples t-test results show that the mean difference in Internet-banking experience between male and female (gender) is statistically insignificant. In other words, Internet-banking experience does not vary between male and female customers in case of four cities selected for the study.

Internet Banking Experience – Analysis Based on Respondents' Education Level

It is identified that there is a significant difference in Internet-banking experience among respondents with different education levels. Hence, the alternate hypothesis is accepted. It can be concluded that there is significant difference in Internet-banking experience among respondents across various education levels selected for the study. In simple terms, Internet-banking experience varies with different education levels selected for the study.

ANOVA results show that the variance in Internet-banking experience by education is statistically significant. In other words, Internet-banking experience varies with different educational levels in case of four cities selected for the study.

Means for groups in homogeneous subsets are displayed.

(a) Uses Harmonic Mean Sample Size = 32.216.
(b) The group sizes are unequal. The harmonic mean of the group sizes is used. Type I error levels are not guaranteed.

Table 9. Independent sample test results for internet-banking experience by gender

		Levene's Test for Equality of Variances		t-test for Equality of Means			
		F	Sig.	t	df	Sig. (2-tailed)	Mean Difference
IB - EXP	Equal variances assumed	2.234	.136	1.211	416	.227	.15769
	Equal variances not assumed			1.211	406.520	.226	.15769

Table 10. ANOVA results for internet-banking experience by level of education

	Sum of Squares	df	Mean Square	F	Sig.
Between Groups	5738.531	3	1912.844	7.779	.000
Within Groups	101802.943	414	245.901		
Total	107541.474	417			

Respondents with Master degree and above (M.Phil./Ph.D.), and those with Bachelor degree scored more than those who stopped education after Intermediate and high school & below. Therefore, it has been concluded that Internet banking experience has increased with an increase in the respondent's education levels.

Table 11. Post Hoc test results for education regarding internet-banking experience

Education	N	Subset for alpha = 0.05	
		1	2
High School & Below	11	112.3214	
Intermediate	26	114.2698	
Bachelor degree	191	119.5000	119.5000
Others (M.Phil./Ph.D.)	42	121.4923	121.4923
Master degree	147		124.6000
Sig.		.081	.221

INTERNET BANKING EXPERIENCE – MARITAL STATUS WISE ANALYSIS

It has been identified that there is no significant difference in Internet-banking experience based on the marital status of the respondents. Hence, the Null hypothesis is accepted. It can be concluded that Internet-banking experience does not differ by marital status. In simple terms, Internet-banking experience does not vary in terms, of married and unmarried respondents.

Independent samples t-test results show that the mean difference in Internet-banking experience between married and unmarried (marital status) is statistically insignificant. In other words, Internet-banking experience does not vary with married and unmarried respondents in case of four cities selected for the study.

INTERNET BANKING EXPERIENCE – OCCUPATION WISE ANALYSIS

It is observed that there is a significant difference in Internet-banking experience among respondents with different occupation levels. Hence, the alternate hypothesis is accepted. It can be concluded that there is a significant difference in Internet-banking experience among respondents across various occupations selected for the study. In simple terms, Internet-banking experience varies with different occupation levels selected for the study.

ANOVA results show that the variance in Internet-banking experience by occupations is statistically significant. In other words, Internet-banking experience varies with different occupations in case of four cities selected for the study.

Table 12. Independent sample test for internet-banking experience by marital status

		Levene's Test for Equality of Variances		t-test for Equality of Means			
		F	Sig.	t	df	Sig. (2-tailed)	Mean Difference
IB - EXP	Equal variances assumed	5129	.633	.419	533	.850	.35497
	Equal variances not assumed			.440	651.077	.849	.35497

Table 13. ANOVA results for internet-banking experience by occupation

	Sum of Squares	df	Mean Square	F	Sig.
Between Groups	11697.772	4	2924.443	12.602	.000
Within Groups	95843.702	413	232.067		
Total	107541.474	417			

Table 14. Post Hoc test results for occupation regarding internet-banking experience

Occupation	N	Subset for alpha = 0.05		
		1	2	3
Self-employed	32	110.1622		
Govt. Employee	91		118.6495	
Student	68			120.6667
Business owners	156			122.8571
Private Employee	70			125.0000
Sig.		1.02	2.060	.308

Means for groups in homogeneous subsets are displayed.

(a) Uses Harmonic Mean Sample Size = 31.499.
(b) The group sizes are unequal. The harmonic mean of the group sizes is used. Type I error levels are not guaranteed.

There is a significant difference in internet banking experience scores among respondents with different occupations. Private employee respondents scores are high compared to respondents falling under the category of business owners, students, government employees and self-employed. Therefore, it has been concluded that Internet banking experience was varying among respondents with different occupations.

INTERNET BANKING EXPERIENCE – AGE WISE ANALYSIS

It is identified that there is a significant difference in Internet-banking experience among respondents with different age groups. Hence, the alternate hypothesis is accepted. It can be concluded that there is a significant difference in Internet-banking experience among respondents across various age groups selected for the study. In simple terms, Internet-banking experience varies with different age groups selected for the study.

ANOVA results show that the variance in Internet-banking experience by age is statistically significant. In other words, Internet-banking experience varies with different age groups in case of four cities selected for the study.

Table 15. ANOVA results for internet-banking experience by age

	Sum of Squares	df	Mean Square	F	Sig.
Between Groups	16977.092	4	4244.273	19.355	.000
Within Groups	90564.382	413	219.284		
Total	107541.474	417			

Table 16. Post hoc test results for age regarding internet-banking experience

Age	N	Subset for alpha = 0.05		
		1	2	3
Above 50 yrs.	8	107.7188		
42-50 yrs.	127		120.3333	
34-41 yrs.	44		121.9600	
Under 25 yrs.	138			123.0000
26-33 yrs.	100			124.0000
Sig.		.100	.231	.398

Means for groups in homogeneous subsets are displayed.

(a) Uses Harmonic Mean Sample Size = 28.938.
(b) The group sizes are unequal. The harmonic mean of the group sizes is used. Type I error levels are not guaranteed.

There is a significant difference of internet banking experience among respondents of different age groups. Respondents under 25 years and between the age groups 26 to 33 years have better score compared to rest of the respondents. Therefore, it has been concluded that Internet banking experience scores decrease as the respondent's age groups increased. Age group of under 25 years respondents have moderate experience scores, while respondents between 26-33 years have high experience scores. And rest of the respondents have low experience scores.

INTERNET BANKING EXPERIENCE – INCOME WISE ANALYSIS

It is identified that there is a significant difference in Internet-banking experience among respondents with different income levels. Hence, the alternate hypothesis is accepted. It can be concluded that there is a significant difference in Internet-banking experience among respondents across various income levels selected for the study. In simple terms, Internet-banking experience varies with different income levels selected for the study.

Table 17. ANOVA results for internet-banking experience by income

	Sum of Squares	df	Mean Square	F	Sig.
Between Groups	13194.044	5	2638.809	11.523	.000
Within Groups	94347.430	412	228.999		
Total	107541.474	417			

ANOVA results show that the variance in Internet-banking experience by income is statistically significant. In other words, Internet-banking experience varies with different income levels in case of four cities selected for the study.

Means for groups in homogeneous subsets are displayed.

(a) Uses Harmonic Mean Sample Size = 50.288.
(b) The group sizes are unequal. The harmonic mean of the group sizes is used. Type I error levels are not guaranteed.

There is a significant difference in Internet banking experience among respondents with different income levels. Respondents with monthly income levels >Rs. 45, 000 and between Rs.35, 001-Rs. 45, 000 have better score compares to rest of the respondents. Therefore, it has been concluded that Internet banking experience scores increase as the respondents' monthly income levels increase. Respondents with monthly income levels >Rs.45, 000 have high Internet banking experience scores, while respondents with monthly income between Rs.35, 001 and Rs.45, 000, Rs.25, 001 and Rs.35, 000 and Rs.15, 001-Rs.25, 000 have moderate experience, whereas respondents with monthly income up to Rs.15, 000 have low Internet banking experience scores.

Table 18. Post hoc test results for income regarding internet-banking experience

Monthly Income	N	Subset for alpha = 0.05			
		1	2	3	4
Up to 15000	35	111.3721			
15001-25000	64	116.4375	116.4375		
25001-35000	76		118.0000	118.0000	
35001-45000	98			121.3846	121.3846
>45000	144				124.1429
Sig.		.094	.605	.054	.631

Summary of test of hypotheses for ANOVA with post hoc (Duncan) on internet banking experience

Research Hypotheses	Sig.	Decision
There is a significant difference among the respondents of different geographic locations in terms of overall Internet banking experience.	.454	Not Supported
There is a significant difference among the respondents with different levels of education in terms of overall Internet banking experience.	.000	Supported
There is a significant difference among the respondents with different occupations in terms of overall Internet banking experience.	.000	Supported
There is a significant difference among the respondents of various age groups in terms of overall Internet banking experience.	.000	Supported
There is a significant difference among the respondents with various income levels in terms of overall Internet banking experience.	.000	Supported

Demographic Profile Analysis Findings of Internet Banking Experience

- The results indicate that the variance in Internet banking experience across geographic locations is statistically insignificant.
- The results indicate that the variance in Internet banking experience by education is statistically significant. Internet banking experience varies with different educational levels. From the Post Hoc (Duncan) test Internet banking experience scores increase as the respondent's education levels increase.
- The results indicate that the variance in Internet banking experience by occupation is statistically significant. Internet banking experience varies with different occupations. From the Post Hoc (Duncan) test Internet banking experience score is high among self-employed compared to students, private employees, and government employees.

Summary of test of hypotheses for independent sample t-test on internet banking experience

Research Hypotheses	Sig.	Decision
There is a significant difference between male and female respondents in terms overall Internet banking experience.	.349	Not Supported
There is a significant difference between married and unmarried respondents in terms of overall Internet banking experience	.734	Not Supported

- The results indicate that the variance in Internet banking experience by age is statistically significant. Internet banking experience varies with different age groups. From the Post Hoc (Duncan) test Internet banking experience scores decrease as the respondent's age increase.
- The results indicate that the variance in Internet banking experience by income is statistically significant. Internet banking experience varies with different income levels. From the Post Hoc (Duncan) test Internet banking experience scores increase as the respondent's monthly income levels increase.

CONCLUSION

Banking self-service technology (e.g., internet banking) is bound to play a significant role in producing superior customer experience in the current scenario of increasing penetration of internet, wide spread deployment of retail banking services related innovative technologies, preference of smartphones by users and rapid developments in information technology that are finding applications in banking industry paramount importance. In the Indian context where there is a clear digital, divide across various cross sections of the society. The of study the Internet banking experience and understand the role of demographics in delivering superior customer experience is very much needed. It is only when the above issues are clearly understood; bank managers could be successful while examining demographics of each individual customer towards creating and delivering superior customer experience to a wide cross section of society.

The results indicate that gender does not have a significant impact on Internet banking experience. The study revealed that the mean scores of Internet banking experience by marital status is statistically insignificant. Cross sectional nature of research implies that results may vary across different countries. However, the study adopted purposive sampling method, which is non-random, and there may be a chance of sampling bias.

REFERENCES

Addis, M. & Holbrook, M. B. (2001). On the conceptual link between mass customization and experiential consumption: an explosion of subjectivity. *Journal of consumer behavior*, *1*(1), 50-66.

Aldás-Manzano, J., Lassala-Navarre, C., Ruiz-Mafe, C. & Sanz-Blas, S. (2009). The role of consumer innovativeness and perceived risk in online banking usage. *International Journal of Bank Marketing*, *27*(1), 53-75.

Babin, B. J., Darden, W. R. & Griffin, M. (1994). Work and fun: measuring hedonic and utilitarian shopping value. *Journal of consumer research*, *20*(4), 644-656.

Bagozzi, R. P., Gopinath, M. & Nyer, P. U. (1999). The role of emotions in marketing. *Journal of the academy of marketing science*, *27*(2), 184-206.

Berry, L. L., Carbone, L. P. & Haeckel, S. H. (2002). Managing the total customer experience. *MIT Sloan management review*, *43*(3), 85.

Bitner, M. J. (1990). Evaluating service encounters: the effects of physical surroundings and employee responses. *The Journal of Marketing*, 69-82.

Calhoun, J. (2001). Driving loyalty by managing the total customer experience. *Ivey Business Journal*, *65*(6), 69-73.

Carbone, L. P. (1998). Total customer experience drives value. *Management review*, *87*(7), 62-63.

Carbone, L. P. & Haeckel, S. H. (1994). Engineering customer experiences. *Marketing Management*, *3*(3), 8.

Dabholkar, P. A. (1999). Implications for Self-Service and Service Support. *Handbook of services marketing and management*, 103.

Devlin, J. F. & Gerrard, P. (2004). Choice criteria in retail banking: an analysis of trends. *Journal of Strategic Marketing*, *12*(1), 13-27.

Gentile, C., Spiller, N. & Noci, G. (2007). How to sustain the customer experience: An overview of experience components that co-create value with the customer. *European Management Journal*, *25*(5), 395-410.

Holbrook, M. B. & Hirschman, E. C. (1982). The experiential aspects of consumption: Consumer fantasies, feelings, and fun. *Journal of consumer research*, *9*(2), 132-140.

Jamal, A. & Naser, K. (2002). Customer satisfaction and retail banking: an assessment of some of the key antecedents of customer satisfaction in retail banking. *international journal of bank marketing*, *20*(4), 146-160.

Meyer, C. & Schwager, A. (2007). Understanding customer experience. *Harvard Business Review*, 1-12.

Meuter, M. L., Ostrom, A. L., Roundtree, R. I. & Bitner, M. J. (2000). Self-service technologies: understanding customer satisfaction with technology-based service encounters. *Journal of marketing*, *64*(3), 50-64.

Pine, B. J. & Gilmore, J. H. (1999). *The experience economy: work is theatre & every business a stage*. Harvard Business Press.

Pine, J. & Gilmore, J. H. (1999). *The experience economy: work is theatre & every business a stage.* Boston: Harvard Business Press. November 2010).

Verhoef, P. C., Lemon, K. N., Parasuraman, A., Roggeveen, A., Tsiros, M. & Schlesinger, L. A. (2009). Customer experience creation: Determinants, dynamics, and management strategies. *Journal of Retailing*, *85*(1), 31-41.

Zineldin, M. (1996). Bank strategic positioning and some determinants of bank selection. *International Journal of Bank Marketing*, *14*(6), 12-22.

In: Strategic Rethinking
Editors: Rajagopal et al.
ISBN: 978-1-53616-835-8

Chapter 8

SELF-IMAGE CONGRUENCE TOWARDS VOGUE BRANDS AMONG MILLENNIALS: A STUDY OF CONSUMER BEHAVIOR IN MEXICO

Ananya Rajagopal
Department of Administrative Sciences, EGADE Business School
Tecnologico de Monterrey,
Santa Fe Campus, Mexico City, Mexico

ABSTRACT

Millennial consumers are dynamic, innovative, and personality oriented. Buying behavior of millennial consumers is widely influenced by self-image congruence, social self-concept, psychodynamics, and vogue. This study focuses on exploring the consumption behavior among millennial consumers in reference to self-image congruence, consumer relationships, and consumption experience leading to their buying behavior of vogue brands. The study revealed that the vogue brands develop emotions and me-too-feeling. Vogue brands inculcate social identities among millennial consumers and establish the concept of 'self' to drive anthropomorphic emotions. Millennial consumers tend to share their brand experience on digital space to create effective psychodynamics and brand sovereignty.

Keywords: millennial consumers, self-image congruence, social self-concept, vogue brands, purchase intentions, Mexico

INTRODUCTION

Most consumers exhibit satisfaction as a materialistic output instead of gaining perceptual value based on self-congruity, motivations, and consumption experience derived through consumer relationships (Schmitt et al., 2015). Millennial consumers exhibit consumption behavior towards possessing vogue brands, and engaging in new trends in social dynamism (Rindfleisch et al., 1997; Rahinel and Redden, 2013; Giesler and Veresiu, 2014), which distinguishes them as pro-vogue consumers versus mass consumers. Conventionally, consumers tend to be more responsible in acquiring comprehensive information about brands for making buying decisions in reference to perceived satisfaction and societal values. However, millennial consumers exhibit subjectivity in adapting to vogue brands and the transformative consumption experience (Giesler and Veresiu, 2014).

The buying behavior of millennial consumers is widely influenced by self-perceived expectations, psychodynamics, vogue, and socio-personal interactions. Consumer expectations are portrayed for self-image revelation,and play a major role in making buying decisions and determining the consumer behavior. Vogue brands are generally positioned as high-end products. They motivate middle- and upper-class consumers for experimentation,and develop a social pattern-based consumption spread across spatial and temporal dimension (Gofman et al., 2010). Self-congruity theory explains that the congruence resulting from a cognitive comparison involving the product, user image, and the self-concept of consumers, affects the consumer behavior (Sirgy et al., 2000) Millennial consumers are largely influenced by the market vogue, they develop their perceptions on brands in reference to peer consumption experiences. The extrinsic values associated with consumption experiences build self-congruence among the potential consumers of the vogue brands in the marketplace. Consumers explore motivations to derive consumption experiences to support their self-congruence (Plewa and Palmer, 2014). Brand communication motivates consumers by using rich conceptual and application driven vocabulary which distinguishes the brand meaning and the associated relationships. Consumers explore brands, and analyze social relationships with brands to validate self-congruity and brand experience (Fournier, 1998).

Product consumption among millennials signifies symbolism, which can be explained as exhibition of personal attributes motivated by vogue. Consumers today live at par with the contemporary social patterns. Symbolic consumption reflects the personality and lifestyle of consumers, expressing social distinctions (Hosany and Martin, 2012). Consumers symbolize consumption in reference to self-congruity and brand personality. They experience symbolic consumption by anthropomorphizing with social endorsements of brands and their attributes (Fournier, 1998; Brown 1991). Consumers tend to make buying decisions promptly, and avoid the temporal gaps in order to gain experience on consumption matching with their self-congruence (Kumar and Gilovich, 2015). Self-congruence leads to satisfaction by developing consumer values in reference to the attributes of products and services comprising referred experience, image, and brand reputation. Millennial consumers develop self-congruence on brands in view of the peer-culture, and the contemporary social values. The peer motivation drives them to assimilate to their social group by conforming on identity-signaling attributes such as premium brands, uniqueness attributes such as color, and the price-affordability ratio (Chan et al., 2012; Dalton and Huang, 2014).

This study contributes to the existing literature by revisiting the self-congruity theory in explaining behavior of millennial consumers in reference to adapting to vogue brands. The research explored in this study develops convergence between self-image congruity and 'me-too-feeling' for the vogue brands among millennial consumers. Such relationship explained in this research validates the relationship of vogue brands with self-image congruity and brand image congruity studied by Hosany and Martin (2012). This study further explains the new dimension of psychodynamics in reference to social self-concept, which integrates with the consumer experience shared through the social media. This study contributes in exploring further the research propositions laid by Hosany and Martin (2012) and Ibrahim and Najjar (2008), using 'me-too-feeling' cognition as a driver for anthropomorphic satisfaction among consumers on vogue brands.

Literature Review and Research Propositions

Millennial consumers exhibit intensive behavior towards the changing social-dynamism and consumption of vogue brands, as compared to the other consumer generations. Their relationship with the current market trends and fashion industry appears to be linear and sustainable. Millennial consumers tend to restore their consumption behavior for vogue brands in reference to 'boom and bust' fashion trends growing in the emerging markets. Therefore, the relationship of millennial consumers with vogue brands contributes significantly to the fashion industry. The consumer behavior of millennials is constituted by self-congruence, social-dynamics, vogue, and emotions leading to 'me-too-feeling'.

Self-Image Congruence

Self-image congruity in millennial consumers is observed in the context of self-image exhibition, which refers to the cognitive match between the self-concept indicating the ideal-self and the social-self perspectives in relation to brand image (Hosany and Martin, 2012). Self-image congruence analyzes the cognitive dimensions of attention (self and social), interest, desire, and derived satisfaction that develop preferences for brands among millennial consumers (Beerli et al., 2007). Consumption of vogue brands symbolizes personal attributes, motivations, and social patterns. They also reflect on personality and lifestyle of the consumers, expressing social distinctions and self-expressions (Ibrahim and Najjar, 2008). Self-image congruence affects positive attitudes towards brands built through advertising effectiveness (Bjerke and Polegato, 2006), market and social influence on consumer preferences (Quester et al., 2000), peer attitude, perceived quality, and brand preferences (Kressmann et al., 2006). Reviewing the discussions in the previous studies stated above, the following proposition can be framed as:

P_1: Consumer association with vogue brands depends on the self-image congruity and anthropomorphic expressions of the brand.

Self-image congruence is related to the self-concept of consumer and the social significance of vogue brands that determine the market trends. The millennial consumers therefore prefer vogue brands to their ideal social self-concept (Rhee and Johnson, 2012). A positive relationship between the self-image congruence and high-end vogue brands develops consumer preferences towards buying and getting associated with such brands in the long- run. The exclusive brands stores and high-end department stores patronize millennial consumers to inculcate self-image congruence to develop convergence with consumer behavior and vogue brands (Sung and Huddleston, 2018). Convergence of self-image congruence and social significance of vogue brands facilitates self-expression of millennial consumers. In view of the above discussion the following research proposition has been formed:

P_2: Social self-concept, social trends, and brand personality traits affect self-image congruity on vogue brands among millennial consumers.

Self-image congruence influences brand preference, brand satisfaction and purchase intentions. Besides innovative launching practices of vogue brands, the inter-relationship between self-image congruence and perceived quality helps in developing purchase intentions towards vogue brands. The quality perceptions not only develop purchase intentions, but also inculcate affinity of consumers with vogue brands (Kwak and Kang, 2009).

Vogue Brands

Corporate advertising involving visual merchandising and user-generated contents on social media develop consumer perceptions, purchase intentions and emotional attachments on vogue brands in the luxury fashion markets. Consumer engagement in corporate advertisements, social diffusion of functional benefits, and symbolic benefits leading to anthropomorphic satisfaction have significant impact on associating with vogue brands among millennial consumers (So et al., 2013). The millennial consumers derive perceptions on vogue brands and their attributes in the context of store image. The perception of luxury store image helps in pushing the image of vogue brands among millennials. In addition to the store image, the advertisement and brand campaigns of vogue brands develop symbiotic loyalty over store and vogue brands (Herstein et al., 2013). Referring to the above discussion, the following research proposition has been structured:

> **P_3:** Corporate advertising, and brand endorsements of vogue brands affect purchase intentions of millennial consumers.

Consumers' perception on status consciousness related to vogue brands enhances social relationships and individual satisfaction. Millennial consumers feel privileged to pay premium price for a specific vogue brand to enhance their personality and social status (O'Cass and Siahtiri, 2014). Social status consciousness of consumers about vogue brands influences perceived fitness of consumer personality with social trends,and contributes value to augment the satisfaction and social enlightenment. Perceived fit between self-image congruence and attributes of vogue brands develop positive effect on purchase intentions (Kim and Chung, 2012).

Consumer personality, social consciousness, and self-image congruity are strong predicators of brand attitude and brand loyalty of vogue brands among millennial consumers. Both social consciousness and self-image congruity significantly affect the sustainable attitude towards vogue brands and derived social benefits (Liu et al., 2012). Vogue brands are intertwined with dynamic consumption patterns and socially driven consumer personalities. Effective advertisements, fashion events, and vogue campaigns by luxury brands tend to develop four types of involvements comprising consumption involvement, inter-personal communication; product attributes, and purchase decision. Such involvement among millennial consumers strengthen brand affinity in reference to personality manifestation of consumers. The involvement of millennial consumers in vogue brands is gender insensitive, but is sensitive to personality portrayal (Power and Hauge, 2008; Khare and Rakesh, 2010). Accordingly, the following research proposition has been structured:

> **P_4:** Effective consumer relationship established through inter-personal communication revealing social status affects consumer cognition on purchase intention.

Interactive media usage helps millennial consumers in determining the social significance of vogue brands in the current marketing environment. Millennial consumers indicate significantly high involvement in interactive media channels, and diffuse perceptions on socially laudable fashion brands (Moore, 2012).

Millennial Consumer Behavior

The vogue brand companies employ ethnic marketing tactics by highlighting the social and economic advantages of brands to attract millennial consumers, and help in sharing their experience on social media (Grotts and Johnson, 2013; Bonaparte, 2017). The consumer value associated with vogue brands develops relationship between consumer identity and perceived image congruity. The vogue brands are valued by millennials in reference to their social, ethnic, and contemporary cultural dynamics. Such value perceptions have significant implications towards using the vogue brands and deriving a longitudinal satisfaction (Ross and Harradine, 2011). Reviewing the previous studies, the research proposition has been developed as astted below:

> **P_5:** Ethnic promotions and digital marketing strategies influence self-image congruence on vogue brands, and develop purchase intentions.

The millennial consumers prefer consumption of ethnic vogue brands in the marketplace. Such behavior of millennial consumers attracts companies in the fashion industry to refine target markets, and create ethnic brand image through conventional and digital media channels (Meyers and Morgan, 2013).

Consumer Cognition on Vogue Brands

Millennial consumers are dynamic, innovative, and personality oriented. These attributes are very important for companies in fashion industry to determine the cognitive potential of millennials towards decision making in a pre-determined market segment. The shopping styles, diffusion of fashion trends, and associated endorsements of celebrities for vogue brands determine the role of the above-mentioned cognitive attributes of consumers in building brand associations (Park et al., 2010). Vogue brands tend to create unique shopping experiences and diffuse fashion trends to motivate purchase intentions. These brands focus on self-shopping, peer shopping, and shopping for others to purchase novelty gift items. The vogue brands expand the scope of shopping from utilitarian to luxury, and personal to social contexts (Gillison and Reynolds, 2016). The discussion on shopping styles and consumer sovereignty motivates the structure of following proposition:

P_6: Shopping styles, diffusion of fashion trends, and consumer sovereignty influence purchase intentions of vogue brands among millennial consumers.

Millennial consumers express sovereignty within consumers of their age groups, and develop a particular trend of consumption of fashion products. The consumer sovereignty supports the cognitive process towards purchase and consumption of trendy products. Effective advertisements and celebrity endorsements to promote fashion trends lower cognitive defenses, and increase intentions of millennial consumers towards buying vogue brands (Wesson, 2009).

THEORETICAL MOTIVATION AND RESEARCH QUESTIONS

Self-image congruity and purchase behavior patterns have been discussed in length in the previous literature. It establishes that consumer perceptions, consumer relationship, and brand communications help in developing self-image congruity for a vogue brand among millennials (Hosany and Martin, 2012). There are appropriate evidences available in the previous research, which show that self-image congruence and consumer behavior are predictable. In determining the behavioral patterns on vogue brands, satisfaction significantly co-relates with self-image, destination image, and brand image congruity (He and Mukherjee, 2007; Hosany and Martin, 2012). Self-image congruity in reference to social dynamics and consumer personality drives the self-conceptualization on vogue brands among millennial consumers (Beerli et al., 2007).

The relationship between self-image congruence and cognitive variables such as consumption experience, satisfaction, and brand value affects the consumer behavior towards vogue brands. A socially upheld consumption experience on vogue brands creates positive psycho-dynamism, and attracts potential consumers (Hosany and Martin, 2012). The self-image congruity is also affected by the dimensions of 'actual-self' and 'ideal-self' dimensions. The vogue brands try to develop consumer cognition in reference to the above-mentioned dimensions to generate 'me-too-feeling' and purchase intentions (Ibrahim and Najjar, 2008; Kwak and Kang, 2009). These studies focus on the relationship between self-image congruence and purchase intentions of consumers.

The self-concept describes individuals' ideas and perceptions concerning a brand. The self-concept includes perceived abilities public image, and personality. These attributes are well constituted in the vogue brands, which motivate millennial consumers towards developing self-image, and relating to the brands with anthropomorphic satisfaction (Rhee and Johnson, 2012). The vogue brands create high consumer involvement, and develop emotional attachments when consumers find the brand attributes matching with self-image congruence (Malar et al., 2011; Rhee and Johnson, 2012). Consumers express their self-image through the brand personality, which attributes to emotions, and perceived satisfaction of fashion brands. Therefore, brand manifestation plays key role in driving consumer cognition towards trendy and unfamiliar brands (Su and Reynolds, 2017).

Consumers develop consistent behavior on consumption of vogue brands to define their identity and societal values (Rahinel and Redden, 2013). Attitude towards a brand depends on the consumer's overall evaluation of the brand based on his own perceptions. Most researchers suggest that brand image and brand equity develop brand attitude among potential buyers (Shimp, 2010; Liu et al., 2012). Vogue brands use corporate alliances of high brand equity like Chevrolett Camaro SS (Transformers movie brand) and Nike (Michael Jordan celebrity) to enhance the effect of brand value. The fashion brands are increasingly using the brand alliances of celebrities, popular movies, and successful technologies like Intel. Such brand alliances help millennial consumers in developing self-image congruence in relation to their personality and societal value of brands (Kim et al., 2018).

Research Questions

Self-congruity on fashion brand among millennial consumers is a function of contemporary values in society, brand motivation, perceived quality, and perceived satisfaction. Therefore, vogue brands are strategically designed to stimulate self-image congruity and brand manifestation in public. Accordingly, dynamic consumer cognition involves development of affinity with the vogue brands (Lu and Xu, 2015). In view of the review of previous studies on self-congruence, this research addresses the following question:

RQ$_1$: How do vogue brands influence self-image congruity among millennial consumers?

Social self-concept is influenced by inter-personal communications, and consumer interactions with self-expressive brands. Such brands are driven by word-of-mouth, consumer psychodynamics, and user generated contents. Social network motivates consumer affinity towards specific brand communities, which are self-expressive, and socially identifiable (Ruane and Wallace, 2015). The previous research in this context indicate the following relevant research question for this study:

RQ$_2$: What is the relationship between social trends of vogue brands, and social self-concept among millennial consumers?

The consumer affinity towards vogue brands is developed by brand endorsements, expressive advertising, affordable prices, and effective inter-personal communications. Dynamic portfolios of vogue brands use these attributes to highlight brand identity, attract consumers, and develop loyalty towards vogue brands among consumers (Nguyen at al., 2018). Vogue brands tend to develop buying attitude in young consumers by inculcating higher perceived value and purchase intentions. High perceived value derived from fashion brands build self-image congruence and social self-concept that drive consumer affinity towards vogue brands (Naseem et al.,

2015). Considering the previous studies in the above-mentioned context, the research question for this study is structured as:

> **RQ$_3$:** Which drivers affect the brand affinity and consumer purchase intention in vogue brands?

Fashion products companies develop pro-consumer business models by integrating investment on consumer-brand relationships based on brand reliability and brand fidelity. The positive relationship between brands and consumer services develop brand affinity and purchase intentions among consumers (Kwak and Kang, 2009; Hess et al., 2011). Therefore, the research question in this context is framed as:

> **RQ$_4$:** How is consumer-brand relationship constituted in reference to vogue brands, considering societal value and consumer expression on brands?

Consumer attitudes towards vogue brands in reference to user-generated-contents encourage positive consumer behavior towards vogue brands and unfamiliar brands. Consumers manifest brand sovereignty within the consumer portfolios specifying age, gender, and common interest groups to develop a particular trend of consumption. The opinions of consumer community towards purchase and consumption of trendy products endorse consumer sovereignty (Wesson, 2009; Ho et al., 2017). In view of the discussion on the above-mentioned attributes in the literature review section, the following research question has been framed:

> **RQ$_5$:** How do shopping patterns and consumer sovereignty on vogue brands influence consumer cognition?

RESEARCH MODEL

This study aims at exploring the consumer behavior for vogue brands, which influence millennials through various socio-economic and cognitive dimensions. The buying behavior of vogue brands is a result of consumer-brand relationships that influence self-image congruence, and develops satisfaction by establishing anthropomorphic and social values. The attributes of vogue brands discussed above develop compulsive buying behavior among millennial consumers (Shoham and Brencic, 2003). Fashion brands are driven by emotional attachments and brand loyalty when corporate advertising for branding is effective and sustainable (So et al., 2013). Accordingly, the research model has been exhibited in Figure 1, which explains the relationship among various dimensions of the study and their associated attributes in reference to the research propositions derived from the research questions.

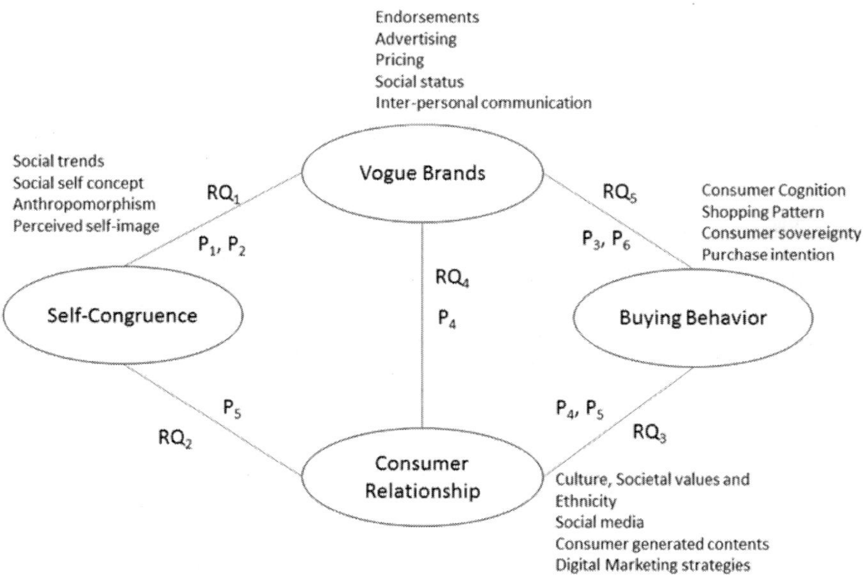

Figure 1. Research model.

The research model exhibited in Figure 1 shows linear relationship between self-image congruence, vogue brands and buying behavior which is moderated by consumer relationship. The self-image congruence encompasses perceived self-image, brand personification, social self-concept, and social trends (Hosany and Martin, 2012). These attributes of self-image congruence are affected by vogue brands, which influence consumer cognition and purchase intentions through reinforcement of effective advertising, brand endorsements, affordable pricing, and inter-personal communications (Bjerke and Polegato, 2006; Khare and Rakesh, 2010). The buying behavior of millennial consumers for vogue brands is the resultant of self-image congruence of consumers, and attributes of the vogue brands. The consumer relationship is determined as a moderating driver that affects self-congruence and buying behavior through dynamic stimulus of vogue brands (Schmitt et al., 2015). The research model discussed above has been used to develop research instrument covering the attributes of all domains of this study. The research propositions constructed in this study have been analyzed using qualitative data.

Study Design

Sampling

This study is based on the qualitative information collected from 72 purposively selected respondents, using semi-structured instrument to conduct in-depth interviews in Mexico City. The respondents belong to a mixed segment representing students and young executives within the age group of 18-30 years who are highly influenced by the vogue brands, and their social status. The respondents were located in Santa Fe (Mexico City) Corporate geo-demographic belt, which has several corporate offices and private higher education institutions. The respondents constituted 64 percent females and 36 percent males in the total sample population. This sample population has shown homogeneous buying behavior towards vogue brands. The respondents were influenced by shopping styles, fashion trends, celebrity endorsements of vogue brands, and social status among peers and the community. The shopping destinations and point of sales promotions have also influenced the respondents towards developing purchase intentions. The summary of consumer profiles with pseudonyms has been exhibited in Table 1.

Table 1. Profile of respondents

(N=72)

Pseudonym (Gender is indicated in parentheses)	Perceptual Segment (Total number of respondents is indicated in parentheses)	Age	Occupation (Number of respondents are indicated in parentheses)
Alberto (M), Javier (M), Marcus (M), Monse (F), Penelope (F), Ricardo (M), Marisela (F), Margarita (F), Ambar (F), Alan (M), Jose (M)	Self-image congruity (11)	23-29	Fashion Industry (2), Sales Executive (2), Student (3), Media and Advertising (2), Event Management (2)
Allison (F), Maria Fernanda (F), Orlando (M), Rachel (F), Sussane (F), Viky (F), Salvador (M), Santiago (M), Isaias (M), Brunno (M), Sara (F), Irma (F)	Ethnic promotions (12)	25-30	Marketing Planning (2), Fashion Industry (3), Media and Advertising (4), Event Management (3)
Andrea (F), Ivonne (F), Paola (F), Patricia (F), Rocio (F), Marcelo (M), Betty (F), Fabio (M), Fabiola (F), Jessica (F), Ximena (F), Mari Cruz (F), Tania (F), Valeria (F)	Shopping style (14)	22-30	Event Management (5), Fashion Industry (2), Media and Advertising (4), Marketing Planning (3)
Angelica (F), Icela (F), Katia (F), Lourdes (F), Roberto (M), Lauro (M), Axel (M), Leo (M), Alondra (F), Tadeo (M), Sophia (F), Frida (F)	Consumer relations (12)	18-27	Fashion Industry (6), Student (4), Financial Executive (2)
Daniel (M), David (M), Fernanda (F), Leticia (F), Marisol (F), Lesly (F), Ian (M), Angelica (F), Erika (F), Nancy (F), Diana (F), Gaby (F)	Social self-concept (11)	19-30	Media and Advertising (3), Marketing Planning (2), Event Management (2), Student (2), Sales Executive (2)
Diana (F), Erick (M), Kevin (M), Pamela (F), Vania (F), Miriam (F), Cynthia (F), Diego (M), Daniel (M), Gabriel (M), Delfin (F), Sebastian (M)	Advertising and purchase intentions (12)	22-28	Fashion Industry (2), Financial Executive (2), Student (3), Media and Advertising (5)

Data Collection

The qualitative data has been collected by employing both structured verbal interviews, and liberal association techniques (Danes et al. 2010). These qualitative research methods have been used to assess consumer perceptions derived from the conventional scale-based approaches (Arora and Stoner, 2009). During the pilot data collection process, it has been observed that respondents experienced cognitive, rational, emotional, and social and cultural attributes in reference to vogue brands. Such behavioral attributes justify adapting qualitative research methods for conducting this research (Cooper, 1999, Hooper, 2011).

The data was collected by taking prior appointments with the respondents, and by administering structured instrument. The data collection process also prompted for in-depth interviews with the respondents on specific questions of their interest. The interview process for each respondent lasted over 90 minutes at a stretch. The continuity and uninterrupted interview process has reduced the redundancy of information by narrowing down the biasness in responses. The interview transcripts were repeatedly discussed with the respondents to identify concurrent views on the social trends on vogue brands, to ascertain the consumer involvement in fashion and preferences for the vogue brands. Only the recurring responses from each domain of the instrument were analyzed in the study.

A focus group was conducted as an exploratory qualitative research approach in order to understand the self-image congruity and purchase intentions on vogue brands. The focus group exercise also helped in acquiring the background information about the consumption pattern and preferences on unfamiliar fashion brands. Researcher's observation pool has been created during the conversations with respondents in the focus group session. Focus group discussions provided insights in understanding the complex behavior of consumers, and the intrinsic and extrinsic motivations (Herstein and Zvilling, 2011; Wei et al., 2015). The response trend for the prescribed sample respondent was 100 percent. The quality of information complied with the pre-determined norms of data collection. The responses were largely comprehensive, and none of the observations were outright rejected for the purpose of data analysis. However, by employing the validity filters, the information was refined and subjectivity-led redundancies were narrowed down (Qu and Dumay, 2011; Robinsson, 2014).

Quality Assurance Criteria

Predetermined criteria were established to ensure the quality of information eliminating information redundancy in reference to subjectivity, external prompting, and biasness. These criteria include refining the instrument in tune to the realistic market environment and cognitive dynamics among millennials towards vogue brands. This action has helped to develop viable research instrument, conceptualization of research questions, clarity of expressions, and consistency of information during the interview process. Simultaneous validation of research questions during the focus group session was carried out to protect the quality of instrument.

A researcher's log for each interview was maintained by earmarking date, time, and contextuality of discussion. Retrieving information from the researcher's log helped in streamlining the qualitative information, transcripts of verbal discussions, and peripheral information on relevant questions. This process also helped in eliminating duplication and inconsistency of information. Accordingly, the quality of information was ensured throughout the data collection process. Many questions were dissected to validate multiplicity of responses by using intercept questions, and response conformity questions in some interviews as deemed fit. The internal consistency of data was maintained by eliminating information anomalies, and introducing appropriate coding technique without interrupting the cognitive base of the responses. All care was taken to avoid any conflict of interest during the process of data collection.

Findings and Discussion

Social dynamics in fashion industry create vogue. The millennial consumers are motivated by the fashion trends through peer interactions, social dynamics, and brand advertisements. These attributes develop social self-concept among consumers to reinforce their personality and societal values by using vogue brands. The social self-concept motivates anthropomorphic values of consumers, which in turn, builds self-image congruity to validate consumer association with vogue brands. The social self-concept propositions significantly influence purchase intentions and perceived value in vogue brands (Ketron and Williams, 2018). The vogue brands are conceptualized by the companies considering the age, gender, and affordability of consumers to drive emotions and me-too-feeling. Louis Vuitton, Pineda Covalin, Chanel, and Versace brands referred in this study have witnessed effective psychodynamics as vogue brands among millennial consumers in reference to self-image congruity and social self-concept. Of the total female respondents, 85.7 percent of women shared their views that they intend to buy vogue brands. These respondents showed homogeneity in determining values led by self-congruity, societal appreciation for vogue brands, anthropomorphic satisfaction across age, occupation, and socio-economic profiles.

> "…women cannot exclude vogue and self-concept in the society to live a normal life. consider the success of brands, which could build self-esteem and public image, and derive vogue into life. Brand awareness in conjunction with the social values drive consumers to get involved with the vogue brands…" (Penelope, 25)

The societal values of vogue brands were found to be of higher significance for women to get associated with the brands. This effect has influenced personality traits and self-image congruence for 90.5 percent. However, 77.7 percent men disagreed with women on determining the brand value of vogue brands in reference to societal attributes. These respondents emphasized that the perceived self-image for adapting to vogue brands has higher influence on purchase intentions than the motivations engrossed in the brand advertisements. However, both social self-concept and self-image congruity play significant role in determining the purchase intentions and consumer behavior towards vogue brands. It has been revealed by 85.7

percent women and 66.6 percent men that Louis Vuitton, Pineda Covalin, and Chanel brands are experienced as self-image builders, and help in developing sustainable buying behavior. Some respondents emphasized the role of brand attributes in developing the sense of vogue among consumers.

> "...the commitment of vogue brands is reflected in its popularity in society that influences consumers to develop affinity, and adapt to the image of the brands..." (Monse, 23)

> "...men are attracted to vogue brands if they fit into their personality and elevate their status in reference to appearance, economic value, and social dignity. No matter how unfamiliar is the vogue brand, its association with consumers depends on its social and personality orientation..." (Javier, 26)

Therefore, the attributes of vogue brands should converge self-image congruity and anthropometric expressions to deliver high value to the consumers. Pineda Covalin brand uses Mexican models to enhance the emotions of consumers, and develop high self-image congruity and anthropomorphic values. In view of the discussion above, the proposition P1 may be considered as established.

The affinity towards vogue brands is largely seeded in the social trends that develop social self-concept endorsing the self-image congruity of millennial consumers. Vogue brands that symbolize the consumer personalities, and live to the expectations of social recognition, are preferred by the millennials. The combination of above-mentioned attributes generates brand affinity, and sustainable social self-perceptions endorsing the vogue.

> "...vogue is a dynamic perception, which is periodically injected in the society. Women carry out the image of vogue in the society, and drive the trend in the market. Therefore, social trends are built by women and followed by others as social self-concept. For women, self-image often drives the affordability of vogue brands..." Leticia, (19)

Vogue appears as a dynamic driver in socially related self-concepts, attributions for personal success, and developing peer relationships. The respondents were inquired to reveal their perceptions on their inclinations in adapting to the vogue brands. Upon reviewing the responses carefully, and removing the redundancy and biasness of information, it has been found that 86.6 percent of total respondents revealed that social self-concept is the key for adapting to the vogue brands. Some of the respondents categorically stated their views on vogue brands in the context of self-concept, social trends, and brand personality as documented below.

> "...I feel that a vogue brand can be successful if it converges with social values, enhances self-esteem, and brings the feeling of self-actualization among young consumers who aim at establishing their social image. Celebrity endorsements do inculcate self-image congruity, but the social appreciation of vogue brands takes them to the heights of success..." David (29)

> "...my recurring dream is to follow social trend, and become a brand ambassador to diffuse social trends with personality traits against socio-economic odds. I like to develop unique self-image congruity on fashion brands to match with the rising social-concept..." Daniel (30)

Identities developed with vogue brands stay on the top of mind of people, which delivers high self-actualization and perceived self-image. Social identities developed by consuming vogue brands establish social relations, work-place acknowledgements, and social group memberships that establish the 'self' of a person. The discussion given above substantiates the proposition P2.

Corporate advertising of vogue brands through celebrity endorsements affects purchase intentions of millennial consumers. In the context of brand advertisements of vogue brands, 76 percent of female respondents revealed that celebrity status, gender, age, and reviews on social media endorse the brand value, while 55.5 percent of male respondents stated that popularity and social posture of male celebrities revealing masculinity appeal the advertisement of vogue brands. The emotional contents of verbal and nonverbal advertisements appeal the purchase intentions of young consumers by modifying their self-image congruity in tune with the celebrity images. The statement above was endorsed by 66.6 percent of female respondents who emphasized that the posture of advertising anchors induces purchase intentions. On the other hand, 77.7 percent of male respondents stated that the emotions in advertisements of vogue brands should be blended with ethnic and trendy values. The following statements of respondents validate the discussions above to a large extent:

> "I like the essentialist concept of Louis Vuitton emphasizing the liberty, value, and lifestyle, which convinces the self-actualization of women today," Pamela, (22)

> "Vogue brands portraying male identities should exhibit confidence, vigor, and masculinity to socially differentiate and empower men. In my view, these attributes deliver immense satisfaction by making me feel like a model," Erick (24)

Self-concepts are cognitive structures that include personal and social attitudes, and focus on personality and goals. Association of millennial consumers with vogue brands depends largely on the quality and contents of advertisements, effective brand endorsements, and their relationship with anthropomorphic expressions. The views of respondents as discussed above appear to be consistent with proposition P3. Further opinions of respondents by segment have been exhibited in Table 2.

Effective consumer relationship for vogue brands helps consumers in defining social self-concept and self-image congruity. Consumer-centric brand relationships of vogue brands generate high-perceived satisfaction among millennial consumers, as they feel brands are rewarding in building their social identity. Such consumer relationships determine social status and self-actualization of consumers in the context of luxury brands (Hanslin and Rindell, 2014). Versace brand has been successful in the luxury products categories due to its effective advertising, and consumer-brand relationship strategies. Inter-personal communication of such brands through digital and print media generates consumer involvement with the brand, which builds purchase intention and social status among millennials. The following statements of respondents validate the above discussion on consumer-brand relationships:

> "...consumer-brand relationship of luxury perfume 'Eros' of Versace brand appeals to me, as it links to philosophical cognition about Greek mythology convincing the brand romanticism. Such inner feeling makes me passionate to go with the mythological storytelling, and relating it to the real life...," Angelica (24)

Table 2. Respondents selected views on various segments trigger questions

Pseudonym	Segment	Opinion	Trigger question
Penelope (25)	Self-image congruity	...vogue and self-concept in the society [...] builds self-esteem and public image [...] social values drives consumers to get involved with the vogue brands.	How does social self-concept help consumers in involving with vogue brands?
Monse (23)	Self-image congruity	...the commitment of vogue brands [...] influences consumers to develop affinity and adaptation to the brands...	Which attribute of vogue brands creates affinity among consumers?
Javier (26)	Self-image congruity	...men are attracted to vogue brands if they fit into their personality and elevate their status in reference to self-image, economic value, and social dignity...	What attracts men to go with vogue brands?
Leticia (19)	Social self-concept	...vogue is a dynamic perception [...] women carry out the image of vogue in the society [...] social trends are built by women and followed by others as social self-concept...	How do you describe the role of women in commercializing vogue brands?
David (29)	Social self-concept	...I feel that a vogue brand can be successful if it converges with social values, enhances self-esteem, and brings the feeling of self-actualization among young consumers who aim at establishing their social image...	How do you describe the role of vogue brands in portraying social image of consumers?
Pamela (22)	Advertising and purchase intentions	...I like the essentialist concept [...] emphasizing the liberty, value, and lifestyle, which convinces the self-actualization of women today	Which notion of vogue brands appeals to you?

Pseudonym	Segment	Opinion	Trigger question
Erick (24)	Advertising and purchase intentions	...Vogue brands portraying male identities exhibit confidence, vigor, and masculinity to socially differentiate and empower men...	How do you describe the deliverables of vogue brands?
Angelica (24)	Consumer relations	...consumer-brand relationship of luxury perfume 'Eros' of Versace brand appeals to me as it links to philosophical cognition about Greek mythology convincing the brand romanticism...	How do you explain cognitive appeal in vogue brands?
Roberto (27)	Consumer relations	...this brand is of Mexican origin, ethnic, and inculcates masculinity feeling. I also feel proud to use this brand as it blends patriotism with fashion...	How do vogue brands inculcate emotions?
Allison (29)	Ethnic promotions	...ethnicity in vogue brands builds my posture unique and boosts my self-confidence in the society and workplace as well [...] A tinge of ethnicity in fashion with the above-mentioned attributes allows me to get accepted in to elite circles ...	How does ethnicity in vogue brands contribute to societal status?
Rachel (30)	Ethnic promotions	... I get attracted to ethnic promotions as I visualize my social postures with the ethnic vogue brands [...] to be a face in the modern crowd...	In your view, how do vogue brands deliver personal values?
Paola (18)	Shopping style	...I am actively involved in social media and Facebook is my favorite virtual space [...] I express my consumption sovereignty on this channel by striking 'likes' and commenting...	How do you describe consumer sovereignty for vogue brands?
Ivonne (21)	Shopping style	...I watch selectivity in brands observing the social trends in informal social interactions, in-store demonstrations, and simulations to develop self-image congruity. I get involved with vogue brands [...] that offer new shopping styles and consumption experience...	How do value and lifestyle determine the performance of vogue brands?

> "…social media and peer values generated by Pineda Covalin brand for men's wear and accessories drive me to get associated with the brand, as this brand is of Mexican origin, ethnic, and inculcates masculinity feeling. I also feel proud to use this brand as it blends patriotism with fashion…," Roberto (27)

Fashion industry uses digital space comprehensively to build consumer-brand relationships which allows consumers to participate in brand-building through sharing user-generated contents. Therefore, successful vogue brands co-create consumer relationship strategies in revealing the social status, which stimulates consumer cognition towards purchase intentions (Confos and Davis, 2016). Hence, the proposition P4 is consistent with the discussion given above.

Commenting on the ethnicity of vogue brands, a respondent revealed that "…ethnicity in vogue brands builds my posture unique, and boosts my self-confidence in the society, and the workplace as well […] A tinge of ethnicity in fashion with the above-mentioned attributes allows me to get accepted in to elite circles …" (Allison, 29). Vogue brands with ethnic promotions are high priced, and are promoted through fashion events, visual merchandising, and non-verbal advertisements. Consumers are attracted to ethnic promotions by developing eco-fashion images among matured women, and the female workforce engaged in fashion industry. The following statements of respondents have been documented in the above-mentioned context:

> "…blending ethnicity with fashion symbolizes not only fashion, but also expresses the social dignity. Such attributes in fashion bring elegance among modern women with affinity to the social culture. I am deeply involved in fashion that exhibits ethnic designs…," Sussane (28)

> "… I get attracted to ethnic promotions as I visualize my social postures with the ethnic vogue brands. A woman adorned with ethnic fashion accessories appears to be a face in the modern crowd…," Rachel (30)

Promoting vogue brands through multi-ethnic advertising is increasingly used for regional and global brand communications using various destination-models. Such advertisements supported with appealing verbal and nonverbal elements not only develop visual attraction, but also connect to brand-contextualization, brand-anthropomorphism, and brand-etymology. Multi-ethnic advertising develops homogeneous markets within niche, and creates brand-inclusivity (Strebinger et al., 2018). Therefore, ethnic promotions and digital marketing strategies influence self-image congruence on vogue brand among millennials, leading to purchase intentions. The discussion above is consistent with proposition P5.

The shopping styles illustrate consumer preferences for preferred brands in different retail ambiances. The millennial consumers prefer to shop in exclusive brand stores located in shopping malls to enjoy diversity and recreation. Consumer sovereignty is a cognitive process influenced by peer motivation and consumption patterns. Brand experiences shared by consumers through inter-personal communications and on digital media build sovereignty among consumers for luxury brands. Social reviews on brand commitment, celebrity endorsements, and peer motivations also affect consumer sovereignty, and influence brand affinity among millennial consumers (Wesson, 2009). The following statements endorse the on role of shopping styles and consumer sovereignty discussed above:

> "…I am actively involved in social media, and Facebook is my favorite virtual space to get aligned with social trends and look for joining the peers by affiliating with new brands. I express my consumption sovereignty on this channel by striking 'likes' and commenting…," Paola (18)

> "…I look for selectivity in brands observing the social trends in informal social interactions, in-store demonstrations, and simulations to develop self-image congruity. I get involved with vogue brands to integrate with social trends. However, I choose to visit exclusive vogue brand outlets that offer new shopping styles and consumption experience…," Ivonne (21)

Table 3. Contextual responses on vogue brands

		(N=72)
Segment	Contextual opinions	Response trend (%)
Self-image congruity (11)	self-esteem, public image, social values, brand affinity and adaptation, and economic value	Male: 54.55 Female: 45.45
Ethnic promotions (12)	Social acceptance, self- confidence, public image	Male: 41.67 Female: 58.33
Shopping style (14)	consumption sovereignty, experience sharing, atmospherics marketing	Male: 14.29 Female: 85.71
Consumer relations (12)	Brand etymology, in-store promotions, advertisements, consumer emotions	Male: 41.67 Female: 58.33
Social self- concept (11)	Social dynamics, self-actualization, social image	Male:18.18 Female: 81.82
Advertising and Purchase Intentions (12)	liberty, value, and lifestyle, gender sensitivity, self - confidence	Male: 50.00 Female: 50.00

Total number of respondents is indicated in parentheses.

The emotions associated with vogue brands are largely supported by the shopping styles which empower consumers in evoking the sense of 'self' and social importance. The shopping ambiance and brand experience develops purchase intentions, attitude, and consumption behavior over time. Such experience was endorsed by a respondent, who stated, "…I like shopping, I like trendy brands, and I like a 'Wow' that reinforces my self-actualization to stay with super elites […] I feel happy to contribute to the sovereignty of vogue brands, and stay as a vogue icon in my social group…" (Andrea, 30). Therefore, shopping styles, diffusion of fashion trends, and consumer sovereignty influence purchase intention of vogue brands among millennial consumers. Reviewing the opinions of respondents documented in the above-mentioned context, the proposition P6 stands established.

The narration stated above illustrates selective opinions of the respondents on various segments of the research which establishes all propositions of this study. These results were further endorsed by similar views expressed by the respondents as exhibited in Table 3. The contextual opinions presented in Table 3, represents the consolidated views of respondents in reference to various segments of consumer and brand attributes of vogue brands.

MANAGERIAL IMPLICATIONS AND CONCLUSION

Analyzing qualitative data of this study, several managerial implications can be drawn to improve the performance of vogue brands. The companies in fashion industry should develop consumer association with new trends in fashion prior to launching the brands. This strategy should be supported with effective verbal and nonverbal communications, brand events, and dissemination of vogue culture through digital space to motivate millennial consumers. Prior awareness of fashion trends helps consumers develop appropriate self-image congruity, social self-concept, and anthropomorphic expressions on the brands.

Effective social advertisements, and interactions of young consumers on digital channels help in aligning social trends with vogue, and develop purchase intentions. Ethnicity, and embedding cultural values in advertising vogue brands develop brand emotions and affinity. As consumers always explore new shopping styles, the vogue brands should be able to provide recreational shopping infrastructure and scope for self-revelation in the trial rooms. Such strategy would encourage consumers to anthropomorphize their personality with the vogue brands.

This study has been conducted among millennial consumers to explore their dispositions on consumption of vogue brands in Mexico City. The data has been collected by administering a semi-structured instrument, and qualitative information has been analyzed considering logical differentials in responses. The study revealed that the vogue brands develop emotions and me-too-feeling. Millennial consumers tend to share their brand experience on digital space to create effective psychodynamics and brand sovereignty. Most consumers opined that their affinity towards vogue brands is resultant of self-image congruity and social self- concept.

Vogue brands inculcate social identities among millennial consumers, and establish the concept of 'self' to drive anthropomorphic emotions. The emotions on vogue brands are largely driven by advertising appeals embedded with ethnicity, personality, cultural values, and patriotic feelings. The advertisements of vogue brands with such consumer relations blend modernity with ethnicity among millennial consumers. The advertising appeals of vogue brands are strengthened through celebrity endorsements and storytelling beyond several emotional blends. Therefore, the vogue brands with ethnic promotions are high priced, and are launched in the competitive marketplace through fashion events, visual merchandising, and informal communication. Vogue brands are marketed with consumer convenience strategies, which include recreational shopping and exclusive in-store trial suits, to provide consumers an opportunity to reveal their image and self-expression with the brands.

Limitations of the Study

Alike other qualitative research studies, this study also has some limitations in reference to the research methodology, sampling, data collection, and generalization of the findings. In this study, there are possibilities of subjectivity in the responses, which may lead to some regional biases if the findings of this study are reviewed in reference to a different study region. The samples drawn for the study may not be enough to generalize the study results. However, the results of the study may indicate consumer behavior of millennial consumers towards vogue brands are confined to the reference period of this study. Other limitations include the qualitative variables used in the study, which might have reflected on making some causal statements. However, future studies could avoid these limitations by using data from several countries, representative samples, and additional variables.

Future Research Prospects

The principle idea of this study is to examine the effects of consumer-brand relationship on self-image congruity of millennial consumers. This study reviews relevant previous contributions based on emerging research questions for analyzing the qualitative data. There are not many empirical studies available in reference to the study region that address the questions raised in this study. The cognitive determinants of consumption of vogue brands can be further explored in reference to value and lifestyle management and determining social trends.

Consumer attitudes towards vogue brands in reference to user-generated-contents encourage positive consumer behavior towards vogue brands and unfamiliar brands. The future research may also be conducted in reference to analyzing the impact of user-generated-contents on age, gender, and common interest consumers to develop a particular trend of consumption. Millennial consumers are dynamic, innovative, and personality oriented. These attributes are very important for companies in fashion industry to determine the cognitive potential of millennials towards decision making in a pre-determined market segment. Therefore, the prospective research concerning millennials may be directed towards exploring the impact of changing shopping styles, diffusion of fashion trends, and influence of celebrities towards consumption of vogue brands.

In view of increasing market competition of vogue brands and rapidly changing panoramic fashion perceptions, millennial consumers are often inconsistent about their brand preferences. Such behavior represents consumer cynicism among millennials, which drives indecisiveness about consumption of vogue brands and inculcates inconsistent buying behavior. These cognitive dimensions among millennials affect marketing of vogue brands, therefore, future research may be intended to explore the effect of intricacies and paradoxical buying decisions of millennial consumers on vogue brands.

The present study finds that women are attracted to vogue brands as they affect their personality, social-status, and value and lifestyle (VALS). The future research may supplement the findings of the study by expanding the scope of research in a multi-region and multi-attribute models of vogue brands. The social recognition factors, and determinants of consumer cognition towards vogue brands may also be explored in a longitudinal study over spatial and temporal dimensions.

REFERENCES

Beerli, A., Meneses, G. D., and Gil, S. D. (2007), Self-congruity and destination choice, *Annales of Tourism Research*, 34 (3), 571-587.

Bjerke, R. and Polegato, R. (2006), How well do advertising images of health and beauty travel across cultures? A self-concept perspective, *Psychology and Marketing*, 23 (10), 865-884.

Bonaparte, Y. L. (2017), Impacting ethnic marketing practices in the pharmaceutical industry: A qualitative study of transformative African American women leaders, *Journal of Cultural Marketing Strategy*, 2 (2), 114-123.

Brown, D. E. (1991), *Human Universals*, New York; McGraw Hill.

Chan, C., Berger, J., and Boven, L. (2012), Identifiable but not identical: combining social identity and uniqueness motives in choice, *Journal of Consumer Research*, 39 (3), 561–573.

Confos, N. and Davis, T. (2016), Young consumer-brand relationship building potential using digital marketing, *European Journal of Marketing*, 50 (11), 1993-2017.

Dalton, A. N. and Huang, L. (2014), Motivated forgetting in response to social identity threat, *Journal of Consumer Research*, 40 (6), 1017–1038.

Fournier, S. (1998), Consumers and their brands: developing relationship theory in consumer research, *Journal of Consumer Research*, 24 (4), 343-373.

Giesler, M. and Veresiu, E. (2014), Creating the responsible consumer: Moralistic governance regimes and consumer subjectivity, *Journal of Consumer Research*, 41 (3), 840-857.

Gillison, S. and Reynolds, K. (2016), Shopping for yourself versus shopping for someone else, *Journal of Consumer Marketing*, 33 (4), 225-234.

Gofman, A., Moskowitz, H. R., Bevolo, M, and Mets, T. (2010), Decoding consumer perceptions of premium products with rule-developing experimentation, *Journal of Consumer Marketing*, 27 (5), 425-436.

Grotts, A. S. and Johnson, T. W. (2013), Millennial consumers' status consumption of handbags, *Journal of Fashion Marketing and Management*, 17 (3), 280-293.

Hanslin, K. and Rindell, A. (2014), Consumer-brand relationships in step-down line extensions of luxury and designer brands, *Journal of Fashion Marketing and Management*, 18 (2), 145-168.

He, H. and Mukherjee, A. (2007), I am, ergo I shop: does store image congruity explain shopping behavior of Chinese consumers, *Journal of Marketing Management*, 23 (5/6), 443-460.

Herstein, R., Gilboa, S., and Gamliel, E. (2013), Private and national brand consumers' images of fashion stores, *Journal of Product and Brand Management*, 22 (5/6), 331-341.

Hess, J., Story, J. and Danes, J. (2011), A three-stage model of consumer relationship investment, *Journal of Product and Brand Management*, 20 (1), 14-26.

Ho, H. C., Lado, N., and Torres. P. R. (2017), Detangling consumers attitudes to better explain co-branding success, *Journal of Product and Brand Management*, 26 (7), 704-721.

Hosany, S. and Martin, D. (2012), Self-image congruence in consumer behavior, *Journal of Business Research*, 65 (5), 685-691.

Ibrahim, H. and Najjar, F. (2008), Assessing the effects of self-congruity, attitudes, and customer satisfaction on behavioral intentions in retail environment, *Marketing Intelligence and Planning*, 26 (2), 207-227.

Ketron, S. and Williams, M. (2018), She loves the way you lie: size-related self-concept and gender in vanity sizing, *Journal of Retailing and Consumer Services*, 41, 248-255.

Khare, A. and Rakesh, S. (2010), Predictors of fashion clothing involvement among Indian youth, *Journal of Targeting Measurement and Analysis for Marketing*, 18 (3-4), 209-220.

Kim, S. and Chung, H. (2012), The impacts of perceived fit, brand familiarity, and status consciousness on fashion brands extension evaluation, *International Journal of Fashion Design, Technology, and Education*, 5 (3), 203-211.

Kim, P., Vaidyanathan, R., Chang, H., and Stoel, L. (2018), using brand alliances with artists to expand retail brand personality, *Journal of Business Research*, 85, 424-433.

Kressmann, F., Sirgy, M. J., Hermann, A., Huber, F., Huber, S., and Lee, D. J. (2006), Direct and indirect effects self-image congruence on brand loyalty, *Journal of Business Research*, 59 (9), 955-964.

Kumar, A. and Gilovich, GT. (2015), To o do or to have, now or later? The preferred consumption profiles of material and experiential purchases, *Journal of Consumer Psychology*, 26 (2), 169-178.

Kwak, D. H. and Kang, J. H. (2009), Symbolic purchase in sport: the roles of self-image congruence and perceived quality, *Management Decision*, 47 (1), 85-99.

Liu, F., Jianyao, L., Mizerski, D., and Soh, H. (2012), Self-congruity, brand attitude, and brand loyalty: a study on luxury brands, *European Journal of Marketing*, 46 (7-8), 922-937.

Lu, J. and Xu, Y. (2015), Chinese young consumers' brand loyalty towards sportswear products: a perspective of self-congruity, *Journal of Product and Brand Management*, 24 (4), 365-376.

Malar, L., Krihmer, H., Hoyer, W. D., and Nyffenegger, B. (2011), Emotional brand attachment and brand personality: the relative importance of actual and ideal self, *Journal of Marketing,* 75 (), 35-52.

Meyers, Y. J. and Morgan, A. J. (2013), Targeted marketing and African American millennial consumers, *Journal of Research in Interactive Marketing*, 7 (1), 6-17.

Moore, M. (2012), Interactive media usage among millennial consumers, *Journal of Consumer Marketing*, 29 (6), 436-444.

Naseem, N., Verma, S., and Yaprak, A. (2015), *Global brand attitude, perceived value, consumer affinity, and purchase intentions: a multi-dimensional view of consumer behavior and global brands*, in Stottinger, B., Schlegelmilch, B. B., and Zou, S. (ed.) International marketing in the fast-changing world, London: Emerald Group Publishing Limited, 255-288.

Nguyen, H. T., Zand, Y., and Calantone, R. J. (2018), Brand portfolio coherence: scale development and empirical demonstration, *International Journal of Research and Marketing*, 35 (1), 60-80.

O'cass, A. and Siahtiri, V. (2014), Are young adult Chinese status and fashion clothing brand conscious?, *Journal of Fashion Marketing and Management*, 18 (3), 284-300.

Park, J. E., Yu, J., and Zhou, J. X. (2010), Consumer innovativeness and shopping styles, *Journal of Consumer Marketing*, 27 (5), 437-446.

Plewa, C. and Palmer, K. (2014), Self-congruence theory: towards a greater understanding of the global and malleable selves in a sports specific consumption context, *International Journal of Sports Marketing and sponsorship*, 15 (4), 26-39.

Power, D. and Hauge, A. (2008), No man's brand- brands, institutions, and fashion, *Growth and Change*, 39 (1), 123-143.

Quester, P. G., Karunaratna, A., and Goh, L. K. (2000), Self-congruity and product evaluation: a cross cultural study, *Journal of Consumer Marketing*, 17 (6), 525-535.

Rahinel, R. and Redden, J. P. (2013), Brands as products coordinators: Matching brands make joint consumption experiences more enjoyable, *Journal of Consumer Research*, 39 (6), 1290-1299.

Rhee, J. and Johnson, K. K. P. (2012), Investigating relationships between adolescents' liking for an apparel brand and brand self-congruence, *Young consumers: insight and ideas for responsible marketers*, 13 (1), 74-85.

Rindfleisch, A., Burroughs, J. E., and Denton, F. (1997), Family structure, materialism and compulsive consumption, *Journal of Consumer Research*, 23 (4), 312-325.

Robinsson, O. C. (2014), Sampling in interview based qualitative research: A theoretical and practical guide, *Qualitative Research in Psychology*, 11 (1), 25-41.

Ross, J. and Harradine, R. (2011), Fashion value brands: the relationship between identity and image, *Journal of Fashion Marketing and Management*, 15 (3), 306-325.

Ruane, L. and Wallace, E. (2015), Brand tribalism and self-expressive brands: social influences and brand outcomes, *Journal of Product and Brand Management*, 24 (4), 333-348.

Schmitt, B., Brakus, J. J., and Zarantonello, L. (2015), From experiential psychology to consumer experience, *Journal of Consumer Psychology*, 25 (1), 166-171.

Shimp, T. A. (2010), *Advertising, promotions and other aspects of integrated marketing communications*, 8th ed. Boston, MA: South Western.

Shoham, A. and Brencic, M. M. (2003), Compulsive buying behavior, *Journal of Consumer Marketing*, 20 (2), 127-138.

Sirgy, M. J., Grewal, D., and Mangleburg, T. F. (2000), Retail environment, self-congruity and retail patronage: an integrative model and research agenda, *Journal of Business Research*, 49 (2), 127-138.

So, J. T., Parsons, A. G., and Yap, S. F. (2013), Corporate branding, emotional attachment and brand loyalty: the case of luxury fashion branding, *Journal of Fashion Marketing and Management*, 17 (4), 403-423.

Strebinger, A., Guo, X., Klauser, F., and Hay, P. G. (2018), Is multi-ethnic advertising a globally viable strategy for a western luxury car brand? A mixed-method cross-cultural study, *Journal of Business Research*, 82 (1), 409-416.

Su, N. and Reynolds, D. (2017), Effects of brands personality dimensions on consumers' perceived image congruity and functional congruity with hotel brands, *International Journal of Hospitality Management,* 66, 1-12.

Sung, E. and Huddelston, P. (2018), Department vs discount retail store patronage: effects of self-image congruence, *Journal of Consumer Marketing*, 35 (1), 64-78.

Wei, F., Ren, S., and Di. Y. (2015), Locus of control psychological empowerment and intrinsic motivation relation to performance, *Journal of Managerial Psychology*, 30 (4), 422-438.

Wesson, D. (2009), Suggestibility as an operant factor in advertising effects, cognitive defences and the issue of consumer sovereignty, *Journal of Customer Behavior*, 8 (4), 347-359.

In: Strategic Rethinking
Editors: Rajagopal et al.
ISBN: 978-1-53616-835-8

Chapter 9

ROLE OF ETHICS AND VALUE SYSTEM IN HIGHER EDUCATION WITH SPECIAL REFERENCE TO PROPOSED NEW EDUCATION POLICY

Karunesh Saxena[1,*], Vandana Gupta[2] and Ashish Mathur[3]

[1]Faculty of Management Studies,
Mohan Lal Sukhadia University, Udaipur
[2]Faculty of Commerce & Management Studies,
Lachoo Memorial College of Science & Technology,
(Autonomous) Jodhpur
[3]Indira Gandhi National Tribal University, Amarkantak

ABSTRACT

India is considered to be a developing country with a rapidly growing economy. The Indian higher education system plays a vital role in it.

* Corresponding Author's Email: karuneshsaxena@gmail.com.

Higher education is very important for the development of the economy as well as for the society. To cater to the need of the society and the nation, the Government of India has drafted an education policy to educate both urban and rural people. The first National Education Policy was formulated in 1968, and later, in 1986. The policy which was formed in 1986 was modified and the new policy was framed in the year 1992. After 15 years of that policy, a new education policy was proposed in September 2015 in Ambedkar University, Delhi. It was a welcome step by the Government of India. This proposed education policy has several good points like focusing on governance reforms for quality; technology enabled learning, internationalization of higher education, etc. The present paper is an attempt to highlight the role of ethics and value system in higher education of India. Some of the recommendations given by the author are that there should be a compulsory paper about ethics and values in the curriculum of schools, imparting value based education and the establishment of a value cell in colleges.

Keywords: higher education, ethics, values, spirituality, morality, promoting

INTRODUCTION

Education and public health are possibly the two most important development vectors in a democracy (Subramanian, 2016). The reality over the past two decades in India is that these have not received a fraction of the importance and focus they deserve. India is considered to be the developing country having growing economy and Indian higher education system plays a vital role in it. Higher education is very important for development of economy as well as for society. The aspirant of higher education is youth. Higher education educates people and made them knowledgeable as well employable. Initially India followed 'Gurukul' system for imparting education to people but the British gave a new system of imparting education i.e., school, colleges, etc. The main aim of education is to make people civilized and provide the means through which they can earn a livelihood. Higher education fulfils both the aims. Employability ensures better standard of living and an increase in cash inflow in the country. Indian higher education system should be improved as it is not fulfilling the job demands of the citizens. To cater to the need of education by the society as well the nation, it has become the duty of the government to draft a policy through which higher education can reach the masses, which include both urban and rural people. The first policy on education was formed in the year 1968 and that policy was known as National Policy on Education.

In a competitive society, parents naturally desire that their children get a good education. However, linking the development of skills in vocational fields, and bringing in an academic equivalence to vocational accomplishments, has not been seriously attempted. This also means that the avenue for horizontal and vertical mobility has not been provided in adequate degree. Fostering dignity and social acceptability to quality vocational training are important task demanding urgent attention (Subramanian, 2016). Against this backdrop an attempt is made in the present research paper:

- To trace the evolution of education policy in post independence era.
- To showcase the salient features of National Education Policy.
- To conceptualize the framework of ethics and value system.
- To emphasize the role of ethics and value in higher education.
- To throw light on Seven Blunders of the World.

Evolution of Education Policy in Post Independence Era

The National Policy on Education (NPE) is formulated by the Government of India to promote education amongst India's people. The policy covers elementary education to colleges in both rural and urban India. After the nation's independence, the government sponsored a variety of programs to address the problems of illiteracy in both rural and urban India.

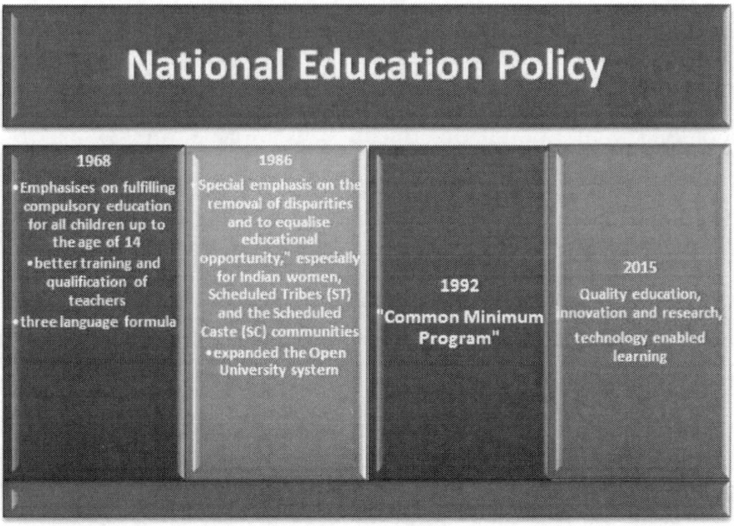

Figure 1. Evolution of education policy of India (artistic creation by author).

The first National Policy on Education (1968) is called for a "radical restructuring" and equalise educational opportunities in order to achieve national integration and greater cultural and economic development. The policy emphasises on fulfilling compulsory education for all children up to the age of 14, as stipulated by the Constitution of India, and the better training and qualification of teachers.

According to National Council of Educational Research and Training, the policy focused on learning of regional languages, outlining the "three language formula" to be implemented in secondary education. Language education was seen as an essential element to reduce the gulf between the intelligentsia and the masses.

The new policy (1986) called for "special emphasis on the removal of disparities and to equalise educational opportunity," especially for Indian women, Scheduled Tribes (ST) and the Scheduled Caste (SC) communities (National Informatics report, 2012). The policy expanded the Open University system with the Indira Gandhi National Open University, which had been created in 1985. The policy also called for the creation of the "rural university" model, based on the philosophy of Indian leader Mahatma Gandhi, to promote economic and social development at the grassroots level in rural India. The policy emphasises on creation of the "rural university" model, based on the philosophy of Indian leader Mahatma Gandhi, to promote economic and social development at the grassroots level in rural India (National Informatics Centre. 2011)

The 1986 National Policy on Education was modified in 1992 and adopted a new policy based on the "Common Minimum Programme" which envisaged conduct of a common entrance examination on all India basis for admission to professional and technical programs in the country (National Policy on Education, 2011). This also solves problems of overlaps and reduces physical, mental and financial burden on students and their parents due to multiplicity of entrance examinations.

All the above stated policies have one thing in common that they want to spread education to the masses. But then the question arises that does education alone improve the quality of life? The answer is no because education alone cannot help to achieve the aforesaid goal. Morality, spirituality, ethics and value system has a significant role in attaining the quality of life. An individual's quality of life is jeopardized due to the day to day mundane routine due to which people are suffering from various psychological diseases.

Spirituality is a sense of connection to something bigger than us, and it typically involves a search for meaning in life while Morality is principles concerning the distinction between right and wrong or good and bad behaviour. Ethics are the moral principles that govern a person's behaviour or the conducting of an activity & the value system is a set of consistent values used for the purpose of ethical or ideological integrity. When spirituality, morality, ethics and value system combined with education then only quality of life will be achieved.

Salient Features of Proposed National Education Policy-2019

The Government of India would like to bring out a National Education Policy to meet the changing dynamics of the population's requirement with regards to quality education, innovation and research, aiming to make India a knowledge superpower by equipping its students with the necessary skills and knowledge and to eliminate the shortage of manpower in science, technology, academics and industry (MHRD, 2016)

- To develop the Universities of Multi disciplinary, HRDCs will be merged with Universities.
- Establishment of a National Research Foundation and DST, ICSSR, etc like funding agencies also will also function in addition to NRF.
- Private institutions also will get funding for projects.
- UGC will be replaced by NHERA (National Higher Education Regulatory Authority)
- NHERA shall be the sole regulator for higher education, including professional duration
- All bodies like AICTE, NCTE, etc. will be transformed to Professional Standard Setting Bodies PSSBs.
- In higher Education, the system will be modified as Type I, Type II, Type III.
    - Type I- Research Universities will include all research and teaching activities
    - Type II- Teaching Universities
    - Type-III- Teaching Colleges
- Boards will be constituted with autonomy for colleges/Type I, II, III institutions.
- MOOC will be given special preference.
- Open and Distance Learning also will be covered under NAAC, only qualified institutions will be permitted to Conduct ODLs.
- There will be Yes/No- recognition by NAAC, instead of Grading.
- Affiliation structure will be closed- all will be individual intuitions of any one type. All colleges will be transferred to Type III.
- All Type I, II, III institutions will have B.Ed., four year programs to link Higher Education with school Education.
- There will be a common examination for MBBS at the final stage of exit also as NEET.

- Levels will be introduced between Assistant, Associate and Professor cadres.

1. Establishment of a National Research Foundation:
   A National Research Foundation (NRF) will be established to promote and support the grant/funding for outstanding research proposals across all disciplines, as determined by peer review and success of proposals. Most importantly, it will aim to seed, grow, and facilitate research at academic institutions where research is currently in a nascent stage, through systems of mentoring by active research scholars, who may have retired or be near retirement at top research institutions.
2. Funding for the National Research Foundation: The NRF will be given an annual grant of Rs. 200 billion.
3. Eligibility for receiving National Research Foundation funding: Researchers from all educational institutions, universities, colleges and schools, both public and private, as well as from research institutions, will be eligible to compete for funding from the NRF.
4. Other funding agencies: Institutions that currently fund research at some level, such as DST, DAE, DBT, ICAR, ICMR, UGC, as well as various private and philanthropic organizations, will continue to independently fund research according to their priorities and needs.
5. The National Research Foundation will fund competitive peer – reviewed grant proposals of all types, across all disciplines.
6. Types of proposals: Proposals of various types will be allowed, including:
   (a) Research projects to be conducted by a single principal investigator (PI);
   (b) Collaborative grants for inter- and intra-institutional projects;
   (c) Initial capacity building by a mentor researcher and mentee institution;

(d) Capacity building to push institutions that are already conducting research into a higher orbit;
(e) Well-envisioned consortia and conferences that are likely to move forward research in the country;
(f) Research facilities of national and international importance;

7. Research proposals would generally be for projects of three-years duration; however, for truly outstanding proposals of high impact, proposals of five years or even longer in exceptional cases would be considered. Projects will be provided a mentor-(retired pesons of any age, no age limit), they will get salary in addition to their pension. In addition to project work they have to teach at least one subject.
8. It is the vision of this Policy that all HEIs evolve into one of these three types of institutions, which we will refer to as Types 1, 2, and 3; research universities, teaching universities, and colleges respectively.
9. Type 1: Research universities:
   These will focus equally on activities of research and teaching. They will dedicate themselves to cutting-edge research for new knowledge creation while at the same time offering the highest quality teaching across undergraduate, masters, Ph.D., professional, and vocational programs. Many graduate and research institutions do not currently offer undergraduate education, which is essential for ensuring that knowledge from the best institutions gets passed on, on a wide scale, to the next generation. These institutions will be encouraged to introduce undergraduate programs as well. It is expected that, over a period of two decades, a couple of hundred institutions, say 150–300, will belong to the Type 1 category, and each will aim for on-campus enrolments between 5000 to 25000 or more students. They will aim to become world-class research universities and compete with global institutions.

10. Type 2: Teaching universities:
    These will focus on both teaching and research but will focus primarily on high quality teaching across disciplines and programs, including undergraduate, master's and doctoral, professional, vocational, certificate and diploma programs, while also significantly contributing to cutting-edge research. Such institutions will target enrolments between 5,000 and 25,000 or more on their campuses. It is expected that there will be several hundred such universities, say, between 1000 to 2000, created over a period of two decades. As they begin to achieve higher quality in research and the range of programs offered, some of them may aim to join the ranks of Type 1 institutions.
11. Type 3: Colleges:
    These will focus almost exclusively on the goal of high quality teaching. These institutions will largely run undergraduate programs, in addition to diploma and certificate programs, across disciplines and fields, including vocational and professional. A large number of such autonomous colleges, say 5,000–10,000, will provide high quality liberal undergraduate education, with a target of on-campus enrolments of 2,000–5,000 or higher. These colleges will also be expected to offer certificate, diploma, and degree courses in vocational education, and in some fields of professional education. Given that teaching is strengthened through research and vice- versa, faculty at these colleges will be encouraged to apply for research funding and conduct, and be able to give senior undergraduate students a flavor of research. Over time, such autonomous colleges can begin to conduct quality research across disciplines and introduce graduate programs, and may thereby aim towards becoming either Type 2 or Type 1 institutions.
12. The private HEIs will have equal access to NRF funding for research support as public institutions.

13. By 2032, all higher educational qualifications – including all degrees and diplomas – shall be granted only by accredited (see Section 18.2) Type 1, 2, or 3 institutions.
14. All affiliating universities will transition to a Type 1 or 2 institution, with one or more campuses. Universities will have no affiliated colleges.
15. All (currently) affiliated colleges, must develop into autonomous degree granting colleges (Type 3) by 2032, or merge completely with the university that they are affiliated to, or develop into a university themselves (Type 1 or 2). These transitions will be a part of State level plans for developing the new higher education institutional architecture
16. The present complex nomenclature of HEIs in the country as 'deemed to be university', 'affiliating university', 'unitary university', and so on will be phased out. Universities will be characterized only as public, private, or private-aided; and as multidisciplinary research universities (Type 1) or comprehensive teaching universities (Type 2).
17. Private HEIs will offer scholarships ranging from 100% to 50% for at least half of their students
18. The MHRD will be re-designated as the Ministry of Education (Moe). [2019]
19. HRDCs will be allowed to train teachers of private HEIs, and charge for the same.
20. The HRDCs will be integrated into the Universities presently hosting them, instead of remaining external entities.
21. MHRD will provide for the expenditure of HRDCs in two separate parts: funding for (I) the centre and the staff as part of the university budgets, and (ii) professional development programs.
22. The number of HRDCs will be expanded by funding new ones within the multidisciplinary universities.
23. Both traditional and open and distance learning modes to be offered by institutions: All Type 1 and Type 2 institutions will

be encouraged to offer innovative ODL programs with the help of the very best teachers at their institutions. Existing programs of high quality may be used to develop ODL programs with similar learning goals. These institutions may also offer programs exclusively in the ODL mode – again when equivalence to standards of the highest quality in-class programs at the institution can be ensured. Type 3 institutions may also offer ODL, based on receiving appropriate accreditation for the same.

24. Recognition and accumulation of credits earned by MOOCs. A mechanism for the recognition and accumulation of credits earned through MOOCs will be put in place by the GEC as part of the NHEQF. MOOCs offered by universities anywhere in the world will be suitably recognized, after ascertaining the alignment of their contents with the NHEQF, and appropriate checks on their delivery methods, modes of interaction with students, and assessment procedures. HEIs may allow their students to take part of their total requirement in a particular semester (especially for subjects not yet represented at the HEI) through recognized MOOCs, as per their choice. The details will be left to individual HEIs to specify as per their needs.
25. Online education: Departments of Education must also be able to offer programs that are blended and part time, to enable practicing teachers to continue their higher education studies and aspire for professional mobility. They must develop courses and activities for in service teachers as well as mentoring programs for beginning teachers. All courses offerings must be available in a range of formats including part time, evening, blended and online, in addition to full time programs. Working professional teachers need to be seen as an important student clientele of education departments, and programs that meet their research and higher education interests should be

developed and offered in the online as well as face-to-face modes.

26. The four-year program, the BLA or BLE in the chosen major and minors, will provide students the opportunity to experience the full range of liberal arts education. The three-year program will lead to a Bachelors degree. Both programs may lead to a degree "with Research", if the student completes a rigorous research project as specified by the HEI. HEIs may choose to call their three-year undergraduate degree a Bachelor of Arts, or Science, or Vocation, or the appropriate professional field. Certain professional streams (e.g., teacher education, engineering, medicine, law) may only have programs of a four-year duration (or more) for the undergraduate degree.
27. Undertaking a PhD shall require either a Master's degree or a four-year Bachelor's degree with Research.
28. The M.Phil program shall be discontinued.
29. Faculty profile: The faculty profile in Departments of Education will necessarily have to be diverse. Not everyone would be required to have a PhD, but teaching experience and field research experience will be highly valued. Faculty with training in areas of social sciences that are directly relevant to school education (e.g., psychology, child development, linguistics, sociology, philosophy/political science) as well as from science education, mathematics education, social science education, and language education programs will be attracted and retained in teacher education institutions, to strengthen multidisciplinary education of teachers and provide rigor in conceptual development. It is desirable to have faculty who have researched/worked with children and teachers, and to ensure that a minimum of at least 50% of faculty come with such experience. It is also desirable for faculty to have at least one degree in Education (M.Ed. or a Master's degree or Doctorate in Education) but this will not be mandatory for faculty. The focus of the Departments of Education will be on

creating a well-rounded faculty with a diversity of expertise and experience.

30. Professional development of faculty: The Departments of Education at the respective universities must also offer continuing education programs for the professional development of faculty. Research will not be mandatory for all teachers in the shorter run, and emphasis will be shifted towards teaching methodology, classroom innovations and student motivation in evaluating teachers. Writing of textbooks and translation of literature between different languages also needs support and encouragement.
31. Appointments will be made to individual institutions; faculty will not be transferable across Institutions.
32. The evaluation of research will ensure that the quality of work is assessed rigorously, and will not be driven by mere number of publications, being especially careful about the credibility and reputation of the publication platforms (journals, etc.), ensuring that no credence is given to low quality (some being 'fake') journals.
33. Academic staff would have three levels - Assistant Professor, Associate Professor and Professor - across which promotions may happen depending on evaluation of individual faculty members as mentioned earlier. Within each of these levels there would be a wide compensation range, with some overlap across the levels. The HEI may decide the overall structure and levels of staffing.
34. Donations from industry: It is suggested that all public and private sector enterprises will contribute a small percentage, say at least 0.1%, of their annual profits to research (such as donations for research to the NRF). This could be done within or outside CSR funds, and such contributions would come with suitable tax incentives.
35. Recognition of truly outstanding research through awards and national seminars: The NRF will institute a system of awards

for truly successful research taking place in the nation, and in particular for research funded by the NRF. The awards will be given across divisions and subjects, and in a number of categories, e.g., for postdoctoral fellows and young un- tenured faculty, and for institutions (and the people involved) for successful efforts in seeding and growing research where it was previously limited. The NRF will also organize national seminars and public lectures on outstanding research to encourage the award-winning researchers as well as other scholars and members of the public to get involved in the important issues that the research addresses.

36. Closure of substandard and dysfunctional teacher education institutions: Substandard and dysfunctional TEIs that do not meet basic educational criteria will be closed. This effort will be launched in a mission mode by MHRD with strong political will, positive administrative intent, and an effective implementation strategy. All TEIs will be held accountable for adherence to the basic criteria of approval of their programs; after giving one year for remedy, if any breaches are found, they will be shut down if the breaches are not remedied. There must be a sound legal approach developed to make sure this enforcement is carried out effectively. By 2023, India should have only educationally sound teacher preparation programs in operation, developing professionally competent teachers - all others must be shut down.
37. Exposure to pedagogy during PhD programs: All fresh PhD entrants, irrespective of discipline, will be required to have taken 8-credit courses in teaching/education/pedagogy related to their chosen PhD subject, during their doctoral training period. Exposure to pedagogic practices, designing curriculum, credible evaluation systems and so on, is desirable since many research scholars will go on to become faculty. They must also have a minimum number of hours of actual teaching experience gathered through teaching assistantships and other

means. PhD programs at universities around the country must be reoriented for this purpose. Opportunities for PhD students to assist faculty as teaching assistants must be created as part of all PhD programs.

38. There will be Board of governors for each higher education institution with autonomy for governance.
39. Separation of functions: The functions of regulation, provision of education, funding, accreditation and standard setting will be separated, and will not be performed by the same institution or institutional hierarchy. These will all be dealt with by independent and empowered bodies.
40. The National Higher Education Regulatory Authority will be the only regulator for all higher education including professional education.
41. The regulatory architecture: NHERA shall be the sole regulator for higher education, including professional education (see P18.1.4). The NAAC shall develop an ecosystem of multiple AIs and oversee the accreditation processes. The HEGC shall be responsible for disbursing developmental grants and fellowships across the entire higher education sector including professional education - the current UGC shall transform to the HEGC.
42. For the next 10 years, the graded accreditation (GA) of HEIs with concomitant graded autonomy, as per the system already in place, will continue. This will be reviewed for improvement by 2020. After 10 years (by 2030) there shall only be a "Yes or No" accreditation - Binary Accreditation (BA). It is this step that shall fully empower HEIs and give them autonomy. The BA system should be introduced at the earliest, certainly by 2022. Till 2030, HEIs would be free to choose between the GA or BA regime.
43. All the other current regulatory authorities such as NCTE, AICTE, MCI, BCI, etc. shall transfer their regulatory function to NHERA which shall become the sole regulator for higher

education. These bodies may transform themselves into PSSBs. the PSSBs may devise a curricular framework which shall facilitate this process in the HEIs.

44. Categories for new higher education institutions: All new colleges started from 2020 onwards must only be autonomous colleges (Type 3). No new affiliated colleges shall be started after 2020. After 2030 there shall be no affiliated colleges in existence - all colleges must develop to become autonomous degree granting colleges or a university.
45. An autonomous National Educational Technology Forum (NETF) will be set up to facilitate review of initiatives related to the use of technology in education along with sharing of best practices. [2020]

CONCEPTUAL FRAMEWORK OF ETHICS AND VALUE SYSTEM

Ethics are the moral principles that govern a person's behaviour or the conducting of an activity with the rightness or wrongness of human actions. Ethics refers to the most important values and beliefs of an individual or a society. These belief help shape the character of the people in that society, teaching them what is good and bad. It implies knowledge of these basic principles and the responsibility to make appropriate choice when necessary. Many philosophers argue that ethics implies values that are universal and are not ties to one society or time period. Ethics is concerned with what is good or right for society. These principles of ethics are based on practice.

The value system is a set of consistent values used for the purpose of ethical or ideological integrity. Value means worth, to be strong. As per dictionary meaning value gives the following meaning: relative worth, utility or importance, degree of excellence, quality, intrinsically valuable. Values are set of principles or standards of behaviour that are regarded as desirable, important and held in high esteem by society. They are based on the moral norms or standards.

Ethics is manifestation of morals and values in the form of decisions. It is an applied moral science.

ROLE OF ETHICS AND VALUES IN HIGHER EDUCATION

Ethics, spirituality, values and morality are basically the guidelines which guide the human behaviour. The world is fighting a crucial war against terrorism, corruption, scandals, scams and many unethical practices. As a social, political, and economic cancer, these unethical activities destroys economies and makes it impossible for a healthy recovery. It comes in many shapes and sizes, and much of it does not involve financial gain.

For example, Corruption is not just an exchange of money between two people. It is misuse of public office for private gain. There is no denying the fact that there is widespread corruption in India. Petty corruption which affects the basic rights, services and society of the common man is highly rampant besides the grand corruption scandals which break out every now and then. The important causes of unethical activities in India are absence of value based education system, poor regulatory framework, exclusivist process of decision making aggravated by discretion and official secrecy, rigid bureaucratic structures and processes; and absence of effective internal control mechanism. Social acceptability and tolerance for the activities and absence of a formal system of inculcating the values of ethics and integrity further propagates it. It is the duty of education providers to imbibe the moral standards, spirituality, values and ethics in young generation of India.

Recommendations for Improving Proposed New Education Policy (2019)

The Government has identified the need of higher education in improving the value system of society; it had sponsored many seminars, workshops, etc. in many parts of the country for eradication of many unlawful activities from the society. Author culled out some recommendations for improving proposed new education policy (2015). Some of these measures are as follows:

1. This is a time to call for inculcating human values in the University students, like quest for peace, adherence to truth and right conduct, non-violence, compassion, tolerance, love for all living beings, respect for the Motherland and the glory of its culture and traditions, in order to promote societal concern and responsible citizenship; so that such an effort is in the interest of the students, society and the nation. The new education policy may take up the nodal responsibility for this, in pursuance of UGC's X Plan Policy document.
2. It is entirely feasible to inculcate 'values' in the students at the college level and there are several institutions in the country where such value-based education is imparted with impressive results. However, it requires sustained efforts to practice, absorb, and assimilate values. A Cell for Value Education may be established at the MHRD to plan, implement and oversee this requirement. The MHRD along with UGC and NAAC could play a crucial role in realizing this objective.
3. Human values and spirituality are essential for students of all disciplines. Thus it is desirable that it should infuse and form part of the teaching in all disciplines and subjects. Here again, the new education policy can play an important role in spreading this message in the University system in the country.

4. The new education policy to involve the UGC for working towards evolving a syllabus for a compulsory paper of appropriate credits at the undergraduate level of all disciplines, to stress human values and the duties laid down in the constitution [Art. 51 – A], and the same may be suitably supported by the methodology and examination/evaluation criteria facilitating a learner-centric approach. A Committee of Value Education Experts may be constituted by the MHRD for taking appropriate steps in this connection.
5. Human Values should be the guiding parameters for governance processes at higher education institutions. The University system may take note of this. Also, the new education policy may consider taking suitable measures for disseminating this information in the higher education system.
6. Due recognition should be given to the expanding socially relevant role of open education and to explore the methods of communicating and internalizing 'Human Values' among the students. Special attention should also be given to develop appropriate study material for this on a priority basis through proper supportive measures. The new education policy include for the constitution of an Expert committee on Value Education which play a crucial role in this connection. Besides, the Distance Education Council and Indira Gandhi National Open University could also play useful roles (Woods et al., 1988).

CONCLUSION

The new education policy should involve spirituality, morality, ethics and value system as an important part of education and focus should be given them to promote it in masses including both urban and rural people. There is a quest for these educations in the society and it becomes responsibility of new education policy to imbibe it in its framework. Many unhealthy practices like satyam scam, avon scam, etc. can be prevented by imparting it.

We may conclude it by saying that the world is fighting a crucial war against terrorism, corruption, scandals, scams and many unethical practices. As a social, political, and economic cancer, these unethical activities destroys economies and makes it impossible for a healthy recovery. It comes in many shapes and sizes, and much of it does not involve any benefits. The important causes of unethical activities in India are absence of value based education system, poor regulatory framework, exclusivist process of decision making aggravated by discretion and official secrecy, rigid bureaucratic structures and processes; and absence of effective internal control mechanism. Social acceptability and tolerance for the activities and absence of a formal system of inculcating the values of ethics and integrity further propagates it. It is the duty of education providers to imbibe the moral standards, spirituality, values and ethics in young generation of India.

REFERENCES

Covey, Stephen R. *(2009).* Principle-Centered Leadership. *Rosetta Books., pp. 87–93.* ISBN 978-0-7953-0959-5.

Hosmer, LaRue T. (1988). "*Adding Ethics to the Business Curriculum*, pp. 9-15.

http://mhrd.gov.in/sites/upload_files/mhrd/files/NPE-1968.pdf. Retrieved 2016-07-01.

India Today Vol XLI Number 27 For the week June 28-July 4, 2016.

MHRD. (2016). http://mhrd.gov.in/sites/themes_discussions.pdf. Retrieved 2016-07-01.

National Council of Educational Research and Training http://www.ncert.nic.in/html/pdf/FinalNCERT_ProfileBrochures.pdf. Retrieved 2016-06-30.

National Informatics Centre, 38–45 http://www.education.nic.in/policy/npe-1968. pdf. Retrieved 2009-07-12.

"National Policy on Education. (1986). (As modified in 1992)" (PDF). *HRD Ministry*. Retrieved 3 March 2011.

Subramanian. (2016) India Today Vol XLI Number 27 for the week June 28-July 4, 2016).

The Collected Works of Mahatma Gandhi (electronic edition), Vol. *33*, pp. 133-134. ISBN 8123007353, ISBN 9788123007359 OCLC 655798065

Woods, John A., Justin, G. Longenecker. & Joseph, A. McKinney. (1988). *Attitudes of Students and Business Professional: A Study of Moral Reasoning of Business Ethics*, vol. 7, pp. 249.

In: Strategic Rethinking
Editors: Rajagopal et al.
ISBN: 978-1-53616-835-8

Chapter 10

Digitization: A Study of Service Delivery Innovation in Banking Systems

***Khushboo Kumari*[1] *and Rajeev Verma*[2]**
[1,2]Chandragupt Institute of Management Patna (CIMP), India
[2]Fellow of Indian Institute of Management Indore (IIM Indore) and Doctoral Exchange Scholar of ITESM, Mexico City, Mexico

Abstract

The recent growth of new financial services by banking and financial firms has driven service innovation in order to gain sustainable competitive advantage. This study aims to conduct an investigation of the banking sector to study the impact of digitization on service delivery innovation of financial and banking firms. The purpose of this paper is to establish digitization as an effective approach for service delivery innovation of financial institutions in the Indian context. This initiative is based on the government's long-term strategic policy that aims to innovatively reform the Indian Banking System.

So far, the potential of digitization has been investigated only in the context of existing products/services. Digitization potential to aid in future

New Service Development (NSD) has been under studied. Current research model is based on Resource Advantage (R-A) theory and includes the constructs such as New service concept (NS), New business partners (NB), New revenue models (NR), Organizational innovation (OI) and Technological innovation (TI) under one umbrella, as enablers of digitization.

The result of this enabler driven digitization will provide strategies for the sustainable development of India's banking industry and the implementation of changes in response to the impact of the digital revolution. We tested our model based on the responses received from 211 applicants from diverse backgrounds using digital platform. The empirical outcome provides the positive significant relationships for all 5 hypotheses established using six (6) constructs. The results provide evidence that digitization has a positive effect on service delivery innovation. These empirical evidences can help banking industry to further strengthen and improve upon the utilization of digitalization as a useful tool for transparent, efficient and accountable service platform.

Keywords: digitization, new service development, service innovation, banking

INTRODUCTION

The recent growth of new financial services by banking and financial firms have driven these institutions towards service innovation in order to gain sustainable competitive advantage. Digitization is one such phenomenon that has changed the way banking system works with an impact on sectorial profitability. Digitization in banking industry involves the implementation of financial and technological innovations such as cloud computing, big data, and artificial intelligence (Zhao 1, Tsai and Wang, 2019: Cohen and Eimicke, 2002; Jorgensen and Cable, 2002). This combination provides users with more innovative financial services including mobile payments, e-wallets, crowdfunding, peer to peer (P2P) lending, and e-wealth management (Zhao 1, Tsai and Wang, 2019).

Indian banking sector is becoming both more strategically focused and technologically advanced to respond to digitization driven consumer expectations while trying to gain market share against an increasing competition from global firms (Lee, I. and Shin, Y. J., 2018). A great deal of emphasis is being placed on digitizing core business processes and drawing new organizational structures with an intent to be better prepared for the future of banking. This transformation in conventional banking is called as 'digital banking'.

This importance of innovation and developing new solutions that take advantage of data, advanced analytics, digital technologies and new delivery platforms has never been more important. We are seeing organizations innovate in targeting, expanding services, re-configuring delivery channels, delivering proactive advice, integrating payments and applying blockchain technology. These efforts are further increasing as global financial and tech giants revolutionize the financial services arena. Banks are also experimenting with new mobile applications, Robotics and voice-enabled gadgets to enhance both delivery and contextual personalization (Schaupp et al., 2010; West, 2008).

Furthermore, in countries like India e-government services has opened new opportunity to deliver information and services more conveniently and cost effectively to the citizens (Wang and Shih, 2009). With this, more and more regulatory bodies globally are requiring banking organizations to enable customers to share their data securely with third parties to power new financial services and increase competition in the banking industry. By making account and payment data available through secure application programming interfaces (APIs), consumers have greater freedom and control in how they interact with their financial service providers.

However, coming up with these innovative services is not possible without the active support of government. It is the government role to provide policy and technological backbone to further accelerate the digitization process. The continuous development and launching of new service is an important determinant for sustained organizational performance (Atristain and Rajagopal, 2012; Sorescu and Spanjol 2008; Zhou et al., 2005). However, while new products/services open up new growth opportunities, they also involve a substantial amount of risk in terms of technology adoption. Interestingly, the failure rate of new products and services has remained high over the years (Rajagopal et. al, 2011; Crawford and DiBenedetto 2003) and organizations are searching the right solution to address the issue.

So far, the potential of digitization has been investigated only in the context of existing products/services. Digitization potential to aid in future Service Delivery Innovation (SDI) has been under studied (Ernst et al, 2011, Boulding et al., 2005; Reinartz et al., 2004). Hence, current research model is based on Resource Advantage (R-A) theory and includes the constructs such as New service concept (NSC), New business partners (NBP), New revenue models (NRM), Organizational innovation (OI) and Technological innovation (TI) under one umbrella, as enablers of digitization.

The result of this enabler driven digitization will provide strategies for the sustainable development of India's banking industry and the implementation of changes in response to the impact of the Digital revolution. Previous studies (Rana et. al, 2013; Lean et al., 2009; Lin et al., 2011; Loo et al., 2011; Han et al., 1998; Zhou et al., 2005) rarely used factor driven approach to evaluate the service innovation strategies for the banking industry during the Digital revolution. Furthermore, important issues have not been considered, for example, how to enhance the competitive advantage of the banking industry following the risks of competition from the unorganized financial sector. Therefore, this study addresses the concept of service delivery innovation driven by digitization factors such as (new service concepts, new business partners, new revenue models, organizational innovation, and technological innovation) for enhancing the competitive advantages of the banking industry in India.

The contribution of this study for theory and practice is twofold. First, it extends service innovation theory to the context of Digitization. For example, the introduction of the automated teller machine (ATM) or e-wallets changed the way customers undertake banking transactions. Furthermore, based on service innovation theory, this study aims to provide a comprehensive view on how banks are making service improvements by digitizing. A construct of five digitization dimensions is employed to construct a model of service delivery innovation for the banking industry. The model also identifies major service innovation strategies for the industry during pre and post digitization.

Literature Review, Model Development and Hypothesis

Schumpeter (1934) first proposed the concept of innovation as a phenomenon that significantly impacts productivity and competitiveness. Innovation has been described as a fundamental source for competitiveness. Based on an extensive review of the previous literature (Payne and Frow 2005, Jayachandran et al., 2005; Parvatiyar and Sheth 2000, Brown 2000) we define service innovation in terms of three facets, i.e.; strategic technological enhancements, human-technology interface and customer centric applications, especially in terms of service firms such as banking and financial firms. Similarly, digitization was considered mainly as information-technology (IT) enabled customer solutions provider. Today, however digital banking is widely seen as an approach to manage customer relationships to create shareholder value (Ernst et.al, 2011, Payne and Frow 2005 p. 168). An important aspect of digitization led service delivery is that it involves strategic planning and processes that take place between an enterprise/organization and its customers/stakeholders (Jayachandran et al., 2005; Parvatiyar and Sheth 2000).

Digitization combines relationship marketing strategies and appropriate technology for firm sustainable profitability (Ernst et al, 2011). One such example is e-wallets by various banks and BHIM and UPI apps by Government of India wherein, digital platform has not only been used for banking transactions but also for providing subsidies and targeting the goals of rural financial inclusion.

Based on the Resource Advantage (RA) theory and Service Dominant logic (SDL) framework, we develop a strategic framework in the context of digitization and service delivery that focuses on important customer-specific processes of Innovation management, Value management and Multi-channel management for the purpose of identifying customers, differentiating among them, and interacting with them (Parvatiyar and Sheth 2000; Peppers et al., 1999; Zhao 1, Tsai and Wang 2019; Lee, I. and Shin, Y. J.,2018). Our research architecture includes five dimensions of digitization namely, as New service concept (NS), New business partners

(NB), New revenue models (NR), Organizational innovation (OI) and Technological innovation (TI) under one umbrella.

We view digitization as an antecedent for Service Delivery innovation (See Figure 1). We extend previous research by applying each of these five processes to the context of SDI as in our research. These antecedents are as,

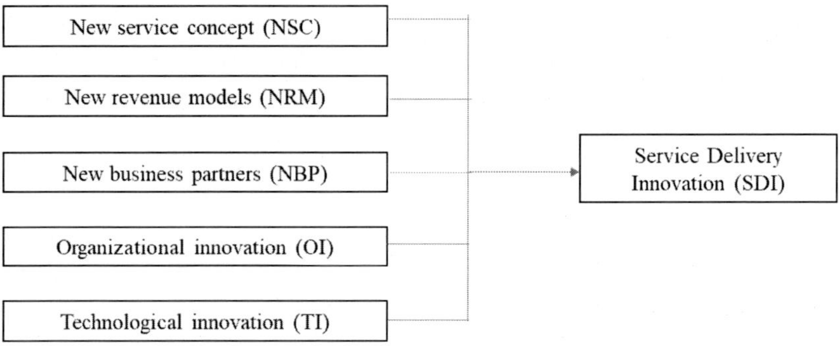

Figure 1. Assessing impact of digitization enablers on service delivery innovation (SDI).

We follow the Resource Advantage view on service delivery and argue that the five above mentioned digitization enablers need to be integrated to achieve an effective execution of a SDI strategy for firm sustainability (Boulding et. al, 2005). Based on our extensive literature review (Zhao 1, Tsai and Wang, 2019; Lee, I. and Shin, Y. J., 2018; Lusch, R. F. and Nambisan, S., 2015), we treat digitization processes as a higher order construct consisting of as New service concept (NS), New business partners (NB), New revenue models (NR), Organizational innovation (OI) and Technological innovation (TI).

Innovation management in view of digitization is the key of new product development Schumpeter, J. A., 1934; Alam, 2002). This customer active process of innovation orientation has been explained by various researchers as organizational openness to new ideas and propensity to change through adopting new technologies, resources and skills (Hurley and Hult 1998; Zhou et al., 2005; Chesbrough 2006). Hereby, we explain the enablers of digitization as,

New Service Concept: New service concept innovation refers to the proposal of a new method or idea to resolve problems (Drucker, P. F., 1985). Service innovation as a novel service concept is to deliver new value-added services to customers hence enhancing firm performance.

New Business Partners: It is defined as an enterprise ability to use its business networks and strategic partnerships for business enhancement and generating new opportunities. For example, banks partner with payment gateways to launch customized credit and debit cards across various business locations, offering free parking to credit card customers, and set up other convenience services aimed at enhancing customers' perceived value.

New Revenue Models: New revenue model innovation concerns organizational changes necessary to facilitate service innovation. Many banks have built their own e-commerce platforms and e-wallets such as Yono, Pay-Zapp etc., to provide customers with convenient capital integration channels.

Organizational Innovation: It refers to the degree of adoption of change in the organization. Organizational innovation is about enabling employees to appropriately execute new services. Organizational structure refers to the interrelationships constructed among various departments and at different levels.

Technological Innovation: Technological innovation emphasizes an integration of various technological advancements for improvising the efficiency of financial services. It includes incorporation of technologies such as big data, cloud computing, and blockchains into traditional financial services to provide customers with innovative and comprehensive business solutions. Therefore, the development of big data analysis, blockchain applications, new payment methods, and digital marketing enhancement are used as evaluation criteria for technological innovation.

Based on the above enablers, we have listed the sub-dimensions for measuring the digitization effort by the banking and financial institution. It comes up as,

Table 1. Enablers of digitization with reference to financial institutions*

New service concept (NS)	Customer-centric (NS1) Service efficiency enhancement (NS2) Reduced credit risk (NS3) Development of scenario finance (NS4)
New business partners (NB)	Alliance with Fintech (NB1) Alliance with offline merchants (NB2) Alliance with financial peers (NB3)
New revenue models (NR)	Multi-faceted business strategies (NR1) Professional business strategies (NR2)
Organizational innovation (OI)	Organizational structure reform (OI1) Employee training and learning (OI2) Organizational innovation culture (OI3)
Technological innovation (TI)	Development of big data analysis (TI1) Development of smart investment management (TI2) Blockchain application (TI3) New payment methods (TI4) Digital marketing enhancements (TI5)

*Adopted from Zhao 1, Tsai and Wang (2019).

Organizations need to collect, comprehend, and apply information about its customers to improve new product/service performance. Hence, we posit,

H1: Digitization led by New Service Concept Impacts Service Delivery Innovation.

H2: Digitization led by New Business Partners impacts Service Delivery Innovation.

H3: Digitization led by New Revenue Models impacts Service Delivery Innovation.

H4: Digitization led by Organizational Innovation impacts Service Delivery Innovation.

H5: Digitization led by Technological Innovation impacts Service Delivery Innovation.

Research Methodology

Sample

To analyse the impact of Digitization on Service Delivery Innovation in the context of banking and financial firms in India, we considered survey as an appropriate research method (Rana, Williams and Dwivedi, 2003). The sample for the present study has been collected from 211 respondents availing digital banking facilities in 5 major Indian public and private sector banks.

In order to test our hypotheses, a large-scale survey was conducted. Anonymity was ensured to all informants. A self-administered questionnaire was found to be suitable as a primary survey instrument of data collection in this research. The sample of the study consists of wide array of respondents from different cities of the State Bihar, India. A total of 400 questionnaires were distributed to the respondents in the seventeen districts in the course of two and a half months duration. The data related to the adoption and usage of the digital banking system were collected only through the adopters of digital banking. This was done purposefully realizing the fact that the system is relatively new. All the respondents were briefed and demonstrated about the functioning of digital banking at one-to-one basis.

A total of 279 completed survey questionnaires were returned to us. The further scrutiny of questionnaires revealed that 68 of them were partially completed and so rejected from the subsequent analysis. Hence, we were left out with 211 usable responses, which made the basis for our empirical analysis for measuring the success of the digital system. The overall response rate was found to be 51%.

Operationalization and Measures

The final questionnaire consisted of total 22 questions including 5 questions from respondent's demographic profiling and 17 questions on the six different constructs (five antecedents and one consequent) of the proposed research model. All these questions were multiple-type, closed-ended and five-point Likert scale type questions. Likert scales (1-5) with anchors ranging from "strongly disagree" to "strongly agree" were used for all non-demographic based questions.

An extensive literature review formed the basis for the specification of the content of the constructs. To fully capture the construct's domain of content, the constructs were revised and pre-tested based on 22 in depth interviews with specialists from digital banking department. Based on this process, scales were refined in terms of wording to better reflect the SDI context. All items were measured on a 5-point scale ranging from "strongly disagree" (= 1) to "strongly agree" (=5) except where indicated. All our constructs were tested for external validity. The summary table for the scales are as,

Table 2. Scale used in the study #

Construct	Variables Studied	Explanation
New service concept (NS)	Customer-centric (NS1) Service efficiency enhancement (NS2) Reduced credit risk (NS3) Development of scenario finance (NS4)	Focus on customer needs to provide personalized and customized services. Mobilize new technologies to expedite transaction speed and improve service efficiency Mobilize new technologies to collect consumer behaviour data to lower credit risk. Combine financial services with new commercial scenarios to develop new services.
New business partners (NB)	Alliance with Fintech (NB1) Alliance with offline merchants (NB2)	Share data with Fintech and e-commerce companies to explore potential customers' financial needs to enhance customer satisfaction.
	Alliance with financial peers (NB3)	Partner with offline businesses to install ATM machines in business premises, provide free parking for credit card holders, and offer other convenient services. Form an alliance with domestic and overseas financial peers to develop service content and scope.

Construct	Variables Studied	Explanation
New revenue models (NR)	Multi-faceted business strategies (NR1) Professional business strategies (NR2)	Operate cross-border banking businesses to develop diversified products or markets such as in-house e-commerce platforms and mobilize business data collected through e-commerce transactions to provide financing services that are convenient. Focus on specific groups to provide more professional products and services.
Organizational innovation (OI)	Organizational structure reform (OI1) Employee training and learning (OI2) implementation of new services. Organizational innovation culture (OI3)	Set up online financial centers and process reform departments to expedite financial innovation, promptly adapt to external changes, and improve decision-making efficiency. Train service personnel to enhance their professional knowledge and skills to ensure smooth functioning. Establish incentive mechanisms to motivate employees to participate in innovation and develop an innovative organizational culture.
Technological innovation (TI)	Development of big data analysis (TI1) Development of smart investment management (TI2) Blockchain application (TI3) New payment methods (TI4) Digital marketing enhancements (TI5)	Utilize big data analytics to construct customer behaviour patterns to explore new customer demands. Employ new technologies to provide customers with effective investment portfolio recommendations Apply blockchain technology to improve transaction security. Adopt Internet-of-Things and biometric identification technology to provide innovative payment methods using, for example, face recognition and voice control. Use digital media, content marketing, and database marketing to enhance the publicity of new services and accelerate customer understanding of these services.

Table has been adopted from Zhao 1, Tsai and Wang (2019).

Analysis Plan

To test the hypotheses and overall model, we used OLS, a useful tool for path analysis with formative indicators (Fornell and Bookstein 1982). External validity has been demonstrated for all constructs. The issue of common method bias was addressed using a procedure suggested by Bagozzi et al., (1991). We calibrated our final model for 211 individuals.

Two aspects of validity were examined: Convergent validity and Discriminant validity. For all constructs, convergent validity, assessed by the average variance extracted (AVE) to meet the criterion of .50 (Fornell and Larcker, 1981). Discriminant validity is confirmed for all latent constructs since the square root of each construct's AVE is greater than the bivariate correlation with the other constructs in the model (Chin 1998).

Table 3. Discriminant validity: correlations of constructs and √AVE

		1	2	3	4	5	6
1	NSC	.72					
2	NBP	.43	.81				
3	NRM	.43	.19	.77			
4	OI	.54	.42	.29	.81		
5	TI	.36	.28	.21	.14	.79	
6	SDI	.03	.23	.07	.15	.29	.62

*Bold main diagonal represent square root of corresponding AVE.

Research Findings

In developing our research instrument, we followed the procedures for conducting research as proposed by Hair, Anderson, Tatham and Black (2006). We also followed the paradigm of Churchill (1979) to test and validate the questionnaire. We performed pre-tests by conducting confirmatory factor analysis using AMOS 18.0. It assessed the construct validity. (Durvasula et al., 1993).

Descriptive Statistics

Prior to administering in the field, the questionnaire was pre-tested and no changes in the wording of the questions were deemed necessary. Before analyzing, the data has been tested against normality. The result suggests no transformation of data, as results are well under the normality limit (Burdenski, 2000).

Model Description, Results and Discussion

The hypothesized relationship as depicted in Figure 1 is tested using the 2-step linear step-wise regression technique. In includes testing of direct relationship between independent and dependent variables.

Testing the Structural Model

The main effect model has also been explored using OLS. SEM takes a confirmatory approach to test the dependence relationships and account for measurement errors in the process of testing the model (Byrne, 2001). The assessment of model fit has been done using the various fit indices as in the Table 4.

Table 4. SEM model fit summary

$\chi 2$/df	AGFI	PGFI	NFI	TLI	CFI	PNFI	RMSEA	RMR
4.11	0.741	0.761	0.912	0.897	0.823	0.85	0.024	0.061

The chi-square/df ratio of 2 to 3 is taken as good or acceptable fit (Bollen, 1989; Gallagher, Ting and Palmer, 2008). The various incremental fit indices include the Normal Fit Index (NFI), comparative Fit Index (CFI) or the Tucker-Lewis Index (TLI), with suggestions for a cut of 0.90 for a good fitting model (Hu and Bentler, 1999). Further the absolute fit index of Adjusted Goodness of Fit Index (AGFI) is greater than the minimal 0.75 cutoff. The multiple R square for the model is 0.61. The path coefficients or standardized regression weights for the predictor relationship are shown in Table 5 as,

Table 5. Path coefficients from the SEM analysis

Hypothesized Relationship			Estimate	P-value
SDI	←	NSC	.346	0.001
SDI	←	NBP	.312	0.000
SDI	←	NRM	.241	0.003
SDI	←	OI	.038	0.050
SDI	←	TI	.451	0.005

It can be seen from the SEM results that all the direct and indirect relationship has been found significant ($p < 0.05$). The findings are consistent with the earlier studies done by Ordanini and Parasuraman (2011). Overall, this study establishes that Service Delivery innovation in the context of Digitization is a theoretically relevant construct for understanding the firm system efficiency. Above results provides useful insights regarding the effectiveness of digitization in generating System Efficiency.

DISCUSSION

The main goal of the current paper is to examine the role of digitization enablers and assessing its impact on the new service delivery innovation process and in-turn its effect on the system efficacy. Our study produced several interesting findings which add to our knowledge in this area. First, our model explained a relatively high degree of New Service delivery innovation (system efficiency) relationship. It substantiates the existing fact that with the new system in existence, lots of improvement has happened in timely delivery of banking services. Our model explains more than 61 percent of the variance in service delivery innovation, thus indicating that digitalization as a rich predictor of new product success.

Our indicators of digitization such as new business partners, new service concept, organizational innovation, technological innovation, and new revenue models are positively related to service delivery with varying degree of relationship strength.

The highest gap (weakest regression coefficient) has been found in the organizational innovation wherein there is a lot of scope in providing timely training to the bank staff and team members about the digital platform. This is alarming as poor knowledge of digital products in the staff itself has led to the lesser customer involvement and sensitization about the issue. New service concept has a very strong impact on system efficiency led by service delivery. It is evident with the high download numbers of e-wallet and banking apps wherein customers have shown interest to use them. However, the usage of the same is different issue and needs to be addressed.

CONCLUSION

Several important managerial implications follow from our study. It is evident from our study that digitization of records and cloud computing can be leveraged to provide important and sorted information about profiling of the customer, which can be used to improve new service performance. Since the new service failure rate has remained high over the years especially in public sector (Crawford and Di Benedetto 2003), digital platforms provide organizations a promising way to address this critical problem. In order to do so it is important to adopt a broader perspective on digital banking (beyond just relationship management). Our study reinforces the conclusion of Ernst et al., 2011that digitization does not simply involve the adoption of the latest digital platform. Its implementation is more complex and involves other elements, especially all stakeholders. It includes all the service seekers and employees of the implementing organizations. On the other hand, solely relying on digital technology is probably not the best way to collect new product ideas from customers. Our study strongly suggests that available digital technology need to be judiciously used to apply for new product development in the context of service delivery innovation.

Limitations and Future Research

Our study represents a first step in examining the utility of digitization as an input into the new service development process. However, there are some limitations within this study. First, the five evaluation indicators were selected from a literature review on banking service innovation. Other methods, such as longitudinal studies and meta-analysis, could have been used to identify other possible indicators.

As such, this study provides a good reference model for banking service innovation and sustainable development following the digital revolution however future research can adopt different approaches to estimate the relative weights of the evaluation criteria on service delivery innovation evaluation in banking.

Further, despite the fact that our measures demonstrated external validity, it would have been more ideal to have a more extensive pre-test of our new items, as it has been used in a different context. These issues need to be explored in future studies.

Acknowledgments

The authors thank Prof. Rajagopal, ITESM, Mexico City for his motivation and encouragement to document this work. Many thanks are also extended to the financial agencies for providing access for data collection.

References

Alam, I. (2002). 'An exploratory investigation of user involvement in new service development'. *Journal of the Academy of Marketing Science*, 30(3), pp. 250-261.

Atristain, C. and Rajagopal (2012), Qualitative determinants of the managerial efficiency toward improving the organisational performance and competitiveness of SMEs in Mexico, *International Journal of Business Competition and Growth*, 2 (4), 370-399.

Boulding, W., Staelin, R., Ehret, M., & Johnston, W. J. (2005). A customer relationship management roadmap: what is known, potential pitfalls, & where to go. *J Mark*, 69(4), 155–166.

Brown, S. A. (2000). *Customer relationship management—a strategic imperative in the world of E-business*. New York: Wiley.

Burdenski, T. (2000) 'Evaluating univariate, bivariate, and multivariate normality using graphical and statistical procedures.' *Multiple Linear Regression Viewpoints,* Vol. 26, No. 2, pp. 15-30.

Carter, L., Shaupp, L. C., Hobbs, J. and Campbell, R. (2011) The role of security and trust in the adoption of online tax filing, *Transforming Government: People, Process and Policy*, 5(4), 303-318.

Cohen, S. and Eimicke, W. (2002) The use of the Internet in government service delivery, In M. A. Abramson, and G. E. Means (Eds.), *E-Government* 2001, 943. Lanham, Maryland: Rowman & Littlefield Publishing, Inc.

Childers, T. L. (1986). Assessment of the psychometric properties of an opinion leadership scale. *J Mark Res*, 23(2), 184–188.

Chesbrough, H. (2006). *Open business models: how to thrive in the new innovation landscape,* Boston: Harvard Business School Press.

Churchill, G. A. Jr. (1979). 'A paradigm for developing better measures of marketing constructs'. *Journal of Marketing Research*, Vol. 16, No. 1, pp. 64-73.

Chen, Ja-Shen, Hung, T. T. and Astrid, Ya-Hui, H. (2009). 'Service delivery innovation: antecedents and impact on firm performance'. *Journal of Service Research*, Vol. 12, No. 1, pp. 36-55.

Chin, Wynne W. (1998). 'The Partial Least Squares Approach to Structural Equation Modeling.' *Modern Methods of Business Research,* Marcoulides G. A. ed. London: Lawrence Erlbaum Associates.

Cooper, R. G., & Kleinschmidt, E. J. (1995). Benchmarking the firm's critical success factors in new product development. *J Prod Innov Manage*, 12(5), 374–391.

Crawford, M. C., & DiBenedetto, A. (2003). *New products management* (7th ed.). Boston: Irwin/McGraw-Hill.

Drucker, P. F. (1985) *Innovations and Entrepreneurship*; Haper and Row: New York, NY, USA.

Durvasula, S., Andrews, J. C., Lyonski, S., & Netemeyer, R. G. (1993). 'Assessing the cross-national applicability of consumer behaviour models, a model of attitude toward advertising in general.' *Journal of Consumer Research*, 19, 626-36.

Ernst, H., Hoyer, W. D., Kraft, M. and Krieger, K. (2011), "Customer relationship management and company performance – the mediating role of new product," *Journal of the Academy of Marketing Science*, Vol. 39 No. 2, pp. 290-306.

Fornell, Claes and David F. Larcker (1981). 'Evaluating structural equation models with unobservable variables and measurement error'. *Journal of Marketing Research,* 18 (1), 39–50.

Gruner, K., & Homburg, C. (2000). Does customer interaction enhance new product success? *J Bus Res*, 49(1), 1–14.

Grönroos, C. (2000). Service marketing and management: a customer relationship management approach (2nd ed.). New York: Wiley.

Han, J. K., Kim, N., & Srivastava, R. K. (1998). Market orientation and organizational performance: is innovation a missing link? *J Mark,* 62(4), 30–45.

Hunt, S. D. (2000). 'A general theory of competition: too eclectic or not eclectic enough? Too incremental or not incremental enough?'. *Journal of Macromarketing*, 20(1), 77–81.

Hung, Y. H., Wang, Y. S. and Chou, S. C. T. (2007) *User Acceptance of E-Government Services,* Pacific Asia Conference on Information Systems.

Hurley, R. F. and Tomas, M. H. (1998). 'Innovation, market orientation, and organizational learning: an integration and empirical examination'. *Journal of Marketing*, Vol. 62(3), 42-54.

Im, S., & Workman, J. P., Jr. (2004). Market orientation, creativity, & new product performance in high-technology firms. *J Mark*, 68(2), 114–132.

Jarvis, C. B., MacKenzie, S. B., & Podsakoff, P. M. (2003). A critical review of construct indicators and measurement model misspecification in marketing and consumer research. *J Consum Res,* 30(2), 199–218.

Jayachandran, S., Sharma, S., Kaufman, P., & Raman, P. (2005). The role of relational information processes and technology use in customer relationship management. *J Mark*, 69(4), 177–192.

Jindal, R. P., Reinartz, W., Krafft, M., & Hoyer, W. D. (2007). Determinants of the variety of routes to market. *Int J Res Mark*, 24(1), 17–29.

Jorgensen, D. and Cable, S. (2002) Facing the challenges of e-government: A case study of the city of Corpus Christi, Texas, SAM-Advanced *Management Journal*, 67(3), 15-21.

King, C. W., & Summers, J. O. (1970). Overlap of opinion leadership across product categories. *J Mark Res*, 7(1), 43–50.

Kohli, A. and Jaworski, B. (1990). 'Market orientation: The construct, research propositions, and managerial implications'. *Journal of Marketing*, Vol. 54, No. 2, pp. 1-18.

Lean, O. K., Zailani, S., Ramayah, T. and Fernando, Y. (2009) Factors influencing intention to use-government services among citizens in Malaysia. *International Journal of Information Management*, 29(6), 458-475.

Lee, I. and Shin, Y. J. (2018) Fintech: Ecosystem, business models, investment decisions, and challenges. *Bus. Horiz*. 61, 35–46.

Lusch, R. F. and Nambisan, S. (2015) Service innovation: A service-dominant logic perspective. *MIS Q*.,39, 155–175.

Lin, F., Fofanah, S. S. and Liang, D. (2011) Assessing citizen adoption of eGovernment initiatives in Gambia: A validation of the technology acceptance model in information systems success, *Government Information Quarterly*, 28(2), 271-279.

Loo, W. H., Yeow, P. H. and Chong, S. C. (2011) Acceptability of Multipurpose Smart National Identity Card: An Empirical Study. *Journal of Global Information Technology Management,* 14(1), 35-58.

Madhavan, R., & Grover, R. (1998). From embedded knowledge to embodied knowledge: new product development as knowledge management. *J Mark*, 62(4), 1–12.

Nonaka, I. (1991). The knowledge-creating company. *Harv Bus Rev*, 69, 96–104.

Ordanini, Andrea and A. Parasuraman (2011). 'Service innovation viewed through a service-dominant logic lens: a conceptual framework and empirical analyses.' *Journal of Service Research,* Vol. 14, No. 1, pp. 3-23.

Panesar, S. S. and Markeset, T. (2008) Development of a framework for industrial service innovation management and coordination. *J. Qual. Maint. Eng.* 2008, 14, 177–193.

Parvatiyar, A., & Sheth, J. N. (2000). The domain and conceptual foundations of relationship marketing. In J. N. Sheth & A. Parvatiyar (Eds.), *Handbook of relationship marketing* (pp. 3–38). Thousand Oaks: Sage.

Payne, A., & Frow, P. (2005). A strategic framework for customer relationship management. *J Mark*, 69(4), 167–176.

Peppers, D., Rogers, M., & Dorf, B. (1999). Is your company ready for one-to-one marketing? *Harv Bus Rev*, 77, 3–12.

Rana, Nripendra; Williams, Michael; and Dwivedi, Yogesh, "Examining Factors Affecting Adoption of Online Public Grievance Redressal System: A Case of India" (2013). UK Academy for Information Systems Conference Proceedings 2013. 31.

Rajagopal, Banks, J., and Rajagopal, A. (2011), Analyzing Cognitive Determinants in Managerial Decision Making, *International Journal of Business Excellence,* 4 (1), 44-60.

Reinartz, W. J., Krafft, M., & Hoyer, W. D. (2004). The customer relationship management process: its measurement and impact on performance. *J Mark Res*, 41(3), 293–305.

Ryals, L. (2005). Making customer relationship management work: the measurement and profitable management of customer relationships. *J Mark,* 69(4), 252–261.

Sawhney, M. S., & Prandelli, E. (2001). Beyond customer knowledge management: customers as knowledge co-creators. In Y. Malhotra (Ed.), *Knowledge management and virtual organization* (pp. 258–281). Hershey: Idea Group.

Schaupp, L. C., Carter, L. and McBride, M. E. (2010) *E-file adoption: A study of US taxpayers' intentions, Computers in Human Beh*avior, 26(4), 636-644.

Schumpeter, J. A. (1934) The Theory of Economic Development: An Inquiry into Profits, Capital, Credit, Interest, and the Business Cycle; Transaction Publishers: Piscataway, NJ, USA.

Siguaw, Judy A., Penny M. Simpson, and Cathy A. Enz (2006). 'Conceptualizing innovation orientation: a framework for study and integration of innovation research.' *Journal of Product Innovation Management,* 23 (6), 556-574.

Sorescu, A. B., & Spanjol, J. (2008). Innovation's effect on firm value and risk: insights from consumer packaged goods. *J Mark*, 72(2), 114–132.

Smith, J. B. (1998). Buyer–seller relationships—similarity, relationship management, & quality. *Psychol Mark*, 15(1), 3–21.

Von Hippel, E. (1986). Lead users: source of novel product concepts. *Managing Science*, 32(7), 791–805.

Van Dijk, J. A. G. M., Peters, O. and Ebbers, W. (2008) Explaining the acceptance and use of government Internet services: A multivariate analysis of 2006 survey data in the Netherlands, *Government Information Quarterly*, 25, 379399.

Venkatesh, V., Morris, M., Davis, G. and Davis, F. (2003) User acceptance of information technology: Toward a unified view, *MIS Quarterly*, 27(3), 425478.

Wang, Y. S. and Shih, Y. W. (2009) Why do people use information kiosks? A validation of the Unified Theory of Acceptance and Use of Technology, *Government Information Quarterly*, 26(1), 158-165.

West, D. M. (2008) *Improving technology utilization in electronic government around the world.* Washington, D.C.: The Brookings Institution.

Wheeler, B. C., and Valacich, J. S. (1996). 'Facilitation, gss, and training as sources of process restrictiveness and guidance for structured group decision making: an empirical assessment'. *Information Systems Research* (7:4), pp. 429-450.

Yeow, P. H. and Loo, W. H. (2009) Acceptability of ATM and Transit applications embedded in multipurpose smart identity card: An exploratory study in Malaysia, *International Journal of Electronic Government Research*, 5(2), 3756.

Yli-Renko, H., & Janakiraman, R. (2008). How customer portfolio affects new product development in technology-based entrepreneurial firms. *J Mark,* 72(5), 131–148.

Zhou, Kevin Z., Gerald Y. Gao, Zhilin Yang and Nan Zhou (2005). 'Developing strategic orientation in China: antecedents and consequences of market and innovation orientations.' *Journal of Business Research,* Vol. 58, No. 8, pp. 1049-1058.

Zhou, K. Z., Yim, C. K., & Tse, D. K. (2005). The effects of strategic orientations on technology- and market-based breakthrough innovations. *J Mark,* 69(2), 42–60.

Zhao 1, Tsai and Wang (2019) Improving Financial Service Innovation Strategies for Enhancing China's Banking Industry Competitive Advantage during the Fintech Revolution: *A Hybrid MCDM Model, Sustainability* 2019, 11, 1419; doi:10.3390/su11051419.

In: Strategic Rethinking
Editors: Rajagopal et al.

ISBN: 978-1-53616-835-8

Chapter 11

INVESTIGATION OF CUSTOMER CO-CREATION IN DEVELOPING NEW AGE BANKING PRODUCTS

Jyoti Verma
Organizational Behavior and Human Resource Management
Chandragupt Institute of Management Patna
Patna, Bihar, India

ABSTRACT

Customer involvement in service design and development has a positive impact on the performance and growth of service sector. Firms can effectively involve customers in New Service Development (NSD) to create radically innovative, high-performing new services. Prior studies recognize importance of customer involvement in service innovation across various sectors such as aviation, IT, banking, health, hospitality and likewise. Yet researchers have not explored the relationship between new age technological advancement in baking industry such as e-service platforms with the firm performance. For example, banking Application Programme Interface (APIs) accelerate innovation and collaboration, with a prime purpose to ease out customer experience. However, it is not possible to co-create unless customer does not allow the sharing of their data. What if, customer refuse to give the consent?

Hence, in the present research, we study the impact of customer driven service innovation medicated by technology advancements for achieving firm performance. This study has been conducted with 143 employees of one of the largest public sector banks in India. Our findings suggest that there is significant relationship between technological advancements, customer co-creation efforts and firm performance.

Customer involvement in the NSD process increases the innovativeness of a new service when customers are involved in the design stage. Ease of technological complexity helps in greater firm performance. Technological complexity also mediates the positive influence of co-creation on the firm performance.

Keywords: customer co-creation, service innovation, NSD

INTRODUCTION

The service industry has become a prominent sector based on the large work force involved into it. Recent advancements in technology coupled with work force abilities has transformed the industry and hence increased the need to better understand New Service Development (Verma and Jayasimha, 2011). However, for long focus on service innovation has neglected a fundamental issue within the service marketplace. This issue is regarding abilities for service co-creation especially in the data driven sectors such as health and banking services. For example, banking Application Programme Interface (APIs) accelerate innovation and collaboration, with a prime purpose to ease out customer experience. However, it is not possible to co-create unless customer does not permit sharing of data and processing of relevant information.

Customer involvement in service design and development has a positive impact on the performance and growth of service sector. Firms can effectively involve customers in new service development (NSD) to create radically innovative, high-performing new services. Prior studies (Zhao, Tsai and Wang, 2019; Lee and Shin, 2018) recognize importance of customer involvement in service innovation across various sectors such as aviation, IT, banking, health, hospitality and like. Yet researchers have not explored the relationship between new age technological advancement in baking sector such as e- service platforms on the firm performance.

Banks need to leverage digital technology to provide simple, easy-to-use, convenient, and cost-effective products and services to customers and improve the productivity of their employees. However, this service blueprint will remain incomplete unless customer play their roles effectively such as, allowing sharing of information over cloud and so on. This paper identifies role of new bank products like mobile banking apps, new methods of client verification, cordless payment, digital payments, and use of data, AI and analytics to improve operations. In the present research, we study the impact of customer driven service innovation medicated by technology advancements with the lens of SD logic and RA theory.

Service dominant logic reflects evolution, research in business and marketing strategy for value co-creation (Madhavaram and Hunt, 2008). Lisa and Mish (2011), has focused on market co-creation leveraging insights from consumer aspirations and service dominant logic.

Currently, retail banking is a connected network for financial and non-financial services with several service providers. UPI (Unified Payment Interface) and BHIM (Bharat Interface for Money), a mobile app based on UPI Interface by the National Payments Corporation of India (NPCI) provides opportunity for innovation led by co-creation. APIs facilitate banks to restructure their IT architecture and work with financial institutions to develop innovative solutions for their clients. Ramaswamy (2009), who claims that it is a transformation that starts from within the organization: "…becoming a co-creative organization is about changing the very nature of engagement and relationship between the institution of management and its employees, and between them and co-creators of value – customers, stakeholders, partners or other employees. In reality, the co-creation journey always begins inside the organization" (p. 32).

Based on (Vargo and Lusch, 2008) the drivers relevant for service innovation in the current context has been identified. It has been found as customer collaboration and business partner collaboration at the firm level. Hence, in the present research, we study the impact of customer driven service innovation medicated by technology advancements for achieving firm performance.

LITERATURE REVIEW, MODEL DEVELOPMENT AND HYPOTHESIS

Based on an extensive review of the previous literature (Payne and Frow, 2005; Jayachandran et al. 2005; Parvatiyar and Sheth 2000; Brown 2000) we define customer co-creation in terms of three facets, i.e., two-way communication channels with customers, active involvement of customer in service creation and provision of customized services at consumer end. Initially, Co-creation was considered mainly as information-technology (IT) enabled customer solutions provider. However, today it has been seen as an approach to manage customer relationships to create shareholder value (Ernst et al., 2011, Payne and Frow 2005 p. 168). An important aspect of service co-creation involves strategic planning and processes that take place between an enterprise/organization and its customers/stakeholders (Jayachandran et al. 2005; Parvatiyar and Sheth 2000).

It combines relationship marketing strategies and technological innovation for firm sustainable profitability (Ernst et al., 2011). By focusing on consumer value in service chain, and product offerings, organizations are acquiring, managing and applying customer information which aids in both understanding and co-creating value with them. One such example is KYC during bank account openings in India wherein, data has not only been used for customer identification but also for providing subsidies and targeting the goals of financial inclusion.

Based on the Resource Advantage (RA) theory and Service Dominant logic (SDL) framework, we develop a strategic co-creational framework in the context of technological innovations and firm performance that focuses on important customer-specific processes of innovation and value management for the purpose of identifying customers, differentiating among them, and interacting with them (Parvatiyar and Sheth 2000; Peppers et al. 1999).

We view service co-creation in a technological innovation context as higher order construct that consists of the three sub-dimensions, as mentioned in the forthcoming table. We extend previous research by applying each of these three processes to the context of SD logic as in our research. The summery of the literature review is as,

Table 1. Listing of sub-dimensions for co-creation, technological innovation and firm performance

Construct	Variables Studied
Service Co-creation (SC)	Two-way communication channels with customers (SC1) Active involvement of customer in service creation (SC2) Provision of customized services at consumer end (SC3)
Technological innovation (TI)	Development of big data (TI1) Development of cloud computing initiatives (TI2) Blockchain application (TI3) E - payment methods (TI4) Digital transaction security enhancements (TI5)
Firm Performance (FP)	Identification of financial parameters (FP1) Identification of non-financial parameters (FP2) Comparison of Revenue on YoY basis (FP3)

We follow the Resource Advantage view on consumer involvement in service creation and argue that the three above mentioned customer-centric processes need to be integrated to achieve an effective execution of a firm strategy for its sustainability (Boulding et al., 2005). Based on our extensive literature review, we treat service creation processes as a higher order construct. Some of the significant work in the above area are as,

Table 2. Summary of important contributions in service co-creation literature (based on RA Theory and SD Logic)

S. No.	Authors	Contribution
1	Boulding et al. 2005 Jayachandran et al. 2005	Identified Customer Information Management (CIM) as one of the key activities of identifying customers and their needs.
2	Payne and Frow 2005	Co-creation can be used to develop new products that are aligned with customer requirements and create value for the firm
3	Parvatiyar and Sheth 2000 Ryals 2005	Customer Value Management (CVM) in addition to CIM, differentiating co-creational activities among customers based on their preferences and value contribution.
4	Ramaswamy 2009	This involves all activities that help to evaluate customers and integrate information about them in organizational processes

Based on our reviewed constructs, the proposed model of the study is as,

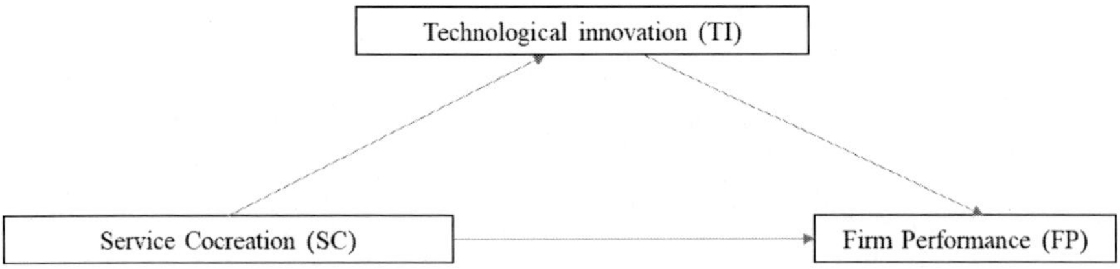

Figure 1. Assessing impact of customer service cocreation (SC) on firm performance (FP).

To approach this purpose, we contrasted R-A theory with S-D logic substantiated by extensive literature review. In doing so, we explicitly studied and compared foundational premises of both the theories and came up with derivative propositions (service co-creation) leading towards firm performance mediated by technological innovations.

In the present research, one of the objectives of service co-creation is to identify and to interact with the most valuable customer segments with regard to firm profitability. Hence, in our framework we treat Technological Innovation (TI) as the mediator for Customer Co-creation and Firm Performance. Studying the overall performance implications of co-creation is important as it has been assumed that co-creation should lead to superior firm performance (Payne and Frow 2005). However previous research has produced inconclusive findings (Ernst et al., 2011, Reinartz et al. 2004; Jayachandran et al. 2005). This may indicate that its success possibly depends on critical mediating effects of technological innovations. Organizations need to collect, comprehend, and apply information about its customers to improve new product/service performance. Hence, we posit,

- H1: Service co-creation has an impact on the technical innovations in a firm.
- H2: Technical innovations has an impact on the overall firm performance
- H3: Service co-creation leads to higher firm performance.

RESEARCH METHODOLOGY

Sample

To analyse the impact of Customer Co-creation on Firm Performance mediated by Technological Innovations, in the context of financial institutions especially banks, we considered survey as an appropriate research method (Rana, Williams and Dwivedi, 2003). The sample for the present study has been collected from 143 respondents serving as middle management employees at one of the largest private sector banks in India. Their demographics are as,

Table 3. Respondent's demographic profiling

Characteristics	Percentage
Gender	
Male	87
Female	13
Qualification	
Graduate	41
Post Graduate	59
Age	
30-40	25
40-50	53
50>	22

In order to test our hypotheses, a large-scale survey was conducted. Anonymity was guaranteed to all informants. A self-administered questionnaire was found to be suitable as a primary survey instrument of data collection in this research.

The sample of the study consists of wide array of respondents serving at different branches of one of the leading public sector banks in India. A consent was taken before sharing a questionnaire with them. A total of 200 questionnaires were shared with the employees serving in twelve branches in Bihar and Jharkhand. First, the respondents were briefed about the questionnaire so as to make familiarity with the research purpose. However, we ensured that no personal bias should come in the mind of respondent while filling in the questionnaire.

A total of 148 completed survey questionnaires were returned to us. The further scrutiny of questionnaires revealed that 5 of them were partially completed and so rejected from the subsequent analysis. Hence, we were left out with 143 usable responses, which made the basis for our empirical analysis for measuring the success of the service co-creation. The overall response rate was found to be 72%.

Operationalization and Measures

The final questionnaire consisted of total 16 questions including 5 questions from respondent's demographic profiling and remaining 11 questions on the three different constructs of the proposed research model. All these questions were multiple-type, closed-ended and five-point Likert scale type questions. Likert scales (1-5) with anchors ranging from "strongly disagree" to "strongly agree" were used for all non-demographic based questions. An extensive literature review formed the basis for the specification of the content of the constructs. To fully capture the construct's domain of content, the constructs were revised and pre-tested based on 12 in depth interviews with specialists from HR and general administration department. Based on this process, scales were refined in terms of wording to better reflect service co-creation. All items were measured on a 5-point scale ranging from "strongly disagree" (=1) to "strongly agree" (=5) except where indicated. All our constructs were tested for external validity. The summary table for the scales are as,

Table 4. Construct indicator variables and scale reliability values

Construct	Variables Studied	Scale Reliability
Service Co-creation (SC)	Two-way communication channels with customers (SC1) Active involvement of customer in service creation (SC2) Provision of customized services at consumer end (SC3)	0.75
Technological Innovation (TI)	Development of big data (TI1) Development of cloud computing initiatives (TI2) Blockchain application (TI3) E - payment methods (TI4) Digital transaction security enhancements (TI5)	0.71
Firm Performance (FP)	Identification of financial parameters (FP1) Identification of non-financial parameters (FP2) Comparison of Revenue on YoY basis (FP3)	0.85

Table 5. Discriminant validity: correlations of constructs and √AVE

		1	2	3
1	SC	**0.72**		
2	TI	0.41	**0.55**	
3	FP	0.23	0.21	**0.61**

Bold main diagonal are square root of corresponding AVE.

Table 6. The correlation table among the variable and cronbach's alpha along the diagonal

		1	2	3
1	SC	.75		
2	TI	.415**	.713	
3	FP	.334**	.216**	.85
	Mean	3.51	4.15	4.61
	Standard Deviation	1.14	0.45	0.12

** Correlation is significant at the 0.01 level (2-tailed), * correlation is significant at the 0.05 level (2-tailed), Note: alpha values are along with the diagonal.

Analysis Plan

To test the hypotheses and overall model, we used OLS, a useful tool for path analysis with formative indicators (Fornell and Larcker 1981). External validity has been demonstrated for all constructs. The issue of common method bias was addressed using a procedure suggested by Burdenski (2000). We calibrated our final model for 143 individuals.

Two aspects of validity were examined: Convergent validity and Discriminant validity. For all constructs, convergent validity, assessed by the average variance extracted (AVE) to meet the criterion of .50 (Fornell and Larcker, 1981). Discriminant validity is confirmed for all latent constructs since the square root of each construct's AVE is greater than the bivariate correlation with the other constructs in the model (Chin 1998).

Research Findings

In developing our research instrument, we followed the procedures for conducting research as proposed by Hair, Anderson, Tatham and Black (2006). We also followed the paradigm of Churchill (1979) to test and validate the questionnaire. We performed pre-tests by conducting confirmatory factor analysis using AMOS 18.0. It assessed the construct validity (Durvasula et al., 1993).

Descriptive Statistics

Prior to administering in the field, the questionnaire was pre-tested and no changes in the wording of the questions were deemed necessary. Before analyzing, the data has been tested against normality. The result suggests no transformation of data, as results are well under the normality limit (Burdenski, 2000).

Model Description, Results and Discussion

The hypothesized relationship as depicted in Figure 2 is tested using the 3 step linear step-wise regression technique (OLS). In includes testing of direct relationship between independent and dependent variables apart from testing for the moderating roles of Technological Innovation. The main effect model has also been explained using the path analysis under SEM.

Testing the Structural Model

The main effect model has also been explored using the structural equation modeling. SEM takes a confirmatory approach to test the dependence relationships and account for measurement errors in the process of testing the model (Byrne, 2001). The assessment of model fit has been done using the various fit indices as in the table,

Table 7. SEM model fit summary

$\chi 2$/df	AGFI	PGFI	NFI	TLI	CFI	PNFI	RMSEA	RMR
3.16	0.761	0.731	0.911	0.931	0.893	0.83	0.033	0.049

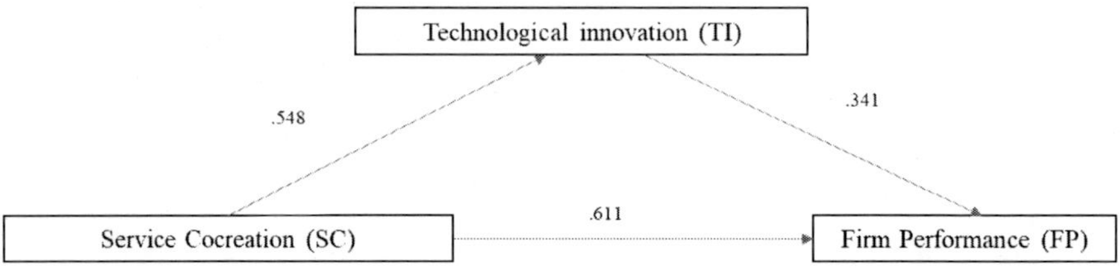

Figure 2. Assessing impact of customer service cocreation (SC) on firm performance (FP).

The chi-square/df ratio of 2 to 3 is taken as good or acceptable fit (Bollen, 1989; Gallagher, Ting and Palmer, 2008). The various incremental fit indices include the Normal Fit Index (NFI), comparative Fit Index (CFI) or the Tucker-Lewis Index (TLI), with suggestions for a cut of 0.90 for a good fitting model (Hu and Bentler, 1999). Further the absolute fit index of Adjusted Goodness of Fit Index (AGFI) is greater than the minimal 0.75 cutoff. The multiple R square for the model is 0.49. The path coefficients or standardized regression weights for the predictor relationship are shown in Table 8 as,

Table 8. Path coefficients from the SEM analysis

Hypothesized Relationship			Estimate	P-value
Technological innovation	←	Service Co-creation	.548	0.002
Firm Performance	←	Technological innovation	.341	0.000
Firm Performance	←	Service Co-creation	.611	0.004

It can be seen from the SEM results that all the direct and indirect relationship has been found significant ($p < 0.05$). The findings are consistent with the earlier studies done by Ordanini and Parasuraman (2011). Overall, this study establishes that co-creation in an innovation context is a theoretically relevant construct for understanding the firm system performance. Above results provides useful insights regarding the management of NSD efforts in generating System Efficiency.

CONCLUSION

The purpose of this research paper is to examine the role of service co-creation for new age service delivery platforms and assessing its impact on the technological innovations and in-turn its effect on the firm overall performance. Our study produced several interesting findings which add to our knowledge in this area. First, our model established that service co-creation in the presence of technological innovations tends to produce better results in terms of firm performance. It suggests that financial firms must aware customers their roles in the delivery of timely services that are highly technology dependent. For example, unless customers are sure about the security issues on the e-platforms, they will not use it. Hence, it's the role of employees to ensure the trust and security of services (led by technological innovations) in the mind of customers. Our model explains more than 49 percent of the variance in firm performance has happened due to customer cocreated services led by technological innovations, thus indicating service co-creation as a rich predictor of new product success.

It is important to note that weakest regression coefficient has been found in the non-mediated effect of service co-creation on firm performance. Proper dissemination of technological innovation is one such parameter wherein there is a lot of scope in providing timely training to the bank staff and team members about the digital platform. This is alarming as poor knowledge of digital products in the staff itself has led to the lesser customer involvement and sensitization about the issue.

Several important managerial implications follow from our study. It is evident from our study that service co-creation in terms of sharing consent about various API's usage and usage of its data for cloud computing can be leveraged to provide important and sorted information about profiling of the customer, which can be used to improve service performance and in turn firm efficiency. Since the new service failure rate has remained high over the years especially in technology led innovations (Crawford and Di Benedetto 2003), co-created digital platforms provide organizations a promising way to address this critical problem. In order to do so it is important to adopt a broader perspective on digital banking (beyond just relationship management). Our study strongly put forward service co-creation as a way to improve to improve service performance of new age technology driven products.

LIMITATIONS AND FUTURE RESEARCH

Our study represents a first step in examining the role of service co-creation mediated by technological innovations as an input into the firm performance. There are several limitations and areas for future research.

First, we have collected our responses from limited number of employees that have exposure into the strategic roles. For example, constructs such as service co-creation mediated by technological innovations are responded based on a limited set of questions. These issues may be further substantiated using some triangulation studies in future.

Second, our study employed a cross-sectional, survey approach to study a dynamic phenomenon. The possibility exists that some of the relationships we investigated may strength then over time. Hence use of longitudinal data followed may be a pragmatic choice in this context.

Further, because of very nature of this study, construct firm performance largely has been measured using non-financial parameters. While conducting this study of a larger magnitude, the incorporation of financial parameters while measuring firm performance will be justified.

ACKNOWLEDGMENTS

Author thank Prof. Rajagopal, ITESM, Mexico City for his motivation and encouragement to document this work. Many thanks are also extended to the bank for providing access for data collection.

REFERENCES

Boulding, W., Staelin, R., Ehret, M., & Johnston, W. J. (2005). A customer relationship management roadmap: what is known, potential pitfalls, & where to go. *J. Mark*, 69(4), 155-166.

Brown, S. A. (2000). Customer relationship management – a strategic imperative in the world of E-business. New York: Wiley.

Burdenski, T. (2000) 'Evaluating univariate, bivariate, and multivariate normality using graphical and statistical procedures.' *Multiple Linear Regression Viewpoints*, Vol. 26, No.2, pp. 15-30.

Churchill, G. A. Jr. (1979). 'A paradigm for developing better measures of marketing constructs.' *Journal of Marketing Research*, Vol. 16, No. 1, pp. 64-73.

Chin, Wynne W. (1998). 'The Partial Least Squares Approach to Structural Equation Modeling.' *Modern Methods of Business Research*, Marcoulides G. A. ed. London: Lawrence Erlbaum Associates.

Durvasula, S., Andrews, J. C., Lyonski, S., & Netemeyer, R. G. (1993). 'Assessing the cross-national applicability of consumer behaviour models, a model of attitude toward advertising in general.' *Journal of Consumer Research*, 19, 626-36.

Ernst, H., Hoyer, W. D., Kraft, M., & Krieger, K. (2011), 'Customer relationship management and company performance – the mediating role of new product.' *Journal of the Academy of Marketing Science*, Vol. 39 No. 2, pp. 290-306.

Fornell, Claes and David F. Larcker (1981). 'Evaluating structural equation models with unobservable variables and measurement error.' *Journal of Marketing Research*, 18 (1), 39-50.

Hunt, S. D. (2000). 'A general theory of competition: too eclectic or not eclectic enough? Too incremental or not incremental enough?.' *Journal of Macromarketing*, 20(1), 77-81.

Jayachandran, S., Sharma, S., Kaufman, P., & Raman, P. (2005). The role of relational information processes and technology use in customer relationship management. *J. Mark*, 69(4), 177-192.

Lee, I. and Shin, Y. J. (2018) Fintech: Ecosystem, business models, investment decisions, and challenges. *Bus. Horiz.* 61, 35-46.

Madhavan, R., & Grover, R. (1998). From embedded knowledge to embodied knowledge: new product development as knowledge management. *J. Mark*, 62(4), 1-12.

Ordanini, Andrea and A. Parasuraman (2011). 'Service innovation viewed through a service-dominant logic lens: a conceptual framework and empirical analyses.' *Journal of Service Research*, Vol. 14, No. 1, pp. 3-23.

Parvatiyar, A., & Sheth, J. N. (2000). The domain and conceptual foundations of relationship marketing. In: J. N. Sheth & A. Parvatiyar (Eds.), *Handbook of relationship marketing* (pp. 3-38). Thousand Oaks: Sage.

Payne, A., & Frow, P. (2005). A strategic framework for customer relationship management. *J. Mark*, 69(4), 167-176.

Peppers, D., Rogers, M., & Dorf, B. (1999). Is your company ready for one-to-one marketing? *Harv. Bus. Rev.*, 77, 3-12.

Ramaswamy V. (2009); Leading the transformation to co-creation of value; Strategy & Leadership, 37 (2).

Rana, Nripendra; Williams, Michael; and Dwivedi, Yogesh, "Examining Factors Affecting Adoption of Online Public Grievance Redressal System: A Case of India" (2013). UK Academy for Information Systems Conference Proceedings 2013. 31.

Reinartz, W. J., Krafft, M., & Hoyer, W. D. (2004). The customer relationship management process: its measurement and impact on performance. *J. Mark Res.*, 41(3), 293-305.

Verma and Jayasimha (2012), Linking resource-advantage (R-A) theory and service-dominant (S-D) logic: an integrative framework of service innovation research, *International Journal of Business Competition and Growth (IJBCG)*, Vol. 2, No. 4, 2012.

Zhao 1, Tsai and Wang (2019) Improving Financial Service Innovation Strategies for Enhancing China's Banking Industry Competitive Advantage during the Fintech Revolution: A Hybrid MCDM Model, Sustainability 2019, 11, 1419; doi:10.3390/su11051419.

In: Strategic Rethinking
Editors: Rajagopal et al.

ISBN: 978-1-53616-835-8

Chapter 12

Study on Transactional Leadership: Findings from an Empirical Survey in Three ITC Divisions

Subba Rao Tulasi*[*] *and S. Suman Babu*[†], *PhD
GITAM Hyderabad Business School,
GITAM (Deemed to be University), Hyderabad, India

Abstract

The purpose of this paper is to explore the relationship between Transactional leadership and outcomes measured in terms of extra effort, effectiveness and satisfaction through an empirical survey in three Indian industry segments based in AP and Telangana.

Transactional leaders use rewards to promote the agenda of leaders and followers in a given situation. Transactional leadership is based on bureaucratic authority and legitimacy in the organization. Transactional leaders emphasize work standards, assignments, and task-oriented goals. They also focus on task completion and employee compliance and rely quite heavily on organizational rewards and punishments to influence

---

[*] Subba Rao Tulasi, Research Scholar, GITAM Hyderabad Business School.
[†] S. Suman Babu, Assistant Professor, GITAM Hyderabad Business School.

employee performance (Edward E. Smith, Capella University, June 2009). The survey established correlation between "Contingent Reward" and outcomes in terms of extra effort, effectiveness and satisfaction.

Keywords: transactional leadership, leadership constructs, multifactor leadership questionnaire

INTRODUCTION

Throughout human evolution, human kind has spent countless hours developing a more thorough understanding of what makes leaders more successful. Globalization has moved through several change phases from capitalistic philosophy to democratic business notions involving stakeholders in the process of business growth. An important component of the stake holders is the employees who need to be constantly inspired, motivated and encouraged to perform the best at all times. The opportunities for global businesses are expanding with the support of rapidly emerging product markets, the global race for innovation, technology, and most importantly, talent management. The multinational companies today are striving to remain "relevant" through continuous innovations and build new business models. Top Leaders establish a vision of the future and align people and resources through any number of leadership approaches, inspiring and directing others. Best leaders are not necessarily the most intelligent, courageous, or intuitive. Good leaders, however, possess the ability to absorb, digest, and use information to motivate others into action. Leadership is about relationship building, challenging the status quo, and the ability to not only visualize one's own perspective, but also the desires and dreams of others. Leaders are expected to establish a course, set standards, challenge current processes and realities, build trust, and encourage right action. The challenge that most leaders face is to transform organizational mediocrity into competitive advantage through effective and ethical leadership. But equally important and in fact more challenging is the ability of the middle level management to translate the vision to reality through "entrepreneurship" in their day to day work style. Because of its essential role in initiating the process of production, some economists identify entrepreneurship as a "fourth factor of production," alongside land, labor and capital.

OBJECTIVES OF THE RESEARCH

Movement from Public sector to a large paper manufacturing facility in private sector in a backward region near River Godavari opened new horizons in understanding cost management. As years progressed, the author moved to General management cadre and could experience *leadership phenomenon* at senior levels. He had noticed many a time that Middle level managers when confronted with difficult and embarrassing questions about organizational policies, conveniently pass on the buck to the "top management" which may be, in fairness to them, true but does not absolve them of their responsibility in implementing the Organizational policies. He was thus emboldened to study the phenomenon of *Leadership* at various levels post retirement and read good number of articles.

LITERATURE REVIEW

Performance is a prerequisite for companies, particularly in an increasingly competitive market exacerbated by the economic difficulties, which Organizations have to face during turbulent times. Situations that leaders and would-be-leaders must face are highly complex, constantly changing, and difficult to interpret. More than ever before, managers of firms, which operate in the global arena, face fierce and rapidly changing international competition. The business environment, both today and in the near future, is rooted in continual change. Economic and political conditions, global competition, technology, increasingly complex world markets, and the growing scarcity of resources are all "fueling the engine" of continuous change. Transactions that once consumed days, weeks, or months to complete, now come "full circle" with a simple click of a computer mouse

(Scott M Shaw, 2008). The trend toward the global economic village is clear, and the 21st century is already termed as the century of the *global world.* In the past, leaders were traditionally seen in many cultures as those whose heritage gave them advantage, but current theorists and researchers view leadership as a learned behavior.

LEADERSHIP THEORIES

Kirkpatrick and Locke (1991) state that few issues have a more controversial history than leadership traits and characteristics. Popper (2004) claims the first modern attempt to formulate a theory of leadership appears to be that of the Scottish philosopher Thomas Carlyle (1907). Carlyle identified the talents, skills, and physical characteristics of men who rose to power. He claims that general history is essentially the chronicles of the great people who acted in it. Those great people were the leaders of people; they were the ones who created everything that humanity enacted. The leader's influence, according to Carlyle, is not limited to the social and political level. The leader is above all a spiritual leader, and therefore Carlyle assigns leaders and prophets to be his heroes, ranking their outstanding characteristic as genius. Carlyle's hero stands above others in courage, originality and ability to see the truth. Approaching the end of the nineteenth century, the popularity of the "great man" leadership theories peaked; these theories asserted that especially people from the upper class inherited leadership qualities.

Marx and Engels (1968) represent a diametrically opposed approach to Carlyle's "great man" theory. In their view, circumstances are the decisive factors that dictate events rather than the leader's characteristics. Marx and Engels claim that people create their own history; they create it not just as they imagine it, and not in the circumstances they choose for themselves, but in the circumstances in which they find themselves (Duerr, 2009).

Early in the twentieth century, the great man theories evolved into trait theories, which did not make assumptions about whether great men were born or made. Trait theory simply asserted that leaders' characteristics are different from non-leaders. Stogdill's (1948) review of the literature in the mid-twentieth century concluded that a person does not become a leader because they possess some combination of traits, but the pattern of personal characteristics of the leader must bear some relevant relationship to the characteristics, activities, and goals of the followers. Kirkpatrick and Locke indicate that trait theory made a comeback since Stogdill's review. Once more research found that somecore traits significantly contribute to leaders' success, especially when leaders apply those traits in executing organizational actions such as formulating a vision, role modeling, setting goals, etc.

Kirkpatrick & Locke identified the key leadership traits, amongst several others, which include:

- Ambition, drive, energy, tenacity, initiative
- Leadership Motivation personalization vs. socialization
- Honesty and Integrity
- Self-confidence and emotional stability
- Knowledge of the Business

Kirkpatrick and Locke concluded that regardless of whether leaders are born or made or some combination of both, it is clear that leaders are not like other people. Leaders do not have to be great men or women by being intellectual geniuses or omniscient prophets to succeed, but they do need to have the "right stuff" (Duerr, 2009). Two psychological processes reflect different mechanisms and profoundly different approaches to understanding leadership. The first, which is *leader- centric,* argues that leaders, particularly charismatic ones, are highly influential and affect organizational outcomes. These are related to *follower-centric* perspective, which states that leadership is a social construction. Observers use organizational outcomes, a presumed indicator of a leader's competence – whether or not caused by the leader, to decide if a leader is effective (Calder, 1977; Lord et al., 1978; Meindl and Ehrlich, 1987; Jacquart, 2012).

Various leadership theories were touched above while explaining leadership styles according to Kirkpatrick and Locke and also while detailing the views of Marx and Engels. Several authors developed theories on leadership, which can be classified into three main groups i.e., traits, behavior and situation. While several other leadership theories are also detailed here such as Charismatic and Transformational, theories too do make use of these attributes and explain them in detail.

Transformational and Transactional Leadership Styles

The two Leadership styles that would attract attention are transformational leadership and transactional leadership. Both of them are complimentary and can coexist in an Organization. In fact, they need to, as the top management needs to practice "Transformational" style while the middle management comprising department/section heads need to adopt transactional style.

Practitioners and scholars of management have long been captivated by the characteristics of the CEO as a crucial predictor of firm success (Katz & Kahn, 1978; Waldman & Yammarino, 1999). Yet, the complexity of creating and carrying out the strategic decisions of an entire organization demands more skill and effort than a single leader can effectivelyprovide. Instead, it requires the collective eability and motivation of a dominant team of leaders within the firm (Cyert & March, 1963; Finkelstein & Hambrick, 1996; Hambrick & Mason, 1984). Consistent with this view, Hambrick noted that leadership of a complex organization is a shared activity (Hambrick 2007; Colbert et al., 2014). Performance of an Organization is thus influenced by the "entire management team" not just the CEO. It is further argued that leadership is not limited to executives at top levels of organizations. Hersey and Blanchard (1998) argued that leaders at all levels of the organization should have the diagnostic ability and adaptability if they are to be successful in leading across diverse situations (Flemming, 2009).

Transactional Leadership and Its Importance

According to Avolio et al., (1991) transactional leadership is the most common form of effective leadership found in organizations, where leaders specify what will be done, how it will be done, and the reward received for completing the objectives. Hierarchically structured entities are well suited for transactional leadership which is conceptualized as the *exchange relationship* between leaders and their followers (Burns, 1978). Experts draw a sharp distinction between transactional and transformational leadership. A transaction implies an exchange of some kind. Therefore, a transactional leader-follower relationship yields *measurable* outcomes: tasks are completed and a salary is paid; a job is well done and the employee receives a bonus or some other reward. Unlike a transformational leader, a transactional leader does not intensely focus on follower needs or respective development. Transactional leadership presents a quid pro quo construct (Bass and Avilo 1994). Transactional leaders use rewards to promote the agenda which is common of leaders and followers in a given situation. Transactional leadership is based on bureaucratic authority and legitimacy in the organization. Transactional leaders emphasize work standards, assignments, and task-oriented goals. They also focus on task completion and employee compliance and rely quite heavily on organizational rewards and punishments to influence employee performance (Smith, 2009). The leader encourages followers to excel in their responsibilities by providing them with resources and rewards in exchange for motivation, productivity and effective task accomplishments. The transactional leadership theory further asserted that the followers rely greatly on the leader to receive certain valued outcomes when they comply with their leader's expectations. The argument is that when the job or the work environment of the follower fails to provide the necessary impetus such as motivation, direction and satisfaction, the leader will be effective by providing the necessary compensation for the deficiencies experienced by the follower (Hartog et al., 1997; Flemming, 2009).

Despite the arguments in favor of transactional relationships in achieving performance, an exclusive focus on such exchanges and transactions with followers has been blamed for low expectations of followers and for minimal performance in organizations. It was further asserted that transactional contracts do not inspire followers to aim for excellence in whatever they do; rather, they focus on short-term, immediate outcomes instead of the long-term commitment exhibited by transformational leadership.

However, Transactional and transformational leadership have been widely recognized as not being mutually exclusive. Bass had described that Transactional and Transformational leadership as a continuum of leadership behavior. The transformative relationship builds on the transactional foundation (Bass, 2008). Avolio (1999) suggested that transactions are at the base of transformations. In this relationship, leaders guide their followers toward higher levels of performance and purpose by integrating the notion of a shared vision, goal or organizational mission. This elevating factor is a hallmark of transforming leadership (Burns, 1978). The transformational leader is an *enriched transactional leader*, through the effects of shared vision and charisma to accomplish more than the expected, insofar as the extraordinary work is intrinsically motivating for the collaborators. However, Bass (1998) argued, "transformational leadership does not substitute for transactional leadership" (p. 21). Transformational leadership is perhaps possible only if underpinned and strengthened by the foundation of transactional leadership. In Bass's (1985) original conceptualization, the transactional leadership outcome is that the followers meet leader expectations, fulfill their part of the contingent exchange, and thus are rewarded. Bass (1988) suggested that transformational leadership is necessary to motivate followers *to exceed* expectations which implies that in the absence of a foundation provided by the transactional leadership, transformational leadership and its effects may not be visible. A leader's transactional skills are the foundational starting point of transformational skills; and thus *transactional skills come first and transformational leadership skills come second*. Transactional leaders honor an agreed-upon exchange system between leader and individual follower, but without the transactional support in place, a transformation may not occur.

Organizational transformation and human resources motivation begin when the follower overrides individual interests, such as receiving an individual paycheck for individual work performed, to focus on the collaborative group goal, or even a step beyond, to focus on the envisioned organizational goals and values. Bass (1998) stated that there are theoretical reasons to believe that transformational leaders will use transactional leadership because consistent honoring of transactional agreements builds trust, dependability, and perceptions of consistency with leaders by followers, each of which are a basis for transformational leadership. This implies that if the day-to- day management (transactional leadership) is present in an organization, with the added benefit of a transformational leadership style, individual employees may start to view themselves as a team and strive towards the overarching vision or mission statement of the organization. Individuals are transformed from thinking independently towards focusing as a group or team on the big picture, big goal, or organizational vision. Bass (1999) suggests that the best leaders are both transformational and transactional. In reality, Transformational leadership builds on the transactional framework to enhance leadership effectiveness. Without transactional leadership skills, even the most inspirational leader would fail to accomplish his mission (Avolio et al., 1998). Hence, if a transactional leader also has transformational leadership traits, then the leader can use either style, or augment leadership styles, when the situation calls in an effort to lead an organization and its human resources toward exemplary levels.

A transformational leader is characterized as one who articulates a vision of the future and shares with peers and subordinates and intellectually stimulates subordinates. He would pay elevated attention to individual differences among people through the construct- individualized consideration. In contrast, the transactional leader focuses on the details and proper exchange of resources for the job completed. If transformational leadership results in followers identifying with the needs of the leader, the transactional leader gives followers something they want in exchange for something the leader desires. Where transactional leaders see task and relationship orientations as opposing, the transformational leader sees them as complementary with both being necessary and not individually sufficient. Burns (1978) suggests that the transformational leader is dependent on the relationship rather than the position of authority.

Thus the transactional leader is mired in daily affairs, focusing on the details of getting the job done and making a living within the current systems. Bass (1985) characterized the transactional leader as one who operates within the existing system or culture, has a preference for risk avoidance, pays attention to time constraints and efficiency, and generally prefers process over substance as a means for maintaining control.

In transactional leadership, relationship between the leader and follower, is based on contingent reward (Howell & Avolio, 1993; OmerFarukIscana, et al., 2014). With a particular emphasis on transactional leadership, Conger and Kanungo (as cited in Aronson, 2001) state, "transactional leadership is not leadership at all but rather manager ship, implying an emphasis on maintaining the status quo of the organization and ensuring the stable administration of practices and resources essential via strategies of control" (p. 246). Kur and Bunning (2002) assert that managers are more transactional in form, whereas leaders are more transformational. Bass found two important points about transactional leadership. The first is that leaders and followers act in their own self-interest. The second is that the leader and the follower enter into a relationship with each other that is predicated upon tradeoffs or exchanges (William G Woods, Feb 2007).

Constructs that Constitute Transactional Leadership

Transactional leaders display behaviors associated with constructive and corrective transactions. The constructive style is labeled as *Contingent Reward* and the corrective style is labeled as *Management-by- Exception both active and passive.*

Contingent reward refers to the degree to which the leader establishes constructive transactions with followers by clarifying standards or expectations and establishing the rewards for meeting them.

Management by exception is the degree to which the leader takes corrective action based on results of leader-follower transactions. The difference between the active and passive forms of management by exception generally lies in the timing of the intervention (Howell & Avolio, 1993). More specifically, active leaders closely monitor follower behavior, anticipate problems, and take corrective actions before the behavior creates problems, while passive leaders do not respond until the behavior has caused serious problems (Junghyun Lee, Jan 2012). Elaborating the same concept, Northouse (2007) asserted that transactional leadership focuses on two core factors: contingent rewards and management-by-exceptions. Northouse defined contingent rewards as a bartering process among leaders and followers toward an agreed upon compensation. Northouse asserted management-by-exception involves corrective criticism and meaningful feedback to followers. As explained above, Northouse too reported that management-by- exception takes on two forms: active and passive. While the active form is associated with Transactional Leadership, the passive form is termed as "Laisse Faire style of Leadership." Northouse argued that transactional leaders use a reward system such as bonuses, employee recognition, and a merit system to reward subordinates. Lee and Chang (2006) asserted that the degree of trust and loyalty between leaders and followers within a transactional construct is either high or low (Geter, 2010).

Thus, Transactional leadership defines expectations and promotes performance to achieve these levels. Transactional leadership involves an exchange process that results in follower compliance with leader's request but not likely to generate enthusiasm and commitment to task objective. The leader focuses on having internal actors perform the tasks required for the organization to reach its desired goals (Boehnke et al., 2003). The objective of the transactional leader is to ensure that the path to goal attainment is clearly understood by the internal actors, to remove potential barrier within the system, and to motivate the actors to achieve the predetermined goals. In transactional leadership, expected effort and performance outcomes occur because leaders understand the role followers must play to achieve organizational goals. Leaders clarify those goals, and thus give confidence to followers to meet the purposed objectives. Additionally, leaders understand the followers' needs and ensure that those needs are met in exchange for the desired performance expectations (Bass, 1985). Finally, Passive-Avoidant leaders "avoid" specifying agreements, clarifying expectations, and providing goals and standards to be achieved by followers.

TRANSACTIONAL LEADERSHIP OUTCOMES

Transformational leadership outcomes have received much more attention than transactional leadership outcomes, especially because of the augmentation effects of transformational leadership on transactional leadership (Gellis, 2001). Bass criticized Burns' conceptualization that transformational and transactional leadership are opposite ends of a scale (Avolio & Bass, 2004). Instead, transformational components build upon a transactional leadership base to create an augmentation effect (Avolio & Bass, 2004). Reports describing transformational leadership effectiveness generally convey an augmentation effect on contingent transactional leadership (the contingent reward aspect of transactional leadership). Transformational leadership and transactional leadership (contingent reward and active management-by-exception) correlate positively with higher levels of employee effort, perceived leadership effectiveness, and employee satisfaction (Watkins, 2008). The competent transactional leader is prone to be effective in stable, predictable environments. Transactional leaders are influential because it is in the best interest of subordinates to do what the leader wants.

Empirical Survey Using Multi Factor Leadership Questionnaire

In the conceptualization, Bass and Avolio propose that the three broad Leadership categories explained above are better defined by their respective dimensions, described in more detail in the following table which is also popularly known as Multifactor Leadership Questionnaire (MLQ) dimensions.

Table 1. Multifactor leadership questionnaire (MLQ)

Transformational	The leader tries to increase followers' awareness of what is right and important and to motivate them to perform "beyond expectation."
	Idealized Influence (behavior and attributed) is described when a leader is being a role model for his/her followers and encouraging the followers to share common visions and goals by providing a clear vision and a strong sense of purpose. Inspirational Motivation represents behaviors when a leader tries to express the importance of desired goals in simple ways, communicates a high level of expectations and provides followers with work that is meaningful and challenging. Intellectual Stimulation refers to leaders who challenge their followers' ideas and values for solving problems. Individualized Consideration refers to leaders who spend more time teaching and coaching followers by treating followers on an individual basis.
Transactional	A process that is mainly based on contingent reinforcement.
	Contingent Reward refers to an exchange of rewards between leaders and followers in which effort is rewarded by providing rewards for good performance or threats and disciplines for poor performance. Management by-Exception (Active) leaders are characterized as monitors who detect mistakes.
Passive-Avoidant	Absent, unavailable leader
	Management-by-Exception (Passive) leader intervenes with his or her group only when procedures and standards for accomplishing tasks are not met. Laissez-faire or non-leadership exhibits when leaders avoid clarifying expectations, addressing conflicts, and making decisions.

Source: Schiena, et al., (2013).

Note: Definitions are from N. Muenjohn, and A. Armstrong ([13], pp. 3–14).

Assessing Full Range Leadership

Bass developed the Multifactor Leadership Questionnaire (MLQ) in 1985 as a means of identifying transformational and transactional leadership characteristics (Bass & Stogdill, 1990). Bass and Avolio subsequently validated the MLQ over the next several years (Bass & Stogdill, 1990), resulting in the MLQ (Form 5x) to measure full range leadership characteristics (Avolio & Bass, 2004). Nearly 200 theses and doctoral dissertations used MLQ forms as the basis for testing transformational and transactional leadership (Bass & Avolio, 2000). Numerous researchers found that the MLQ is an effective test of transformational and transactional leadership qualities (Avolio& Bass, 1999; Barbuto, 2005; Bass & Avolio, 2000; Bass & Stogdill, 1990; Rowald, 2005; Sarros, Gray, & Densten, 2002). Some researchers raised construct validity concerns with early iterations of the MLQ, however, the MLQ (Form 5x) addressed those concerns (Bass & Avolio, 2000).

Bass and Avolio spent a great deal of effort revising the MLQ and responding to critics of the original 6-factor model proposed by Bass in 1985 (Avolio& Bass, 2004; Bass &Avolio, 2000, 2003). The 6-factor model was revised to the 9-factor model used in the MLQ (Form 5x) to define more precisely the constructs associated with leadership styles and behaviors. The refinements did not negate the relevance or significance of the 6-factor model. The MLQ (Form 5x) has been shown to be a valid and reliable measure of transformational and transactional leadership appropriate for use as a leadership development tool.

The MLQ is available in this validated form of 45 questions for Organisational survey, research purposes and for preparation of individual leader reports. Each question is answered in a Likert scale as follows.

Not at all	0
Once in a while	1
Some times	2
Fairly often	3
Frequently, if not always	4

The questions that assess the two constructs of Transactional Leadership are as follows.

Currently MLQ is owned by Mind Garden, California which also administers the survey questionnaire through internet. As explained above, out of these 45 questions, 36 questions assess Leadership while 9 questions assess outcome. Few Leadership instruments include both Leadership and outcome items. The inclusion of both in MLQ, enables comparison of the Leadership on the one hand with performance outcomes in the same instrument.

Such a survey with MLQ was carried out in three divisions of a large Indian Industrial enterprise (ITC Limited) in the private sector in which around 326 managers participated. Mind Garden accorded permission to administer the MLQ Leader instrument to the selected leaders of three divisions of ITC Limited and the Rater form to those followers and peers/seniors chosen by the leader. Leaders were chosen in three divisions of ITC Ltd viz PSPD (Paperboards and Specialty Papers division), ILTD (India Leaf Tobacco development division) and ABD (Agri Business Division) in consultation with respective Chief Executives. An interactive session was conducted with most of the participating managers (Leaders) before the survey was administered and their queries addressed. They were explained the purpose of the survey and the process. They were further requested to answer the questionnaire in a relaxed atmosphere, preferably at their residence when they are not under any work pressure.

CONCLUSION

MLQ is a useful instrument in measuring effectiveness of Leadership outcomes, with particular reference to people related issues. Out comes in terms of profit, productivity, and market standing are very objective and can be quantified and assessed but quantification is very difficult while assessing people related issues such as job satisfaction and willingness to put in extra effort which are highly subjective. These are assessed by MLQ as direct measures in a survey.

Transactional leadership is assessed by two constructs, which are then correlated with outcomes, and as can be seen from the above survey, interesting conclusions are drawn. While several researches were carried out using MLQ, the current research established correlation between

Transactional Leadership constructs and each of the outcomes in terms of extra effort, effectiveness and satisfaction.

REFERENCES

Bass, B. M. and Avolio, B. J. (1995). *The Multifactor Leadership Questionnaire for Research*. Palo Alto, CA: Mind Garden.

Bond, C. A. (2007). *Leadership training, Leadership style and Organizational effectiveness*. Unpublished Thesis, Boston: MA, Boston University, School of Education.

Colbert, A. E., Barrick, M. R., and Bradley, B. H:. (2014). Personality and Leadership composition in Top Management teams: Implications for Organizational effectiveness, *Personnel Psychology*, 44 (1), 1-26.

Di Schiena, R., Letens, G., Van Aken, E., & Farris, J. (2013). Relationship between leadership and characteristics of learning organizations in deployed military units: An exploratory study. *Administrative Sciences*, 3(3), 143-165.

Duerr, R. A. (2009). *Leadership styles and Organizational outcomes in Engineering Societies' Local Chapters*. Unpublished Thesis, Minneapolis, MN: Capella University.

Faruk İşcan, O., Ersarı, G., and Naktiyok, A. (2014). Effect of Leadership Style on Perceived Organizational Performance and Innovation: The Role of Transformational Leadership Beyond the Impact of Transactional Leadership - An Application among Turkish SME's. *Procedia - Social and Behavioral Sciences,* 150, 881-889.

Flemming, P. L. (2009). *A study of the relationship between Transformational Leadership.*

Jacquart, P. and Antonakis, J. (2015). When does charisma matter for top-level leaders? Effect of attributional ambiguity. *Academy of Management Journal*, 58(4): 1051–1074.

Lee, J. H. (2012). *The Effects of Leadership Behavior on Workplace Harassment, Employee Outcomes, and Organizational Effectiveness in*

Small Businesses. Unpublished Thesis, Washington, DC: George Washington University.

Leon, T. and Geter, S. R. (2010). *A quantitative study in the relationship between Transformational Leadership, Organizational commitment and perception of effectiveness*. Unpublished Thesis, Tempe, AZ: University of Phoenix.

Shaw, S. M. (2008). *Leadership development and the characteristics/traits of ethical and effective leaders: The Delphi technique.* Unpublished Thesis, Minneapolis, MN: Capella University.

Smith, E. E. (2009). *Relationship between Organizational culture, societal culture, and Leadership styles*, Unpublished Thesis, Minneapolis, MN: Capella University.

Traits and Organizational culture types in improving performance in Public sector organizations: A Caribbean perspective, Unpublished Thesis, Minneapolis, MN: Capella University.

Watkins, D. (2008). *The common factors between coaching cultures and Transformational leadership, Transactional leadership, and high performance Organizational cultures.* Unpublished Thesis, Tempe, AZ: University of Phoenix.

Watson, L. T. (2007). *Leadership traits in large volume residential construction*, Unpublished Thesis, Minneapolis, MN: Capella University.

Woods, W, W. (2007). *The effect of Leadership practices on Organizational commitment: An analysis of MBA's in their individual workplace settings*. Unpublished Thesis, Minneapolis, MN: Capella University.

In: Strategic Rethinking
Editors: Rajagopal et al.
ISBN: 978-1-53616-835-8

Chapter 13

EASE OF DOING BUSINESS: A CONVERGENCE BUSINESS MODEL

Venu Kesi Reddy[1,*] and A. Sreeram[2,†]
[1]Hyderabad Business School (HBS),
GITAM (Deemed to be University), Rudram, Hyderabad, India
[2]Econometrics, Hyderabad Business School (HBS), GITAM,
(Deemed to be University), Rudram, Hyderabad, India

ABSTRACT

In this article it is identified that the India stands out this year as one of the 10 economies that improved the most in the areas measured by Doing Business.

Evidence shows that an economic crisis creates a stronger motivation for reform than a change of government. Doing Business focuses on key areas of interaction between the government and entrepreneurs, where policy makers and regulators can directly influence procedures to facilitate these interactions.

* Corresponding Author's Email: kesireddyvenu@gmail.com.
† Corresponding Author's Email: sreeram.atluri@gitam.edu.

Keywords: Ease of Doing Business, OECD, business regulation and economic relevance of the aspects

INTRODUCTION

Doing Business uses 11 indicator sets to measure aspects of business regulation that matter for entrepreneurship. Although good regulatory practices can be found around the world, they are most common in Organization for Economic Coopetaion and Development (OECD) high income economies and the economies of Europe and Central Asia. Sub-Saharan Africa has the widest variation in performance among the areas measured by Doing Business, with Mauritius standing at 25 in the ranking and Somalia at 190. South Asia is the only region not represented in the top 50 ranking for ease of doing business. However, India stands out this year as one of the 10 economies that improved the most in the areas measured by Doing Business.

The regions with the highest share of reforming economies in Doing Business 2018 are Europe and Central Asia, South Asia and Sub-Saharan Africa. Crises are opportunities for reform; economies are more likely to implement regulatory reforms in the areas measured by Doing Business when there is fiscal distress. Evidence shows that an economic crisis creates a stronger motivation for reform than a change of government. Better performance in Doing Business is associated with lower levels of unemployment and poverty.

OBJECTIVES OF STUDY

1. To present the Doing Business measures aspects of business regulation and their implications for firm establishment and operations

2. To study the Doing Business indicator sets capture the effectiveness and quality of business regulation and economic relevance of the aspects of business regulation measured by Doing Business.
3. To discuss the number of reforms and their impact on the distance to frontier score because they provide different information.
4. To draw conclusions emerged from the study of Ease of Doing Business – A Convergence Business Model

NEED OF THE STUDY

The Doing Business indicator sets capture the effectiveness and quality of business regulation and economic relevance of the aspects of business regulation measured by Doing Business. Number of reforms and their impact on the distance to frontier score because they provide different information.

DATA COLLECTION

For the study of the topic the ease of doing business a convergence of business policy secondary data has been taken into consideration.

This year marks the 15th Doing Business report. Since the inception of the project in 2003, the global business regulatory environment has changed dramatically.

Governments around the world have embraced and nurtured advances in information technology to reduce bureaucratic hurdles and increase transparency.

Today, in 65 of the 190 economies covered by Doing Business, entrepreneurs can complete at least one business incorporation procedure online, compared with only nine of the 145 economies measured in Doing Business 2004. Furthermore, in 31 economies it is now possible to initiate a commercial dispute online. This kind of progress can also be observed in the other areas measured by Doing Business.

Doing Business measures aspects of business regulation and their implications for firm establishment and operations. It does not include all the issues that are relevant for businesses decisions, but it does cover important areas that are under the control of policy makers. Governments worldwide recognize the economic and political benefits of improved business regulation. In fact, 119 of the 190 economies measured by Doing Business 2018 enacted at least one business regulation reform in 2016 - 17. Of these, 79.8% implemented at least one reform for a second consecutive year and 64.7% for a third. Business regulation can enable new ideas to come to life. When a software engineer realizes that she/he can develop a better and less-expensive product than is currently available, she/he may choose to start her/his own company to develop the idea. She/he will be more likely to become an entrepreneur in an economy where the rules governing start-ups are accessible, transparent and predictable. Conversely, in an economy where business regulation is cumbersome or ambiguous, she/he may be less willing to start her/his own company. In this case, the economy forfeits a new entrepreneur — as well as the associated capital investment and job creation. In turn, consumers have fewer, lower quality and more expensive product choices. Such a scenario highlights the way in which cumbersome regulation can distort resource allocation by stifling entrepreneurial endeavours in favour of maintaining a less optimal status quo.

Consider the case of the potential software entrepreneur. If she/he were a national of Canada, it would take just two procedures, one and a half days and less than 1% of income per capita to start her/her business in Toronto. First, she/he would need to file for federal incorporation and provincial registration online via Industry Canada's Electronic Filing Centre; this costs 200 Canadian dollars ($159) and is completed within a day. Second, she/he would need to register online for value added tax; this costs nothing and is completed within half a day. She/he can perform these steps online from the comfort of her/his home. As her/his business expands and becomes profitable, she/he would be expected to pay 20.9% of her/his commercial profits in taxes and contributions annually. However, if the same entrepreneur were a national of the Philippines, living in Quezon City, the business incorporation process would require 16 procedures, take 28 days and cost around 16% of income per capita. She/he would need to make 20 different tax and contribution payments and visit multiple agencies in person. Furthermore, her/his business would be expected to pay 42.9% of its commercial profits in taxes and contributions annually. Cumbersome business regulatory structures such as these constrain the ability of entrepreneurs to transform their ideas into viable businesses.

Doing Business measures the processes for starting a business, obtaining a building permit, getting an electricity connection, transferring property, paying taxes, taking a commercial dispute to court, and resolving an insolvency case, as well as credit and equity market regulations and logistics of importing and exporting goods. There are many other factors that influence firm decisions—such as the availability of skilled labour or market size—that are not captured in Doing Business. But Doing Business focuses on key areas of interaction between the government and entrepreneurs, where policy makers and regulators can directly influence procedures to facilitate these interactions. For more information on what is measured and what is not, see the chapter About Doing Business.

The Benefits of Improved Business Regulation

The Doing Business indicator sets capture the effectiveness and quality of business regulation. Research findings substantiate the economic relevance of the aspects of business regulation measured by Doing Business. Recent research, for example, examines the impact of improving business regulation. One study finds that high start-up costs can result in lower overall productivity.

Specifically, incumbent firms are more likely to continue operating despite poor productivity because there is little competition from new, more productive firms. In the absence of effective regulation, firms are also less inclined to leave the informal sector.

In addition, Doing Business measures the coverage, scope and quality of credit information available from credit registries and bureaus. When functioning well, these institutions form an essential element of an economy's financial infrastructure by strengthening access to financial services, particularly credit. By collecting and sharing credit information, such agencies reduce information asymmetries, increase access to credit for small firms, lower interest rates, improve borrower discipline and strengthen bank supervision and credit risk monitoring. Indeed, a study of a credit bureau serving the equipment finance industry in the United States found that better exchange of information between lenders results in improved repayment behaviour by firms, including lower incidences of delinquencies and defaults. This impact was stronger for firms that typically lack informational transparency, such as small and young firms.

Doing Business places emphasis on the quality of legal infrastructure and the strength of legal institutions. The protecting minority investors indicator set, for example, measures the protection of minority shareholders. For businesses to secure equity finance, legal mechanisms are needed to prevent the use of corporate assets by company insiders for personal gain—especially during financial crises or times of market distress. Research has shown that during the 2008 global financial crisis, for example, companies in economies with better investor protections and stronger corporate governance experienced a smaller decrease in their market value. Conversely, firms in economies with weak legal structures saw a more significant decline in value.

The Doing Business indicators on resolving insolvency provide evidence of a strong relationship between regulatory quality and efficient outcomes. The indicator set measures the quality of regulation as the recovery rate for secured creditors and the extent to which domestic law has incorporated certain internationally-accepted principles on liquidation and reorganization proceedings. Efficient outcomes occur when viable businesses are given a chance to survive, while loss-prone, inefficient firms exit the market, putting resources to better use elsewhere in the economy. In the absence of strong legal bankruptcy legislation, however, the balance between firm survival and efficient exit is distorted. This distortion was highlighted by research using data from Hungary, where the majority of firms in bankruptcy were preserved and allowed to continue operating as going concerns—despite generating substantial operating losses and resulting in low recovery rates for creditors. The main cause of this distortion was the inadequate allocation of control rights between secured and unsecured creditors, which decreased the recovery value by not allowing creditors to take important decisions related to the company assets during insolvency procedures. Another cause was the establishment of a compensation scheme for agents managing bankruptcy proceedings based on assets sold and operating revenues of a firm, which created a significant increase in the cost of bankruptcy procedures and reduced creditors' recovery rate. In the area of cross-border trade, Doing Business measures the effectiveness of trade logistics. Several studies have underscored the importance of port automation and efficiency for both trade facilitation and regional economic development. These studies have found that ports that are more automated require less maintenance, are more cost-effective and ensure better worker safety. Furthermore, a study of the determinants of shipping costs from Latin America to the United States found that—for most exporting economies—high transportation costs pose even greater barriers to trade than import tariffs, and that port inefficiencies significantly add to these costs. One of the most striking findings is that by improving port efficiency from the 25th to the 75th percentile, shipping costs are lowered by 12%, substantially increasing the volume of bilateral trade. One of the principal causes of port inefficiency is excessive regulation—precisely what Doing Business advocates to curb.

Destination for Better Business Regulation

The overall measure of the ease of doing business gives an indication of where it is easier for domestic small and medium size firms to do business. Although the economies with the most business friendly regulation in this year's ease of doing business ranking are relatively diverse, the economies within the top 20 share some common features. Fourteen of the top 20 are

OECD high-income economies; three are from Europe and Central Asia and three from East Asia and the Pacific. Eighteen of the top 20 are classified as high-income economies. The top 5 performers are New Zealand, Singapore, Denmark, the Republic of Korea and Hong Kong SAR, China. The former Yugoslav Republic of Macedonia is the only upper-middle-income economy on the list, while Georgia is the only lower-middle-income one (Table 1). To date, no low-income economy has reached the top 20 group. However, being wealthy does not guarantee a front-runner position in the ease of doing business ranking; many high-income economies still have room for progress. Having few bureaucratic hurdles, robust legal institutions and laws and regulations that are based on international good practices is what matters most for a good performance in the ease of doing business ranking. Among the top 20 economies Georgia, with a ranking of 9, has implemented the highest number of business regulation reforms since the launch of Doing Business in 2003. During the same period, Latvia and Lithuania have also actively reformed their business regulatory environments, with 28 and 31 reforms respectively. Among other reforms, Lithuania has made six reforms to its business incorporation processes, five reforms to bankruptcy proceedings and four reforms to its taxation system. Many other top ranked economies have followed this pattern of continuous reform, demonstrating that comprehensive reform efforts can lead to considerable improvements in an economy's regulatory and business environment. Another feature that the top 20 economies have in common—albeit not measured by Doing Business—is that on average they have higher labor force participation rates and lower levels of income inequality. Indeed, the average Gini coefficient 6 of the top 20 economies is 0.3 (with 0 representing perfect equality and 1 representing perfect inequality), compared to 0.4 for the lowest 20.7. What can the Doing Business 2018 data tell us about global patterns? Good regulatory practices are present in almost all of the world's regions. Aside from 28 OECD high-income economies, the 50 highest ranked economies include 13 from Europe and Central Asia, five from East Asia and the Pacific, two from Sub-Saharan Africa and one each from the regions of Latin America and the Caribbean and the Middle East and North Africa.

Table 1. Ease of doing business ranking

DB 2018 Rank	Economy	DTF Score	DTF change	DB 2018 Rank	Economy	DTF Score	DTF change
1	New Zealand	*86.55*	*-0.18*	96	Kuwait	*61.23*	*+1.52*
2	Singapore	*84.57*	*+0.04*	97	Guatemala	*61.18*	*-0.43*
3	Denmark	*84.06*	*-0.01*	98	Dominica	*60.96*	*+0.34*
4	Korea, Rep.	*83.92*	*0.00*	99	Dominican Republic	*60.93*	*+2.52*
5	Hong Kong SAR, China	*83.44*	*+0.29*	100	India	*60.76*	*+4.71*
6	United States	*82.54*	*-0.01*	101	Fiji	*60.74*	*+0.04*
7	United Kingdom	*82.22*	*-0.12*	102	Trinidad and Tobago	*60.68*	*-0.19*
8	Norway	*82.16*	*-0.25*	103	Jordan	*60.58*	*+2.38*
9	Georgia	*82.04*	*+2.12*	104	Lesotho	*60.42*	*+0.54*
10	Sweden	*81.27*	*+0.03*	105	Nepal	*59.95*	*+2.35*
11	Macedonia, FYR	*81.18*	*-0.21*	106	Namibia	*59.94*	*+0.54*
12	Estonia	*80.80*	*+0.05*	107	Antigua and Barbuda	*59.63*	*+0.98*
13	Finland	*80.37*	*-0.11*	108	Paraguay	*59.18*	*+0.06*
14	Australia	*80.14*	*0.00*	109	Papua New Guinea	*59.04*	*+0.17*
15	Taiwan, China	*80.07*	*+0.41*	110	Malawi	*58.94*	*+6.33*
16	Lithuania	*79.87*	*+1.05*	111	Sri Lanka	*58.86*	*+0.13*
17	Ireland	*79.51*	*-0.19*	112	Swaziland	*58.82*	*+0.25*
18	Canada	*79.29*	*-0.09*	113	Philippines	*58.74*	*+0.42*
19	Latvia	*79.26*	*-0.79*	114	West Bank and Gaza	*58.68*	*+3.80*
20	Germany	*79.00*	*-0.19*	115	Honduras	*58.46*	*-0.07*
21	United Arab Emirates	*78.73*	*+1.87*	116	Solomon Islands	*58.13*	*-0.01*
22	Austria	*78.54*	*-0.15*	117	Argentina	*58.11*	*+0.07*
23	Iceland	*78.50*	*+0.01*	118	Ecuador	*57.83*	*-0.01*
24	Malaysia	*78.43*	*+0.96*	119	Bahamas, The	*57.47*	*+0.82*
25	Mauritius	*77.54*	*+2.09*	120	Ghana	*57.24*	*+0.34*
26	Thailand	*77.44*	*+5.68*	121	Belize	*57.11*	*+0.03*
27	Poland	*77.30*	*+0.18*	122	Uganda	*56.94*	*+0.42*
28	Spain	*77.02*	*0.00*	123	Tajikistan	*56.86*	*+0.93*

Table 1. (Continued)

DB 2018 Rank	Economy	DTF Score	DTF change	DB 2018 Rank	Economy	DTF Score	DTF change
29	Portugal	*76.84*	*-0.14*	124	Iran, Islamic Rep.	*56.48*	*+0.26*
30	Czech Republic	*76.27*	*+0.03*	125	Brazil	*56.45*	*+0.38*
31	France	*76.13*	*-0.06*	126	Guyana	*56.28*	*+0.39*
32	Netherlands	*76.03*	*+0.51*	127	Cabo Verde	*56.24*	*+0.42*
33	Switzerland	*75.92*	*+0.19*	128	Egypt, Arab Rep.	*56.22*	*+0.10*
34	Japan	*75.68*	*+0.07*	129	St. Vincent and the Grenadines	*55.72*	*+0.01*
35	Russian Federation	*75.50*	*+0.81*	130	Palau	*55.58*	*+0.46*
36	Kazakhstan	*75.44*	*+1.06*	131	Nicaragua	*55.39*	*+0.09*
37	Slovenia	*75.42*	*+0.99*	132	Barbados	*55.20*	*-0.09*
38	Belarus	*75.06*	*+0.55*	133	Lebanon	*54.67*	*-0.10*
39	Slovak Republic	*74.90*	*-0.25*	134	St. Kitts and Nevis	*54.52*	*+0.18*
40	Kosovo	*73.49*	*+4.98*	135	Cambodia	*54.47*	*+0.23*
41	Rwanda	*73.40*	*+3.21*	136	Maldives	*54.42*	*+0.64*
42	Montenegro	*73.18*	*+1.64*	137	Tanzania	*54.04*	*+0.11*
43	Serbia	*73.13*	*+0.26*	138	Mozambique	*54.00*	*+0.97*
44	Moldova	*73.00*	*+0.20*	139	Côte d'Ivoire	*53.71*	*+2.04*
45	Romania	*72.87*	*+0.17*	140	Senegal	*53.06*	*+3.75*
46	Italy	*72.70*	*+1.15*	141	Lao PDR	*53.01*	*+0.43*
47	Armenia	*72.51*	*+0.59*	142	Grenada	*52.94*	*-0.11*
48	Hungary	*72.39*	*+0.26*	143	Mali	*52.92*	*+0.30*
49	Mexico	*72.27*	*+0.18*	144	Niger	*52.34*	*+2.26*
50	Bulgaria	*71.91*	*+0.10*	145	Nigeria	*52.03*	*+3.85*
51	Croatia	*71.70*	*+0.05*	146	Gambia, The	*51.92*	*-0.01*
52	Belgium	*71.69*	*-0.23*	147	Pakistan	*51.65*	*+0.71*
53	Cyprus	*71.63*	*-0.49*	148	Burkina Faso	*51.54*	*+0.20*
54	Israel	*71.42*	*+0.05*	149	Marshall Islands	*51.45*	*+0.03*
55	Chile	*71.22*	*+0.37*	150	Mauritania	*50.88*	*+1.56*

DB 2018 Rank	Economy	DTF Score	DTF change	DB 2018 Rank	Economy	DTF Score	DTF change
56	Brunei Darussalam	*70.60*	*+5.83*	151	Benin	*50.47*	*+1.85*
57	Azerbaijan	*70.19*	*+3.12*	152	Bolivia	*50.18*	*+0.32*
58	Peru	*69.45*	*+0.01*	153	Guinea	*49.80*	*+0.32*
59	Colombia	*69.41*	*-0.11*	154	Djibouti	*49.58*	*+3.99*
60	Turkey	*69.14*	*+1.16*	155	Micronesia, Fed. Sts.	*48.99*	*+0.01*
61	Costa Rica	*69.13*	*+1.23*	156	Togo	*48.88*	*+0.64*
62	Mongolia	*69.03*	*+1.27*	157	Kiribati	*48.74*	*-0.31*
63	Luxembourg	*69.01*	*+0.35*	158	Comoros	*48.52*	*+0.47*
64	Puerto Rico (U.S.)	*68.85*	*+0.05*	159	Zimbabwe	*48.47*	*+0.80*
65	Albania	*68.70*	*+ 0.96*	160	Sierra Leone	*48.18*	*-0.06*
66	Bahrain	*68.13*	*+0.01*	161	Ethiopia	*47.77*	*+2.08*
67	Greece	*68.02*	*+0.01*	162	Madagascar	*47.67*	*+3.05*
68	Vietnam	*67.93*	*+2.85*	163	Cameroon	*47.23*	*+2.18*
69	Morocco	*67.91*	*-0.03*	164	Burundi	*46.92*	*+0.06*
70	Jamaica	*67.27*	*+0.57*	165	Suriname	*46.87*	*+0.11*
71	Oman	*67.20*	*+0.08*	166	Algeria	*46.71*	*-0.01*
72	Indonesia	*66.47*	*+2.25*	167	Gabon	*46.19*	*+1.33*
73	El Salvador	*66.42*	*+3.54*	168	Iraq	*44.87*	*+0.48*
74	Uzbekistan	*66.33*	*+4.46*	169	São Tomé and Príncipe	*44.84*	*+0.39*
75	Bhutan	*66.27*	*+1.06*	170	Sudan	*44.46*	*+0.17*
76	Ukraine	*65.75*	*+1.90*	171	Myanmar	*44.21*	*+0.30*
77	Kyrgyz Republic	*65.70*	*+0.54*	172	Liberia	*43.55*	*+3.10*
78	China	*65.29*	*+0.40*	173	Equatorial Guinea	*41.66*	*+1.77*
79	Panama	*65.27*	*+1.25*	174	Syrian Arab Republic	*41.55*	*+0.08*
80	Kenya	*65.15*	*+2.59*	175	Angola	*41.49*	*+1.38*
81	Botswana	*64.94*	*+0.07*	176	Guinea-Bissau	*41.45*	*+0.23*
82	South Africa	*64.89*	*-0.08*	177	Bangladesh	*40.99*	*+0.15*
83	Qatar	*64.86*	*+0.61*	178	Timor-Leste	*40.62*	*-0.07*
84	Malta	*64.72*	*+0.43*	179	Congo, Rep.	*39.57*	*-0.52*
85	Zambia	*64.50*	*+3.92*	180	Chad	*38.30*	*-0.28*

Table 1. (Continued)

DB 2018 Rank	Economy	DTF Score	DTF change	DB 2018 Rank	Economy	DTF Score	DTF change
86	Bosnia and Herzegovina	*64.20*	*+0.42*	181	Haiti	*38.24*	*+0.01*
87	Samoa	*63.89*	*+2.06*	182	Congo, Dem. Rep.	*37.65*	*+0.22*
88	Tunisia	*63.58*	*-0.20*	183	Afghanistan	*36.19*	*-1.80*
89	Tonga	*63.43*	*+0.50*	184	Central African Republic	*34.86*	*+0.78*
90	Vanuatu	*63.08*	*+0.02*	185	Libya	*33.21*	*+0.03*
91	St. Lucia	*62.88*	*+0.01*	186	Yemen, Rep.	*33.00*	*+0.06*
92	Saudi Arabia	*62.50*	*+2.92*	187	South Sudan	*32.86*	*-0.33*
93	San Marino	*62.47*	*-0.03*	188	Venezuela, RB	*30.87*	*-0.79*
94	Uruguay	*61.99*	*+0.35*	189	Eritrea	*22.87*	*+0.42*
95	Seychelles	*61.41*	*+1.01*	190	Somalia	*19.98*	*-0.31*

Each region also has a relatively wide spectrum of strong and weak performers. Economies are ranked based on the distance to frontier score. This measure shows the distance of each economy to the "frontier," which represents the best performance observed on each of the indicators across all economies in the Doing Business sample. In OECD high-income economies, for example, New Zealand, Denmark and Korea have the highest overall distance to frontier scores at 86.55, 84.06 and 83.92, respectively.

Conversely, Greece, Luxembourg and Chile have the lowest scores in this group, at 68.02, 69.01 and 71.22. However, the OECD high-income group has the smallest gap between the highest and the lowest scores, of only 18.53 percentage points. Sub-Saharan Africa has the widest gap (57.56 percentage points), with a regional average score of only 50.43—the lowest across all regions. Among the economies of Sub-Saharan Africa, Mauritius has the highest distance to frontier score (77.54), while Somalia the lowest (19.98).

Regional rankings across different Doing Business indicator sets also show large variations.

South Asia, for example—the only region not represented in the top 50 list— scores comparatively well for starting a business, with an average distance to frontier score of 83.27.

In contrast, South Asia's regional average score for resolving insolvency is only 33.04. Indeed, Doing Business data show considerable variation in performance between economies within the same region and within the same regulatory area. Within South Asia, India has the highest score (80) for protecting minority investors compared to Afghanistan's score of 10.

Similarly, there is a substantial difference in scores between economies in the Middle East and North Africa region. Malta, for example, has a distance to frontier score for trading across borders of 91.01, while Algeria only scores 24.15.

Interestingly, all regions have at least one economy in the top 20 ranking on the protecting minority investor indicators and all regions—except the OECD high-income group—have at least one economy in the bottom 20 ranking on the protecting minority investor's indicators. These patterns indicate that there is further room for improvement across all regions and at all income levels.

Most of the Improved Economies with Ease of Doing Business in 2018

Doing Business 2018 captures 264 business regulation reforms across the 10 measured indicator sets. As in previous years, Sub-Saharan Africa is the region with the highest number of reforms (83 in total), followed by East Asia and the Pacific (45) and Europe and Central Asia (44). The regions with the highest share of reforming economies are Europe and Central Asia (79%), South Asia (75%) and Sub-Saharan Africa (79%), while the OECD high-income group has the lowest share (46%). The indicator sets for starting a business and getting credit record the highest number of reforms

(38 each) in 2016 - 17. They are closely followed by the trading across borders indicator set with 33 reforms. The least-reformed areas as captured by Doing Business continue to be the indicators with a legal focus—for example, resolving insolvency (13 reforms) and enforcing contracts (20). Legal reforms are typically slow to advance, mainly because they require long-term political commitments, substantial resources and close collaboration between multiple regulatory agencies and rulemaking institutions.

It is important to look at both the number of reforms and their impact on the distance to frontier score because they provide different information. The number of reforms indicates how many areas an economy chose to target for improvement, while the change in the distance to frontier score indicates the size of the impact those changes had on the Doing Business data. Across all economies, the average distance to frontier score increase is 0.76 percentage points, with the highest regional increase in Sub-Saharan Africa (1.18), although this region does not have the highest percentage of economies implementing at least one business regulatory reform. Nevertheless, there is a strong correlation between the number of reforms and the actual improvement in the distance to frontier score. Doing Business data show that it has become easier for small and medium-size enterprises to do business in 62.6% of economies worldwide (or 119 of the 190 economies measured by Doing Business).

While economies in the Sub-Saharan Africa region show the highest average increase in the distance to frontier score, economies in the OECD high income group have the lowest average increase (0.11 percentage points).

This is not surprising as most OECD high income economies are already near to global good practices. The Doing Business indicator sets capturing the most business regulation reforms across regions in 2016 - 17 are paying taxes and trading across borders. Indeed, the reform agendas of OECD high-income and East Asia and the Pacific economies appear to be dominated by regulatory changes captured by the paying taxes indicator set. Lower-middle-income economies have the highest average reform count at 1.9 reforms each; low-income economies are second highest at 1.3 reforms.

Unsurprisingly, high-income economies recorded the lowest average reform count.

Of the 10 economies showing the most improvement in performance on the Doing Business indicators, three are from SubSaharan Africa, two from East Asia and the Pacific, two from Europe and Central Asia, one from Latin America and the Caribbean, one from the Middle East and North Africa and one from South Asia. Brunei Darussalam, the only high-income economy on the list of top 10 improvers, showed the largest advance toward the global good practice frontier after implementing eight reforms in 2016 - 17 it joins this list for the second year in a row. El Salvador, India, Malawi, Nigeria and Thailand also made impressive strides and joined the 10 top improvers for the first time. Among top improvers, Brunei Darussalam, India and Thailand implemented the highest number of business regulation reforms in 2016 - 17, with eight reforms each. The remaining four economies in the list of top improvers are: Kosovo, Uzbekistan, Zambia and Djibouti. For details on the reforms these countries undertook, see the chapter on reforming the business environment in 2016 - 17.

The database of Doing Business reforms indicates differences in reform momentum, both within topics and across regions. Why are reforms more common in some years than others? When do economies tend to reform in the areas covered in Doing Business? Two main theories explain the timing of regulatory reform. The first suggests that economies reform when they must—that is, when there is no choice but to implement a regulatory change. In this case, an increase in reforms would be more likely during crises. A second theory argues that economies reform when they can—that is, when governments are recently elected and are in the "honeymoon period." Doing Business data can be used to explore which theory is more likely to hold true in practice. Recent research shows that governments are more likely to reform business regulation when their economy is experiencing a fiscal crisis. This is particularly true for regulation concerning resolving insolvency, which showed a spike in reform activity in 2010 - 11, 12 a couple of years after the 2008-09 financial crisis. The reason is that these kinds of reforms take time to be implemented and captured by Doing Business. However, the effect of fiscal crises on reform intensity is less robust when public debt is lower. When a fiscal crisis can be solved — albeit temporarily — by increasing borrowing, the need for reform becomes less urgent. In contrast, the "honeymoon" theory of reforms has less evidence to support it. In general, political change is not associated with more reform unless the political change takes place after the fiscal crisis. Indeed, economies tend to reform when they must, rather than when they can.

IMPACT OF BUSINESS REGULATION ON EMPLOYMENT AND POVERTY

Many factors explain poverty. These can include vulnerability to natural disasters, remoteness, quality of governance, property rights, availability of infrastructure and services, proximity to markets, social relationships, the gender of the head of household, employment status, hours worked, property owned and educational attainment. Several of these factors have a direct link to the areas measured in Doing Business since the Doing Business indicators measure factors such as the quality of governance and property rights. Furthermore, Doing Business can have an indirect link to these factors as improvements to business regulation can drive additional job creation. And ultimately, as a reliable source of income, employment can lift people out of poverty.

Reforming in the areas measured by Doing Business can be particularly beneficial to employment creation when those reforms take place in the areas of starting a business and labour market regulation. Such an assertion, however, is made with some caveats from other research exploring causal relationships between business entry regulation and job creation. Nonetheless, one of the mechanisms through which business regulation can impact employment directly is the simplification of business start-up regulations. Across economies there is a significant positive association between employment growth and the distance to frontier score. While this result shows an association, and cannot be interpreted in a causal fashion, it is reassuring to see that economies with better business regulation, as measured by Doing Business, also tend to be the economies that are creating more job opportunities.16 When it comes to unemployment, the expected opposite result is evident. Economies with less streamlined business regulation are those with higher levels of unemployment on average. In fact, a one-point improvement in the distance to frontier score is associated with a 0.02 percentage point decline in unemployment growth rate.

Doing Business 2017 reported that there is a negative association between the Gini index, which measures income inequality within an economy, and the distance to frontier score. Economies with poor quality business regulation have higher levels of income inequality on average. This relationship can be partially explained by the strong association between measures of poverty and the distance to frontier score. When business regulation is overly cumbersome, entrepreneurs and workers are pushed out of the formal sector and must resort to operating in the informal sector. The informal sector is characterized by a lack of regulation, minimal social protection and increased levels of poverty. Individuals living in poverty are likely to gain the most from smarter and more streamlined business regulation. When bureaucratic hurdles are high, only the most privileged members of society can get things done, either through hiring third parties or paying bribes. In economies with complex company incorporation processes, for example, entrepreneurs tend to hire lawyers to assist with the process of registering their businesses.

The data support this interpretation as there is a strong association between inequality, poverty and business regulation. In fact, economies with better business regulation have lower levels of poverty on average. Indeed, a 10 percentage point improvement in the distance to frontier is associated with a 2 percentage point reduction in the poverty rate, measured as the percentage of people earning less than $1.90 a day. Fragility is also a factor linked to poverty. However, even fragile economies can improve in areas that ultimately reduce poverty levels. Despite their fragile status, several economies implemented reforms as captured by Doing Business 2018.

INFORMATION OF EASE OF DOING BUSINESS IN THIS YEAR'S REPORT

This year's report presents four case studies, two of which focus on transparency. The case study on starting a business analyzes new data about the information available at business registries. It finds that economies with more transparent and accessible information have lower levels of corruption on average.

The case study on registering property analyzes the transparency of information as captured by the quality of land administration index and shows that transparent land administration systems are associated with a lower incidence of bribery.

The case study on dealing with construction permits analyzes private sector participation in construction regulation. It demonstrates that economies which employ some form of private sector involvement in construction regulation tend to have more efficient processes and better quality controls. However, they also exhibit higher costs and a propensity for conflicts of interest. Finally, the case study on resolving insolvency discusses three successful insolvency reforms—in France, Slovenia and Thailand—and the lessons learned that are transferable to other economies.

CONCLUSION

From the study it is concluded that Doing Business focuses on key areas of interaction between the government and entrepreneurs, where policy makers and regulators can directly influence procedures to facilitate these interactions. For more information on what is measured and what is not, see the chapter About Doing Business. Research findings substantiate the economic relevance of the aspects of business regulation measured by Doing Business. Recent research, for example, examines the impact of improving business regulation. One study finds that high start-up costs can result in lower overall productivity. The database of Doing Business reforms indicates differences in reform momentum, both within topics and across regions.

References

A World Bank Group Flagship Report.
www.doingbusiness.org/data/exploretopics/entrepreneurship.
www.doingbusiness.org/reports.
www.doingbusiness.org/methodology.
www.worldbank.org.

ABOUT THE EDITORS

Rajagopal

Email: rajagopal@itesm.mx

Rajagopal is Professor of Marketing at EGADE Business School of Monterrey Institute of Technology and Higher Education (ITESM), Mexico City Campus and Life Fellow of the Royal Society for Encouragement of Arts, Manufacture and Commerce, London. Dr. Rajagopal is also Adjunct Professor at Boston University, Boston, Massachusetts. He has been listed with biography in various international directories. He offers courses on marketing, innovation management, project management, new venture management and other subjects of contemporary interest to the students of undergraduate, graduate, and doctoral programs. He has imparted training to senior executives and has conducted over 60 management and faculty development programs. Dr. Rajagopal holds Post-graduate and doctoral degrees in Economics and Marketing respectively from Pandit Ravishankar Shukla University in India. His specialization is in the fields of Marketing Management, Rural Economic Linkages and Development Economics.

He has to his credit 58 books on marketing management and rural development themes and over 400 research contributions that include published research papers in national and international refereed journals. He is Editor-in-Chief of *International Journal of Leisure and Tourism*

Marketing and International *Journal of Business Competition*. Dr. Rajagopal is also Associate Editor of *Emerald Emerging Markets Case Studies*, published by Emerald Publishers, United Kingdom. He is on the editorial board of various journals of international repute. Currently Dr. Rajagopal holds the honor of the highest level of National Researcher-SNI Level- III. He has been awarded UK-Mexico Visiting Chair 2016-17 for collaborative research on 'Global-Local Innovation Convergence' with University of Sheffield, UK, instituted by the Consortium of Higher Education Institutes of Mexico and UK.

Divya Kirti Gupta

Email: divyakirti.gupta@gitam.edu

Divya Kirti Gupta is working as Associate Professor, GITAM Hyderabad Business School, GITAM (Deemed to be University), Hyderabad, Telangana State, India. She holds Ph.D. in Corporate Social Responsibility (CSR) from Banasthali University and has done MBA from FMS-WISDOM, Banasthali Vidyapith, Rajasthan. She is Ambassador, Academic & Research Group, ISO26000 Stakeholders Global Network (ISO26000 SGN) and Fellow, LEAD (Leadership for Environment and Development) India. As the elected representative of developing countries she was the co-drafter of ISO26000, the International Guidance Standard on Social Responsibility of Organizations. Dr. Gupta has published and presented papers in national and international conferences and has conducted capacity building programmes and MDPs for organizations in India and abroad. She has authored a book on Institution building and her research interests include CSR, Organization Development, e-Democracy, and Management Thought. In addition to being an academic, Dr. Divya Kirti carries rich experience of the grass-root level. In December, 2018 she was awarded for 'Excellence in Teaching and Research' by Higher Education Forum, Bangalore Chapter and Indus Business Academy (IBA), Bangalore.

About the Contributors

Subhash Sharma is an eminent management thinker and author. He holds PhD from University of Southern California, Los Angeles, and Post-graduate Diploma in Management (PGDM) from Indian Institute of Management (IIM) Ahmedabad. He is well known for his significant contributions to management thought, management education, development thinking and spiritual concerns. He is author of the creative and thought provoking books such as, Management in New Age: Western Windows Eastern Doors, Quantum Rope: Science Mysticism & Management, New Mantras in Corporate Corridors, New Earth Sastra: Towards Holistic Development & Management (HDM), New Ideas in Strategic Thinking & Management, and Quantum Bridge between Science & Spirituality. Prof. Sharma has also made significant contributions to innovative institution building as founding member of WISDOM (Women's Institute for Studies in Development Oriented Management) at Banasthali University, Banasthali, Rajasthan; Founding Director, Indian Institute of Plantation Management (IIPM), Bangalore and founding member, Indus Business Academy (IBA) and is currently Director, Indus Business Academy, Bangalore.

Andrée Marie López-Fernandez has received Bachelor's degree in Business Management from the Instituto Tecnológico y de Estudios Superiores de Monterrey, Mexico City Campus, and holds a Doctoral Degree in Administrative Sciences from the EGADE Business School. She is currently a full-time Professor and Researcher at the School of Economics and Business (ECEE) at the Universidad Panamericana and is a member of the Mexican National System of Researchers by CONACYT.

Ananta Kumar Giri is a Professor at the Madras Institute of Development Studies, Chennai, India. He has taught and done research in many universities in India and abroad, including Aalborg University (Denmark), Maison des sciences de l'homme, Paris (France), the University of Kentucky (USA), University of Freiburg & Humboldt University (Germany), Jagiellonian University (Poland) and Jawaharlal Nehru University, New Delhi. He has an abiding interest in social movements and cultural change, criticism, creativity and contemporary dialectics of transformation, theories of self, culture and society, and creative streams in education, philosophy and literature. Dr. Giri has written and edited around two dozen books in Odia (one of the Languages of India) and English.

Pushpa Machani is pursuing her PhD from GITAM Hyderabad Business School, GITAM (Deemed to be University), Hyderabad. She has 13 years of work experience, both in industry and academics. She has taught at R.V. Institute of Management, Bangalore and has worked for Tata Consultancy Services (TCS) as a Software Engineer. Ms. Pushpa's teaching interests include Entrepreneurship, Strategic Management and IT. Her research focuses on Entrepreneurship at Micro, Small and Medium Enterprises. She has presented several papers in national and international conferences. She has published four research papers in the area of entrepreneurship.

Yadavalli Lakshman Kumar (YLK) is Dean & Director of GITAM Hyderabad Business School, GITAM (Deemed to be University), Hyderabad. He has obtained M.B.A, and Ph.D. Degrees with specialization in Brand Management. Professor YLK is also post-graduate in commerce. He has 29 years of experience in Sales Management, Brand Management, Marketing, Teaching, Training, Consulting, Placements, Academics, Examinations and Institution building. Prof. YLK has delivered courses in several reputed business institutes in India including Indian Institute of Technology, Chennai, Institute of Financial Management and Research, Chennai, and Indian Institute of Management, Visakhapatnam as visiting Professor. He has published papers and cases in reputed journals. Prof. YLK was given 'Best Professor Award' for teaching marketing by Dewang Mehata Foundation in the year 2015.

Sadhvi Mehrotra is currently working as an Assistant Professor at Dayanand Academy of Management Studies, Kanpur. She did her Ph.D. from Banasthali University, Rajasthan on "Character Competence of Indian Banking Industry – Conceptual Perspectives and an Empirical Study". She is an MBA from Amity University, Lucknow and has presented and published paper at various national and international research platforms. She has done 'Train the Trainer' program on Retail Analytics designed by Tata Consultancy Services (TCS) and has successfully completed Data Analytics course offered by Christ University, Bengaluru.

Thirupathi Chellapalli has received his PhD in Marketing from School of Management Studies (SMS), University of Hyderabad. He was a UGC JRF scholar. Prior to that he did his MBA from Osmania University and studied BSc in Bio-Technology from Kakatiya University.His broad area of research and teaching interests are Marketing Research, Customer Relationship Management, Customer Experience Management, Self Service Technologies, Internet and Digital Marketing. Before joining GITAM HBS, he worked as Assistant Professor at University of Kalyani. Dr Thirupathi has published research papers in several national and international journals, and presented several acclaimed papers in national and international conferences.

D. V. Srinivas Kumar is presently working as an Assistant Professor at School of Management Studies (SMS), University of Hyderabad. He worked for few years in the Industry before switching over to Academics. His research area includes, Customer Relationship Management (CRM), Customer Experience Management (CEM), Digital and Social Media Marketing, and Business Analytics. He is the coordinator of MBA business analytics program at University of Hyderabad. He has published in various National and International journals of repute.

Ananya Rajagopal is an Industrial and Systems Engineering from Tecnologico de Monterrey, Mexico City Campus. She has been working with commercial banking division at HSBC corporate office in Mexico City since 2006. She has published several papers in international journals of repute, contributed research works in international conferences, and edited books. Currently she is pursuing her doctoral research at EGADE Business School, Tecnologico de Monterrey, Mexico City.

Karunesh Saxena holds Ph.D. degree and serving as Director, Internal Quality Assurance Cell, Director, College Development Council, and MLS University. He holds a total teaching and research experience of more than 30 years. His areas of expertise is spread across Behavioral Sciences with special reference to leadership, emotional intelligence, team building, conflict management, and soft skills and much more. Professor Saxena has directed many doctoral theses. He has to his as many as 115 publications in various journals. He is serves as resource person with various national institutes in India. He has been in the academic administration with high responsibilities at Sukhadia University, India.

Vandana Gupta holds PhD degree and serving as Assistant Professor in the Faculty of Commerce and Management Studies at L M College of Science and Technology, India. She is having teaching experience of 10 years. She presented many paper in various national & international conference. She is an editor of an international journal. She is also author of many books.

Ashish Mathur has obtained Ph. D degree and serving as Associate Professor, Department of Commerce in the Faculty of Commerce and Management Studies at Indira Gandhi National Tribal University, Amarkantak, India. He is having teaching experience of 16 years. He presented many paper in various national and international conference.

Khushboo Kumari is currently a post graduate management student at Chandragupt Institute of Management Patna, India with specialization in Finance. She is an NISM certified professional. She has worked with HDFC Bank, India.

Rajeev Verma is Fellow of Indian Institute of Management Indore (IIM Indore) and Doctoral Exchange Scholar of ITESM, Mexico City. He is a graduate from Forest Research Institute (FRI), Dehradun in the area of Forest Economics. He is currently working as Assistant Professor at Chandragupt Institute of Management Patna (CIMP), Bihar, India. Prior to joining, he had experience working with National Innovation Foundation (NIF), Ahmedabad and Indian Institute of Forest Management (IIFM), Bhopal. His research interest lies in exploring Marketing Information System, Product Management, Rural Development and Inclusive Growth, Customer Experience Management and Marketing Engineering.

Jyoti Verma has completed her Ph.D. in the area of Organizational Behavior and Human Resource Management from Institute of Management, Nirma University, Ahmedabad, Gujarat, India. She is currently working as Assistant Professor at Chandragupt Institute of Management Patna (CIMP), Bihar, India. Her research interest lies in exploring Performance Management System, Knowledge Management, Organizational Development and Strategic Human Resource Management. She has published many papers in journals of national and international repute and conference proceedings apart from winning Best Paper Awards at reputed institutes such as IIM Calcutta, IISc., Bangalore etc. She has imparted corporate training sessions on team building, leadership, organizational commitment, organizational ethics, motivation etc. in various Management Development Programs.

Subba Rao Tulasi holds BTech in Mechanical Engineering from Sri Venkateswara University, Tirupati, MA (Telugu) from Potti Sreeramulu Telugu University, Hyderabad and MBA (Finance) from GITAM, Vishakhapatnam. He has close to 40 years of experience in Operations, Maintenance, Industrial Relations and Human Resource Management in Steel and Paper industries, and held senior positions in companies including Steel Authority of India Ltd (Rourkela and Bokaro Steel Plants), Indo Rayon and Sinarmas (Indonesia) before retiring as Vice-President (HR), ITC Limited, Paperboards and Specialty Papers Division. He has acquired Strategic HR expertise through training in Institutions of repute including XLRI, Jamshedpur, Indian School of Business, Hyderabad and Ross School of Business (University of Michigan, USA). He holds an interest in developing leadership and motivation skills, teaching and facilitation. He is currently pursuing PhD in HR Management from GITAM, Hyderabad campus.

Suddapalli. Suman Babu is Assistant Professor and obtained PhD in organizational behavior. He has nearly 17 years teaching experience and 3 years full-time research experience. He has 28 research papers to his credit and presented 20 research papers in National and International Conferences.

Venu Kesi Reddy is working as Assistant Professor in Department of MBA, Vaagdevi College of Engineering (Autonomous), Warangal Urban (TS), India and is also pursuing his Doctoral Research (as part time) from GITAM Hyderbad Business School, GITAM (Deemed to be University), Hyderabad. The author has contributed various research papers and articles in the area of General Management, Financial Management and Management Information System to various reputed national and international journals and conferences. His teaching area includes Financial Accounting and Analysis, Financial Management, Financial Derivatives and Security Analysis and Portfolio Management.

A. Sreeram has been in Teaching, Research, Consulting and Academic Administration for the past thirty-one years. His teaching interests include Quantitative Analysis, Economics, Finance, Research Methodology and Entrepreneurship development. His Research interests include Entrepreneurship Development, Corporate governance and Behavioral Finance. He has rich experience in Research, paper Publication and Consultancy. He completed two research projects funded by UGC and IIBF. He published several papers, participated and conducted National level Workshops and Seminars. He is also a member of Board of studies, staff selection committees and external paper setter for different colleges and universities.

INDEX

C

D

H

I

J

L

M

N

O

P

Q

R

S

T

U

V

W